A Pictorial History of
WAR
FILMS

A Pictorial History of
WAR FILMS

Clyde Jeavons

special research
by
MARY UNWIN

picture research
by
JOHN KOBAL

Hamlyn

London · New York · Sydney · Toronto

Contents

Published by
The Hamlyn Publishing Group Limited
London·New York·Sydney·Toronto
Astronaut House, Feltham,
Middlesex, England

© Copyright
The Hamlyn Publishing Group Limited 1974
ISBN 0 600 37013 5

Printed in England
by Jarrold and Sons Limited, Norwich

endpapers
The Victors (1963)

half-title spread
They Gave Him a Gun (1937)

title spread
Dunkirk (1958)

contents spread
The Longest Day (1962)

page 10
Henry V (1945)

Introduction

What, one has to begin by asking, *is* a war film?

To those, like me, reared in the front stalls of the local Odeon in the 'forties and 'fifties, it used to be a simple affair of Allied heroics and Nazi come-uppance. Sometimes John Mills, Jack Hawkins, Richard Todd or Kenneth More sent the Germans packing; sometimes John Hodiak, Van Johnson, William Bendix or the ubiquitous John Wayne gave the Japs hell. Either way, it was always the same war.

To those, on the other hand, with less nostalgia for the one-and-nines and a more dispassionate view of cinema, the term 'war film' might mean anything from *The Fall of the Roman Empire* to *The War of the Worlds*, from *The Vikings* to *Soldier Blue*. Men have, after all, been at loggerheads for a very long time.

War films can, in other words, be defined in numerous ways. For the purposes of this book, however, I have considered only those films depicting armed conflict in the twentieth century. Apart from being historically convenient (the technological revolution which spawned the cinema in 1895 also gave birth to modern methods of warfare), this has kept the subject within manageable bounds and avoided awkward encroachments into such limitless genres as period war drama – except in a few instances where obvious modern parallels exist, such as *Henry V, Alexander Nevsky* or *A Time Out of War*.

All the same, the number of films which even this tidy brief embraces is staggering, particularly as one cannot, in a survey pretending to be at all comprehensive, ignore such themes as the Russian Revolution or Nazi Propaganda, or pass too peremptorily over the mass of news films and documentaries which have been a constant salutary reminder of the reality behind the romance of war. Consequently, there has – even allowing for a doubling in length of the book's text between conception and completion – been little room to analyse or moralize; or, more regrettably, to add to the persistent debate on the validity of anti-war films (though René Clair may have had the last word on that subject when he said: 'Nobody yet has made a good anti-war picture because we still have wars.')

The intention, in any case, was not to question the ethics of war films or their effectiveness as statements against war, but simply to describe fully, for the first time, their development since the cinema began, to place them in their political and historical context, and to offer a fair distillation of opinion about them.

The continuing popularity of war films is, one would like to think, as much a healthy reflection of people's curiosity about the history, nature and causes of war as a seeking after sensationalism, a charitable viewpoint supported in part by the increasingly disciplined and intelligent use of archive film in cinema and television documentaries. Perhaps, though, Richard Griffith's half-cynical, half-sage explanation for the undiminished appeal of war films (quoted in Robert Hughes's *Films of Peace and War*) is still the one which comes nearest the truth: 'They are made because they are profitable, and I suspect that their audiences derive from them a nostalgia for the time when it was possible for us to kill each other periodically without the danger of ending the human story forever.'

C.J.

Early Skirmishes

There is, perhaps, the merest hint of prophetic irony in the fact that two of the earliest examples of publicly exhibited cinematography show Tom Merry, a lightning cartoonist, drawing sketches of, respectively, Kaiser Wilhelm and Count Bismarck: one, the instigator of the most senseless and wasteful war in human history; the other, the architect of Prussian militarism. Those brief vignettes of 1895 are no more than parts of a simple, ingenuous stage act reproduced on film, yet they can be taken as an early sign, however embryonic, of what was to become one of the chief preoccupations of the cinema – armed conflict (not surprisingly, since that was also to continue to be one of the enduring preoccupations of nations).

There is, too, an inkling of coincidence in the fact that the technical processes of film-making were devised just in time to record the dawn of modern warfare, with its mud and machines, and its monstrous development into an indiscriminate consumer of human life on a global scale, able now to devour all mankind at a sitting. War, in spite of its outrageousness, is no less photogenic or visually stimulating than the American West, or gangsterism, or any other sphere of violence, and the cinema has never been slow to exploit the fact.

At first, British pioneer film-makers largely ignored war as a suitable theme, although the occasional drama with a military setting was produced, such as R.W. Paul's *In the Name of the Queen* (1898), a brief sketch about a deserter. But the infant cinema soon had an opportunity to cut its teeth on a contemporary combat subject, with the outbreak, in 1899, of the Boer War in South Africa. This ugly product of Late Victorian imperialism, which had been brewing ever since the futile Jameson Raid of 1895, inspired not only the Boy Scout movement but also a rash of films. The importance of these lies in the fact that many of them were genuine actuality shots, taken in the theatre of war – the first newsreels, in fact. They were also immensely popular, inducing producers to augment them with 'faked' scenes and reconstructed events, such as the topicals turned out by Mitchell and Kenyon of Lancashire, for

whom the outskirts of Blackburn became a convenient substitute for the South African veld.

The pioneer of authentic war reportage was an American, Charles Urban. He came to London and formed the energetic Warwick Trading Company, which became known for its travel and interest films and which employed the first war cameramen. Prominent among these were John Bennett Stanford and Edgar M. Hyman (both claimants to being the first to send back genuine footage of the events in South Africa), Sydney Goldman, and, most celebrated of them all, Joseph Rosenthal.

Rosenthal captured the first action pictures of the South African War – advertised as *A Skirmish with the Boers near Kimberley by a Troop of Cavalry Scouts Attached to General French's Column* – and was the first cameraman to film behind the Boer lines. He went on to cover the Boxer Rebellion in China in 1900, the US action in the Philippines in 1901, and the Russo-Japanese War in 1904.

Less adventurous coverage relating to South Africa included the departure and return of troops ('As these troops were some of the first to leave England for South Africa,' commented Warwick delicately of one of its films, 'there are many smiling countenances herein portrayed who we regret to state since met with misfortune'), Boers surrendering to Roberts and Kitchener, and other events far removed from the front line. In fact, most of the on-the-spot film reports were of this dull nature, and it was their lack of action and general failure to live up to the excitement of the front-line press reports reaching the newspapers which led to the 'faking' of so many incidents. R.W. Paul, for instance, produced a series called *Reproduction of Incidents of the Boer War*, depicting British soldiers in Mafeking scoffing at enemy shellfire, and nurses tending the wounds of British and Boers alike, while Gaumont even dared to re-create the *Signing of the Peace at Vereeniging in 1902*, complete with ham portrayals of Kitchener, Smuts and the rest.

The heavy hands of patriotism and propaganda also began to make themselves felt in

Percy Moran as the intrepid subaltern in *Lieutenant Daring Quells a Rebellion* (Charles Raymond, 1912).

13

The fate of a
deserter – *In the Name of
the Queen* (R.W. Paul,
1898).

Charles Urban
(seated), founder of the
Warwick Trading Company
and dynamic pioneer of
the newsreel.

British troops set
up Maxim guns prior to *A
Skirmish with the Boers
near Kimberley by a Troop
of Cavalry Scouts Attached
to General French's Column*
(J. Rosenthal for Warwick,
1900) – the first authentic
action shots of the
Boer War.

Boer War films. Cecil Hepworth produced a jingoistic fantasy, *Wiping Something off the Slate* (1900), to emphasize the heroism of the British soldier, and an 'allegory' called *Peace with Honour* (1902) to celebrate the conclusion of hostilities, with Britannia smiling patronizingly down at a Boer and his British conqueror ('May so end all Great Britain's wars'). And there were several attempts at sentimental dramatization of aspects of the war, most notably Hepworth's *The Call to Arms* and James Williamson's *The Soldier's Return* (both 1902).

It is significant that the Boer War – from which Britain emerged with little credit, and which was, in many ways, a dress rehearsal for the conflicts of the twentieth century, symbolized by the concentration camps first set up by the British to intern Boer women and children – has seldom been treated in films since the actual event, and then only as an incidental part of a different theme (e.g. *Young Winston*, 1972). The one exception, ironically, is the Nazi propaganda film *Ohm Krüger* (1941 – described in a later chapter), a skilful, virulent attack on Britain in the 'thirties using the Boer War as a setting.

At the same time as war was being waged in South Africa, Britain became partly involved in another conflict on foreign soil: the Boxer Rebellion. This attempt by the Chinese to drive all foreigners out of their country attracted some on-the-spot coverage, including a series of non-action pictures taken by Rosenthal, and inspired a number of reconstructed incidents. The most celebrated of these – indeed, the best known of all 'faked' actualities – was Williamson's *Attack on a China Mission* (1900), filmed, with the help of his family, in Williamson's own garden. This shows Boxers attacking and setting fire to a mission-house, killing the missionary, and attempting to abduct his wife; sailors arrive in time to rescue her and capture the Chinamen.

Another, more lurid piece of staging, photographed in long-shot, purported to show a rebel being decapitated by Chinese soldiers, but a blatant jump-cut between the sword falling and the victim's 'head' being removed from his 'body' tells all. (This crude fabrication was later more than compensated for by Urban, who in 1904 came up with authentic footage of a Chinese beheading, catalogued as *Execution of Li-Tang, the Chunchus Chief of Manchurian Bandits* and accurately described as 'gruesome, but faithfully depicting the actual scene'.)

The Boxer Rebellion is another slice of *fin de siècle* history noticeable for its absence as a film theme over the years. The only full-scale treatment occurs in Nicholas Ray's *55 Days at Peking* (1962), a spectacular, old-fashioned tribute to the British imperial spirit, with David Niven (as the British Minister in Peking) coolly refusing to leave the foreign legation when it is besieged by the Boxers and thereby compelling his less heroic colleagues from other Western nations to join his resistance against the rebels until help arrives.

Charles Urban continued to search out disturbed areas of the world in order to satisfy the public's appetite for action footage. In 1901 he sent Captain Ralph P. Cobbold to accompany Emperor Menelik's troops against the 'Mad Mullah' in Abyssinia, and in 1903 he commissioned C. Rider Noble to cover operations by the Bulgarian Army and the insurgence in Macedonia.

A more substantial assignment for contemporary cameramen was the Russo-Japanese War, which broke out in 1904 over territorial claims and resulted in humiliating defeat for Tsarist Russia. George Rogers, an American, covered the conflict for Urban from the Russian side, while Rosenthal worked with the Japanese.

Rosenthal really made his reputation with his pictures of this war. He began with a series of pro-Japanese home-front films, of which *Home Life of the Jolly Jap* was a typical example, and followed up with impressive shots of the siege of Port Arthur (though not before Urban, unable to wait for Rosenthal's authentic footage, had reconstructed the event for his customers).

Again, staged scenes were popular, usually depicting the besting of Russians by Japanese. A characteristic example was the Sheffield Photo Company's *Attack On a Japanese Convoy* (1904), which depicts both Japanese superiority and Russian treachery. Sheffield themselves called it 'without doubt the finest war film on the market . . . the Japanese, Russians and Coolies being perfect representations.'

Production of actuality war films continued whenever there was a conflict to film, and they were often incorporated into the regular newsreels which were then being developed, such as the *Topical Budget*. The troubles in Belfast and Morocco in 1907 were covered. Cameramen spent time with various active armies, such as the Bulgars and the Greeks, and the disturbances in the Balkans in 1912–13 provided them with a dress rehearsal for the major assignment which was to occupy them from 1914 to 1918. Gradually, ciné-reporters became more intrepid, manhandling their unwieldy equipment into the front line in order to achieve the action shots which audiences demanded.

American war films of this early period more or less paralleled, and occasionally overlapped, British productions in type and technique. British films (for the first and last time in their history – Hollywood was soon to reverse the trend with a vengeance) enjoyed a healthy export trade to the United States, and events such as the Boer War attracted considerable attention. The Edison Company, for example, issued familiar actuality material such as *Arundel Castle Leaving for Transvaal with British Troops*, with decidedly pro-British captions ('This picture never fails to deeply impress any observer with any loyalty in his veins'), and, like its English counterparts, readily reconstructed front-line events on home soil, contrasting the humaneness of the British (in *English Army in the Battlefield*) with the

alleged brutality of the Boers (in *Boers Bringing in Prisoners*).

The Boxer Rebellion was also reported – and re-created – with enthusiasm in America. Rosenthal's Shanghai street scenes were shown alongside shots purporting to depict Boxer massacres in Peking and multiple executions ('We are promised,' commented one gullible magazine at the time, 'some vivid, soul-stirring pictures of actual, gruesome war . . . the camera does not lie and we form our judgment of this and that as we watch the magic of the screen'), and in 1901 Ackerman of the American Mutoscope and Biograph Company produced, somewhat esoterically, what was probably the first staged film made in China, *Sixth US Cavalry Assaulting South Gate of Peking*.

At the same time, J. Stuart Blackton and Albert E. Smith, already well known for their patriotic propaganda films, made an ambiguous film allegory of the Chinese rebellion called *The Congress of Nations*, depicting representatives of all the 'civilized' nations attacking a Chinaman, who dissolves and turns into the Statue of Liberty.

Boer War scenes by Warwick (1900), with (*above*) a *War Balloon and Transport Crossing the Vaal River,* and (*below*) cameraman Joseph Rosenthal recording a similar event.

Joseph Rosenthal, doyen of early newsreel cameramen.

The United States was, at this time, becoming acutely conscious of its emergence as a world power, and this was reflected in its reaction to America's contemporary equivalent of the Boer conflict, the Spanish-American War. Blackton and Smith were the first to give visual expression to the common feeling with their intensely patriotic vignette, *Tearing Down the Spanish Flag!* (1897), probably the first-ever intentionally propagandist film. Shot on the roof of their New York studio, it was a tremendous success and spawned endless imitations.

Blackton and Smith and others made numerous topical films of troops and transports leaving for the campaign, and some cameramen actually got to Cuba and took film of the troops landing. But there was, as ever, little authentic action and much compensatory reconstruction. Even the lively series, *The Campaign in Cuba*, with its various scenes showing *Landing Under Fire*, *The Battle of San Juan Hill* and (denoting victory) *Our Flag is There to Stay!*, was shot largely in New Jersey. Edison came up with a disarming euphemism for 'faked' war scenes when his company claimed to have 'improved the occasions'.

The most elaborate reconstruction of the time was Edward H. Amet's re-creation, with detailed models and a bath-tub, of the sinking of Admiral Cervera's fleet at Santiago. Amet's assertion that he shot the actual battle through a telescopic lens at six miles convinced even (it is alleged) the military archivists of Spain.

Military patriotism continued to be a favourite theme throughout the American cinema's formative years, reflecting the country's somewhat imperialistic attitude towards South America and its preoccupation with national defence. In *The Hand of Uncle Sam* (1910) an American plotting to overthrow a South American republic is saved from a firing-squad by the intervention of the mother country and restored to his wife. As they embrace, the American flag waves emotively above them.

The flag was, in fact, a common motif and passion-rouser, occurring frequently in film titles (*Rally Round the Flag*, *For Flag and Country*, etc.), and occasionally getting star billing, as in Vitagraph's *Old Glory*, a series of tableaux recalling the champions of freedom in America's past history and concluding with a display of the Star Spangled Banner, 'emblem of prosperity and peace among the nations of the earth'.

Government-approved films demonstrating the joys of being a soldier or sailor, like *A Day With the Soldier Boys* and *Up the Ladder with Bowline*, were made to stimulate recruiting, while the virtues of bravery and patriotism and the necessity of militarism were stressed in such offerings as *None But the Brave Deserve the Fair*, *The Banner Carrier* and *Destiny is Changeless*.

Liberal attitudes were reserved for events abroad, sometimes to good effect. *Auction of Souls*, dramatizing the suffering of the Armenians at the hands of the Turks, helped to raise money for the starving victims, while *Russia, the Land of Oppression*, 'an undying appeal to humanity', contributed something to awareness of the turbulent Russian situation.

The Mexican Revolution (yet another opportunity for film-makers to show their skill at staging actionful events and passing them off as authentic newsreels) was nearer home and aroused more reactionary attitudes. But these were occasionally countered by liberal sentiments, notably in *The Clod*, which showed how revolution is the inevitable outcome of prolonged tyranny.

Pancho Villa, the legendary Mexican bandit and rebel, later showed himself to be unusually perceptive about the propaganda power of film by inviting the Mutual Film Corporation to cover his campaign. But he tended to hog the camera, and when *The Life of Villa* eventually came to be made, it was shot without him, largely in California, with actuality scenes inserted.

While America was indulging its flag-waving on the screen, Britain in the period up to 1914 took a more sober, objective attitude to soldiering and war. One of the more important and influential projects of 1900 was R.W. Paul's *Army Life, or How Soldiers are Made*, a series of twenty or so short films designed 'to illustrate the life and career of a soldier'. This it did by a combination of actuality shots (e.g. *Cavalry Exercises*, *Quick-Firing Guns*, *Exploding a Submarine Mine*) and staged scenes (*A*

Fantasy and reality . . .

Left: Attack on a China
Mission (James Williamson,
1900), most celebrated of
the early 'faked' actualities.
Below: Authentic Urban
newsreel of the Execution
of Li-Tang, the Chunchus
Chief of Manchurian Bandits
(1904).

Lark in Camp, Defending a Redoubt, etc.), and
the War Office recognized its recruiting potential by making facilities available to Paul
during shooting. One reviewer was impressed
enough to say that it was a film 'of exceptional
merit combining art and actuality'.

In the same year, Hepworth made two similar
series, The British Army and The British Navy,
paying more attention to the latter; then in
1909, he revived the idea with In the Service of
the King, a dramatization of military service
tracing the progress of a single soldier. This
was followed in 1913 by Gaumont's British
Army Film, a repeat exercise, but officially
sanctioned and far more ambitiously filmed.

To complement these, there were some excellent factual films, including Urban's From the
Fighting Top of a Battleship in Action, with
impressive close-up shots of huge naval guns
being loaded and fired, and Cricks and Martin's
A Dreadnought in the Making and The Birth of
a Big Gun.

As has been seen, war films at this time were
mostly geared to actual events, but military
dramas maintained their popularity, and audiences were not averse to an occasional gratuitous assertion of imperialism like Walturdaw's
How a British Bulldog Saved the Union Jack
(1906). Curiously, one of the first stirrings of
the star system occurred in two very successful
military films produced by Williamson in 1908,
Still Worthy of the Name and Raised from the
Ranks, whose leading player, Jack Chart,
attracted considerable female admiration and
caused one exhibitor to wonder if he couldn't
profitably exploit the actor's charms by selling
photographs to his audience.

Early war dramas were mostly naïve, sentimental and lacking in action, but some notable exceptions began to appear after 1910, as often as not from the cameras of Cricks and Martin, one of the livelier production companies at that time. The most popular of their titles, directed either jointly or individually by A.E. Coleby and Dave Aylott, were *The Mighty Atom* (1911), a story about a courageous drummer-boy; *The Pirates of 1920* (1911), an ingenious, futuristic adventure-thriller involving an airship and a dashing lieutenant (which, along with Kineto's *Aerial Anarchists*, pioneered some interesting model work and special effects for its action sequences); and *A Son of Mars* (1912), the exploits of another brave lieutenant, who saves the regiment during a colonial skirmish.

Cricks and Martin had had a popular success in 1909 with *Muggins VC*, about a lowly bumpkin who enlists and wins the highest award for bravery. But heroism was, for the most part, the exclusive preserve of subalterns, as amply demonstrated by a couple of long-running spy series featuring two Bond-like characters, Lieutenant Daring (played by Percy Moran) and Lieutenant Rose (P.G. Norgate), who were kept endlessly busy disposing of enemy agents. These one-reel adventures were entertaining and ingeniously plotted (in *Lieutenant Daring and the Plans of the Mine Fields*, made in 1912, the plans in question are drawn on a girl spy's back) and enterprisingly up-to-the-minute (in *Lieutenant Rose and the Stolen Battleship*, also 1912, the indomitable hero pursues the stolen ship in a Blériot monoplane and forces the spies to surrender by dropping bombs on them).

But even the remarkable exploits of Daring and Rose could not avert the tragic conflict which was about to cast its cloud over Europe, and the most appropriate conclusion to the prewar period was provided by the London Film Company's prestige production of 1914, *England's Menace*. This espionage thriller, skilfully directed by Harold Shaw and strongly cast, visualized a planned invasion of England by a hostile power, and was vividly described in the contemporary trade press as 'the greatest national drama yet produced and . . . not a mere romance. It has something of the gift of prophecy and stirs the blood as only war alarms can. It shows the perils of wireless as well as its safeguards. It illustrates how the invader's warships might approach while England sleeps.' And it proved to be a timely and telling portent of the holocaust that was soon to come.

The Impossible War

Scott Fitzgerald described 1914 and the four disastrous years which followed as the 'noisy dawn of our times'. It was, fortuitously, also the period when the cinema began to grow up, acquire respectability, and form the pattern of its future progress, when commentators first started to use the word 'art' in connection with motion pictures, and when the American film industry rapidly came to dominate the world's screens.

The war itself demonstrated fully for the first time the potential of film as a medium of propaganda, debate and agitation. Much of this early propaganda was primitive, even simple-minded, in technique and approach, but as yet audience responses were equally unsophisticated, and many of the war (and pacifist) films made from 1914 to 1918 appear to have been remarkably effective.

The first rumblings of Scott Fitzgerald's 'noisy dawn' came, appropriately enough, from Belgium, soon to be swallowed up in the first Prussian advance. There, in 1913, the progressive French film-maker Alfred Machin produced his prophetic *Maudite Soit la Guerre* (literally, 'War Be Damned'), a spectacular drama telling of the rivalry between two pilots fighting in a war between imaginary nations.

In France, anticipation of impending conflict and the institution of new conscription laws led to a flurry of patriotism in 1913. This was best exemplified in such offerings as *A Soldier's Honour*, *The Old Sergeant*, *1870–1871* (which recalled the heroism of earlier French armies) and *Hands off the Flag* (which roused receptive audiences with scenes entitled 'The Revenge of a Wretch', 'Theft of the Sacred Emblem', and 'Salute to the French Flag'). Once the war started, however, the country which had pioneered commercial cinematography and which had held a pre-eminent place among film-making nations, lost its momentum entirely and for a while produced few films of any kind.

The making of war newsreels kept the spark alight, though, and led to something like a revival in 1915 when another bout of patriotism found unsubtle expression in such morale-boosters as *Frontiers of the Heart*, *A Sacred Love* ('the most poignant conflict of emotions that could rend the heart of a young Frenchman today'), *The Burgomaster's Daughter*, *The House at the Ferry*, and *The Independence of Belgium from 1830 to 1914*. Escapism, in the form of romances and adventure stories, took over from the more harrowing war themes as the conflict progressed, but production of war films continued, partly to bolster spirits behind the lines, partly to arouse sympathy for the French cause in the United States. Titles included *The Avenging Poilu*, *Sweethearts of 1914*, *La Marseillaise*, *Christmas in Wartime*, *The Angelus of Victory*, *Wives of France* and (from the great Abel Gance) *Paddy's Heroism*. Espionage was an added ingredient of *Kit, the Boche's Daughter*, *The Minister's Daughter*, and Arthur Bernède's prestige production, *The Heart of a Frenchwoman*. Louis Mercanton contributed a celebrated curiosity called *Mothers of France* (1917), which made an admirable bid for authenticity by including actuality scenes photographed at the front, but then blew the effect by having the awesome Sarah Bernhardt don a nurse's uniform in order to make a dramatic plea for her country.

The same chauvinism, sentimentality and heroism were injected into the films of all the main combatant countries throughout the war. Even the blockaded Germany churned out its share of melodramas about nurses, soldiers and bereaved mothers of courageous sons, with titles like *The Fatherland Calls* and *In the Field of Honour*.

In England, the pattern differed slightly in that the sudden mobilization for war did not have the same stunning impact on film production as it had in France and Germany. On the contrary, British companies could not produce war dramas fast enough, while almost any old news or interest films with the merest connections with the war were grist to the mill, be they travelogues of Belgium, military parades, glimpses of national leaders, or shots of warships on peacetime manœuvres.

The initial surge of topical, jingoistic dramas took in the whole gamut of familiar, almost ritual themes. *England's Menace* (already

Charles Rock ('Old Bill'), Hugh E. Wright and Arthur Cleave suffer the rigours of the English Channel in George Pearson's World War I comedy, *The Better 'Ole* (1918), based on Bruce Bairnsfather's famous comic cartoon character.

D.W.GRIFFITH'S "HEARTS OF THE WORLD"

noted) was one which propounded the pet myth that the 'home' side were morally and cerebrally so superior that even their children could outwit the wicked enemy; *England Expects* had a young man's cowardice cured by his wife's faith; in *Called to the Front* an agent warned the War Office of impending invasion; *Lest We Forget* (an early effort by Maurice Elvey, one of the longest enduring of British directors) showed a British girl caught on the Franco-German frontier at the start of the war; in *An Englishman's Home* a pacifist reformed after a taste of foreign invasion (in *For the Empire* the pacifist was a vicar); and *Chained to the Enemy* twisted itself round the idea of a German officer's British wife having to nurse both him and the wounded war correspondent she loved.

The foiling of foreign spies with dastardly plans to blow up the Houses of Parliament (among other things) was a frequently recurring theme during the opening months of the war; examples included *The German Spy Peril*, *The Crimson Triangle* and *Guarding Britain's Secrets*, all uniformly preposterous. Later espionage movies, such as *The Man Who Stayed at Home* (1915) and *A Munition Girl's Romance* (1916), the latter with decent flying shots and hints in its plot of social issues such as the growing freedom of women through factory work, proved more substantial.

The depiction of leaders and heroes was considered a good recruiting angle, as in George Pearson's *The Cause of the Great European War* (1914), an almost instant reconstruction of topical events which contained dramatized portrayals of Kitchener, the Kaiser (both by Fred Payne), Churchill and Franz-Josef, and in *England's Call* (1914), in which famous portraits (Raleigh, Wellington, etc.) came to life and encouraged a 'slacker' to enlist. The slacker, or shirker, was a recurring character,

usually held up to ridicule – sometimes to good comic effect, as in Dave Aylott's very funny *Conscription* (1915): when conscription is announced, Micky (*sic*) and his friends dress up as women, assume infirmities, and even feign death to avoid enlisting, but they are all rumbled by the recruiting sergeant ('We've got to round up the shirkers') and the final message flashes up – 'Don't wait for conscription, but come along and defend . . . YOUR COUNTRY.'

There were numerous candidates for white feathers in these endlessly repetitive war melodramas of 1914 and 1915 – black sheep of all kinds who finally shook off their cowardice or drunkenness, or redeemed minor crimes by volunteering for the front and acquiring an honourable wound. *Saving the Colours* (1914) managed to combine this common ploy with yet another – that of the estranged wife/sweetheart who, by a remarkable coincidence, happens to be the nurse who is on hand to tend the wounds of her heroic husband/lover.

The alleged brutality and caddishness of the enemy in Belgium and France were also frequently dramatized, their atrocities usually including rape, as in Aylott's *War's Grim Reality* and Elvey's *The Bells of Rheims* – although the plucky victims of these unwelcome advances were not always completely helpless, as the heroine of *In the Clutches of the Hun* (1915) demonstrated by retaliating with a paper-knife. As another title of 1915 so succinctly put it – *War is Hell*.

The epidemic of patriotic war dramas ended almost as abruptly as it had begun half-way through 1915 as some of the numbing truth and reality of the war filtered back from the front to temper the flag-waving with despair, and escapism took over. Even the few major features which did retain a war theme tended to add an extra touch of fantasy to evade the grimness of it all: Lawrence Cowen's fairly ambitious *It is*

for England (1916), for example, introduces into its plot a reincarnated saint who unmasks a baronet as a German spy. However, a handful of war-oriented dramas were produced which managed partially to escape the general rut of absurdity and bathos. The up-and-coming Maurice Elvey produced one of several vehicles for his popular star, Elisabeth Risdon, which had a superior look to it; called *It's a Long, Long Way to Tipperary* (1914), it told the story of an Irish Nationalist who gave his life to save his rival, an Ulster Volunteer – a plot with a particularly ironic ring to it sixty years later. Cecil Hepworth's *The Outrage* (1915), written by Albert Chevalier and starring Henry Ainley and Alma Taylor, and the London Film Company's *1914*, although they resorted to the well-worn rape theme, could also claim to be a little more meaningful than the rest of the contemporary product. And (although humorous films about the war were extremely rare at this time) there was the occasional simple satire to relieve the monotony, such as Pimple the Clown's 'merry joke at the expense of our foe', *Pimple Enlists* (1914).

The war drama did not come back into favour in England until 1918, when a brief revival showed that it had at last acquired some maturity and point. Sidney Morgan's otherwise conventional *Democracy* attempted to demonstrate the part played by the war in breaking down class barriers; George Pearson's comedy, *The Better 'Ole*, adapted from the play based by Bruce Bairnsfather and Arthur Eliot on Bairnsfather's own famous comic cartoon character 'Old Bill', undermined the taboos against treating the war humorously and introduced the cockney archetype into British war movies; and *The Kiddies in the Ruins*, also directed by Pearson, and adapted from another play, based on the drawings of the French artist Poulbot, depicted the plight of orphaned children found wandering in the ravaged areas of France.

Two large-scale features produced at this time were the result of official sponsorship by the War Office, and both of them involved 'guest' film-makers from America – Herbert Brenon (director, in 1916, of the controversial *War Brides*, of which more shortly) and D.W. Griffith. Brenon's project, variously titled *The Invasion of Britain* and *Victory and Peace*, was an ambitious attempt at a 'great national film', a prestige drama with stars like Matheson Lang, Marie Lohr and Ellen Terry; but it became a useless extravagance when the ending of the war rendered it (still unfinished) prematurely obsolete, and it was never publicly shown.

Griffith's contribution to the Allied powers' propaganda output was *Hearts of the World*, a lavishly backed production planned when he came to London for the première of *Intolerance*, which had made a big impression on influential members of the Establishment. The theme was the effect of the war on two young lovers living in a small French village occupied by the invading German forces, and Griffith was able to shoot much of it on location, under actual front-line conditions. However, in spite of having witnessed the abstract horrors of armed conflict at first hand and being able to incorporate into his film genuine actuality material, Griffith failed to capture the authentic atmosphere of the war. He over-sentimentalized the personal relationships, and his indictment of the brutality of Prussian militarism was too reminiscent of the outraged melodramatics of the earlier fictionalized anti-atrocity films to cut much ice with audiences by now long bludgeoned by the real depredations of war. Griffith himself acknowledged the shortcomings but failed to grasp the reason for them, merely remarking somewhat insensitively that 'viewed as drama, the war is in some ways disappointing'.

23

His innate humanity was more fairly represented six years later in *Isn't Life Wonderful?*. Nevertheless, in terms of scope, technique (i.e. incorporation of specially shot actuality material) and credentials, *Hearts of the World* remains an important film within the genre, saved from many of its built-in weaknesses by a cast which includes both Lillian and Dorothy Gish, Erich von Stroheim (in one of the first of his Cruel German Officer characterizations) and Noël Coward, making his film début.

Griffith made a second British-backed war film, *The Great Love*, but it was evidently a far less satisfactory project than *Hearts of the World*, stringing together endless scenes of wartime England with unrelated shots of royalty.

While the demagogic dramas of the early months of the war trumpeted their primitive propaganda, then swiftly palled, actuality films proved consistently popular, and in the long term made a firmer contribution to the development of film-making by sowing the first recognizable seeds of the British documentary tradition. Cumulatively, they also formed a bank of invaluable archive material to serve as a perpetual reminder, in later compilations, of the reality and tragic futility of what has ironically been termed the 'impossible war'.

Aside from the simple, rousing recruiting pictures like *England's Call*, the idea of making straightforward factual films about the war, 'its causes, its meaning, and its appeal', to stimulate the war effort, was mooted at an early stage. But for a while, the first eager cameramen such as Geoffrey Malins and E.G. Tong (and, for that matter, their French counterparts) met a dispiriting amount of official opposition towards their efforts to film the war as it was, and they could only manage to send back familiar behind-the-lines scenes which not even the addition of hopeful titles like *A Machine Gun School at the Front* or *War with Our Territorials at the Foot* could prevent from looking unremarkable.

The situation in Germany at the beginning of the war was not dissimilar, but German newsreel cameramen did receive some official blessing, and their factual films were as much a success in neutral countries as in the Fatherland itself. They were also more effective propaganda than the hysterical tirades of indignation and displays of mock heroism being churned out by the Allies. It was an awareness of this, expressed by the German Chief of Staff, General Erich Ludendorff, which led to the setting up of the formidable German film propaganda machine Ufa – a sleeping dog in the closing months of World War I but one that was to bare all its teeth as the Nazis propelled the world into World War II.

Once the Allies recognized how much impact the enemy's films were having, matters rapidly improved for Malins and his colleagues – particularly after the success in America of *Britain Prepared*, a compilation of scenes showing the Army in training, fleet manœuvres in the North Sea, and work at the munitions factories of Vickers and Maxim. Eventually films were officially adopted for propaganda purposes, and were organized under a Cinematograph Committee which found its ultimate home in the Ministry of Information. Cameramen were sent to all fronts, regular newsreels were instituted, informative, well-constructed short documentaries such as *The Making of an Officer* and *The Eyes of the Army* (about the work of the Royal Flying Corps) were produced, and central control of all the footage shot made possible the compilation films of major events of the kind already made famous by Malins and his fellow cameraman J.B. McDowell.

The most celebrated, successful and influential of Malins's and McDowell's feature-length actualities was the first, *The Battle of the Somme*, made on the Western Front in July 1916, and shown at home shortly afterwards as a morale-booster and spur to industrial workers. The film's 'astounding realism' was commented upon, as was the way in which it conveyed 'the wonderful spirit of our men in the face of almost insuperable difficulties'; the King urged the public to see it; and Lloyd George called it 'an epic of self-sacrifice and gallantry'. In fact, the film was far more down-beat than these eulogies indicate; an unwitting study of ordinary soldiers suffering unimaginable discomforts, dying abruptly, and exuding a kind of remote despair under the cheerfulness and endless mud. Indeed, along with most British newsreels of the time (although this was clearly of no consolation to contemporary opponents), the film was far more reticent about showing the blatant horrors of warfare than, say, the vivid footage finding its way into French cameras.

Malins and McDowell compiled three more substantial films of battles or their consequences: St Quentin, The Battle of Ancre (which contained the first thrilling shots of tanks in action), and the somewhat less randomly constructed The Battle of Arras. The effect of these films on a riveted public – then as now – was almost entirely due to their raw content and their unblinking artlessness as they simply recorded the quaking, dishevelled landscape of the war and the sufferings, activities, and sometimes, disarmingly, the self-conscious camera antics of its hapless combatants.

As already observed, once war had broken out, there was only one acceptable subject for an actuality film – the war itself. Even old interest films with no relevance at all to the conflict were reissued and reslanted (a straightforward film about trawling, for example, was given the title In the Mine Strewn North Sea). Then followed a plethora of films depicting the Allied armies (and that of the Germans) in training – Lord Kitchener's New Army, Backbone of England, With the Fighting Forces of Europe, and many others – augmented, until the first newsreels started filtering back from France, by a mass of dramatized official propaganda films and topical dramas. A brave example of the former was Whatsoever a Man Soweth, an exposition by Joseph Best of the evils of venereal disease for showing to the troops; the latter included a number of emotional biographies of contemporary heroes, such as The Life of Lord Roberts (1914), the lavish and imperially tub-thumping The Life of Lord Kitchener (1918), and Maurice Elvey's portrait of Lloyd George, The Man Who Saved the British Empire (1918).

Curiously, the war had a direct bearing on the development of the animated cartoon in Britain. Previously, American artists had made all the running in this sphere of film-making (and in terms of technique continued to do so to a point still unsurpassed). Most notable among them was the highly skilled Winsor McKay, who had introduced his famous Gertie the Trained Dinosaur in 1909, and who went on to make in 1918 the remarkable Sinking of the Lusitania, a serious, vivid cartoon depiction of the disaster, based on an eyewitness account. British animation was still rooted in trick-work and 'lightning sketches', in which an artist's hand would be photographed drawing rapid caricatures.

Once the propaganda possibilities of cartoons had been recognized, however, they quickly

became numerous and popular, if always limited in technique. They were almost exclusively concerned with the war, and were for a long time virtually the only acceptable outlet for making fun of the war, which they did in the form of an endless stream of rudimentary topical lampoons ridiculing the enemy. At first, the trick-artist style was still apparent, as in Harry Furniss's Peace and War Pencillings (which showed a German soldier taking a beating from an Australian kangaroo) and the lightning sketches of Alick P.F. Ritchie. But before long Lancelot Speed had produced the first real British animated cartoons with his Bully Boy series, a lively succession of mildly satirical digs at the Kaiser: among other indignities he is seen changing into a sausage and being eaten by a British bulldog; being humiliated by General French's Contemptible Little Army; having vain Sea Dreams of naval domination; and, in Sleepless, suffering from hallucinatory insomnia.

Speed's example was followed by numerous other artists, prominent among whom were Anson Dyer and Dudley Buxton (together they drew John Bull's Animated Sketch Book, while Buxton produced a series of War Cartoons), Ernest Mills (who depicted the Zeppelins in What London Saw), and G.E. Studdy, the comic-dog artist (who contributed Studdy's War Studies). 'Trick-topicals' continued to compete with the 'purer' cartoons – sometimes most effectively, as in Percy Smith's two curiosities, Kinotank, a nightmarish comic fantasy which anticipated the newfangled 'trench dreadnoughts' (i.e. tanks) with such terrifying realism that the War Office clamped down on it for a while, and The Strafer Strafed, which reconstructed, with models, the downing of a Zeppelin in flames over Cuffley village. Kineto's modest but original War Maps, animated diagrams explaining such events as The Exploits of the "Emden" and The Jutland Battle, were also a popular and noteworthy series. This enthusiasm for British animated films did not, however, long outlast the war.

Numerous official films were devised to

Opposite and above: Scenes from *The Battle of the Somme* (Geoffrey Malins and J.B. McDowell, 1916).

25

Sinking of the Lusitania (1918), Winsor McKay's cartoon reconstruction of the infamous U-boat attack which pushed the United States closer to war with Germany.

encourage recruiting, step up arms manufacture, stimulate the purchase of war loans, and otherwise boost the communal war effort. One of the best known of these socially directed war films was Ralph Dewsbury's dramatized food economy tract, *Everybody's Business* (1917), with Gerald du Maurier and Matheson Lang. This and all the other sermons and exhortations finally confirmed in official eyes the value of moving pictures as a propaganda medium.

But it was the newsreel which emerged as Europe's most valuable contribution to the cinema in the war years, in a historical if not artistic sense: *Allenby's Historic Entry into Jerusalem* (shot by the eminent Jeapes); *The British Offensive, July 1918*; *With the Forces in Mesopotamia* (taken by Varges); *The King Visits His Armies in the Great Advance* – just a small random sample gives an indication of their scope. From this hard-earned footage developed the great Malins/McDowell *Battle* series and the authoritative, factual serials (such as Pathé's *History of the Great War*, *Sons of the Empire* and *Our Empire's Fight for Freedom*) which anticipated the epic TV compilations of the 'sixties. And because of its existence every subsequent generation has had, and will continue to have, a unique, vital and moving record of a grotesque event in history which might otherwise have been impossible to believe. As Malins wrote in his own memoirs, 'How I Filmed the War': 'I have always tried to remember that it was through the eye of the camera, directed by my own sense of observation, that the millions of people at home would gain their only first-hand knowledge of what was happening at the front.'

America, of course, did not enter the Great War until 1917. By that time, a surge of rich creativity, inspired by D.W. Griffith, combined with the disappearance of European competition and the awakening of a massive home market, had made her the world's leading film-producing nation, a position she is still reluctant to relinquish. The war itself saw her pass from indifference, through determined pacifism

and shaky neutrality, to patriotic involvement, a trend accelerated by her war films, most of which contrived to undermine America's early isolationist policy in favour of militarism.

First reactions to the war in a cinema sense, however, were mixed, the only consistent factor being (as in Europe) a rapidly developing awareness of the potential of film as a propaganda medium. An effective demonstration of this power was supplied by Griffith in his monumental review of the American Civil War, *Birth of a Nation* (1915), which, with its emphasis on the ravaging of the Southern States and the redemption of their honour through the efforts of the Ku Klux Klan, was an unequivocal declaration of the inferiority of the Negro. This propaganda element in filmmaking was further amplified by the even more monolithic *Intolerance* (1916), Griffith's answer to the criticisms of his display of prejudice in *Birth of a Nation*. Griffith described this ambitious polemic as 'a protest against despotism and injustice in every form'. What he in effect produced was the first anti-war film of any magnitude. Sadly, it went against the tenor of the times, and was barred in some cities and largely rejected by the American film-going public elsewhere.

The initial effect of the outbreak of war was a glut of political and military films, relevant or otherwise: a random influx of travelogue scenes in foreign cities, portraits of the combatant nations' leading statesmen, and old newsreels. Collectively, these films took up a stance of objective neutrality, even allowing room for the German point of view in such offerings as *The Cruise of the Moewe*, *The Log of the U-35*, *Behind the German Lines*, and the exceptionally successful *The German Side of the War*. The tendency even at this stage, however, was to favour the Allied cause, as exemplified by *The Battling British*, *The Kaiser Challenges*, *The Great War in Europe*, *European Armies in Action*, *England's Menace*, *Germania*, *War is Hell*, and sundry French and British topicals.

To start with, though, idealism held sway

over pragmatism and some potent pacifist films were produced in the years prior to America's entry into the war. Among the first of any significance was *Neutrality*, a plea for harmony among the various nationalities represented in the United States: it showed how a Frenchman and a German living in the USA remained friends in spite of the war. The similarly titled *Be Neutral* was more ambivalent, ending a dramatized argument about neutrality between two men with a senseless killing. Uncertainty was also present in Thomas Ince's *The Coward* (1915), starring Charles Ray as a pacifist in the Civil War who is taken for a coward but is later 'converted'. A firmer stand was taken by foreign imports such as the French *The Horrors of War* (1914), depicting the decimation of a Parisian family in the Prussian siege of 1870, and the Danish *Lay Down Your Arms* (1914); their strength of attitude was adopted in turn by American producers like J. Searle Dawley, whose *One of Millions* (1914) had a wife driven to madness by the sight of her soldier-husband's dead body. But by far the most eloquent of the anti-war films of the period were Herbert Brenon's *War Brides* and Thomas Ince's *Civilization*, both of which appeared in 1916.

Set in a mythical kingdom not a million miles from Germany, *War Brides* attempted to demonstrate the German people's supposed antipathy to the war. Its heroine, Joan (played by Alla Nazimova), is a latter-day Lysistrata whose husband and three brothers-in-law are killed in a war and who campaigns against a government decree instructing women to produce more offspring for future conflicts. When she is told by the king that there will always be war, she kills herself and by so doing strengthens the resolve of her fellow protesters: there will be no more children as long as men persist in going to war. The film was effective and, for a while at least, received considerable acclaim, but when American participation in the war became a certainty, it was suppressed. Official reasoning maintained that 'the philosophy of this picture is so easily misunderstood by unthinking people that it has been found necessary to withdraw it from circulation for the duration of the war'. Thus it went the way of *Intolerance*.

Civilization (subtitled *He Who Returned*) was an enormously successful project which has come to be regarded by many as a great anti-war film. In fact, its neutral stand is compromised a little by the built-in implication that the Germans were the savage aggressors, but it remains a strong, spectacular sermon against the tragedy and wastefulness of war. The theme is similar to that of *War Brides*, including the thinly disguised mythical setting: the spirit of Christ is reincarnated in a war hero, who preaches defiantly against the evils of war in the face of constant persecution, until he is arrested and condemned to death. The film is alleged to have aided the re-election of Wilson as President on the platform 'He kept us out of war', and it certainly stands as a peak of idealism in the pre-war years, notwithstanding a hint of calculated commercialism in its making.

This idealism was, however, being inexorably eroded by pro-war agitation and a growing feeling that there was a need to prepare for war if not actually take part. The champion of this kind of nationalism was the man who had symbolically torn down the Spanish flag on his studio roof a decade and a half earlier, J. Stuart Blackton. This rather extreme patriot came into his own during the war years with a series of pro-preparedness films whose titles alone adequately summarize their sentiments: *Wake Up, America!*; *Womanhood*; *The Glory of the Nation*; *The Common Cause*; *Safe for Democracy*; and *The Battle Cry of Liberty*. The pattern for these fervent calls to arm and to arms was set by *The Battle Cry of Peace*

Alla Nazimova in *War Brides* (Herbert Brenon, 1916).

27

(1915), Blackton's highly controversial adaptation of Hudson Maxim's book 'Defenceless America', which emphasized that an armament programme for America was the only means of maintaining peace. Blackton admitted in retrospect that the film 'was propaganda for the United States to enter the war. It was made deliberately for that purpose.' He revealed that it had the support of his neighbour, Theodore Roosevelt. It was also timely, being released shortly after the sinking of the Lusitania.

The Battle Cry of Peace imagined the 'Germans' besieging New York and being generally frightful, sadists and rapists to a man. The film was vehemently denounced by notables such as Henry Ford, who accused Maxim and other munitions-manufacturers of using it to boost their profits, but the public gave its unequivocal support and so launched a massive output of pro-war films in America.

Among the more curious of them was a singularly peculiar satire on pacifism, *The Fall of a Nation* (1916), by the Reverend Thomas A. Dixon, which depicts the 'betrayal' of the United States by pacifist politicians who refuse to make ready against possible armed attack. When a defenceless America is overcome by barbaric enemy troops, the 'traitors'

are rewarded by the invaders by being made, like rookies on fatigues, to peel potatoes. Eventually, of course, the nation girds itself and drives out the atrocious enemy. Another oddity was *Patria*, a patriotic serial made by William Randolph Hearst which starred Irene Castle and honoured the Du Ponts, a family of munitions-manufacturers. Rather carelessly, it imagined a war in which Mexico and Japan jointly invaded the United States. Japan, however, was at that time an ally of Britain, and the anti-Japanese element caused embarrassment before it was removed under official pressure.

Pro-war propaganda crept into every kind of film. As well as straightforward, clearly labelled appeals to nationalism, such as the series *Uncle Sam's Preparedness*, there were more beguiling persuaders like the Douglas Fairbanks vehicle, *In Again, Out Again*, in which a jingoistic young man converts his pacifist sweetheart by exposing peace-movement leaders as profiteering munitions-manufacturers, disguising their product as more peaceable consumer goods. This kind of dramatic and inevitable conversion from pacifism to preparedness was a common theme in the first flood of pro-war pictures. In *A Man Without a Country* the convert becomes a recruit; in *A Nation's Peril* the scatty heroine (played by Ormi Hawley) gets so carried away by the new cause that she becomes virtually a one-girl press-gang; and in *Perkins' Peace Party* a doddery professor and his pals have a rapid change of heart after undertaking a disillusioning peace mission to Europe.

More direct were what could be described as the 'tabloid editorials', such as *Defence or Tribute?* which strung together relevant bits of history (the oppression of the Jews, Roman conquests, the Charge of the Light Brigade, etc.) and quotations from Wilson and Roosevelt in a rhetorical plea for preparedness. Equally emotive on a simple level were the romanticized espionage dramas which imagined a German agent under every bed: *The Hero of Submarine D-2, The Flying Torpedo, Shell 42, My Country First, As in a Looking Glass, Over Secret Wires* were just a few of them. Even the popular serial stars joined in the act, the queen of them all, Pearl White, making her contribution in *Pearl of the Army*, in which she outwitted oriental spies attempting to destroy the Panama Canal.

The savagery of the Hun began to be emphasized more and more, notably in *On Dangerous Ground*, in which an American is helped to escape from occupied Normandy by a brutally treated French girl, and in Thomas Ince's *Bullets and Brown Eyes*, which marked John Gilbert's film début. Somewhat controversial was *The War Bride's Secret*, a blatant attempt to profit from and up-end Brenon's pacifist *War Brides* by concentrating on the rape-and-plunder element.

There was token resistance to the swell of jingoistic propaganda ('These pictures have not . . .' said one commentator, 'proved to us the hopelessness, the despair, the hunger and

Contemporary poster advertising Thomas Ince's *Civilization* (1916).

J. Stuart Blackton's *The Battle Cry of Peace* (Wilfred North, 1915), with Tom Mills and, in a bit part (*left*), Constance Talmadge.

suffering that have been inevitable consequences of the war . . . have not been logical arguments in favor of Peace' – as indeed they were not meant to be), and such documentaries and newsreels as reached the cinemas (they were not particularly popular) retained some objectivity until relatively late in the day (*Guarding Old Glory* and *Heroic France* were conspicuous exceptions). But public opinion was so vehemently in favour of American participation in the war that even peace organizations were beginning to justify 'persecution of the armed conflict', and by the time the United States officially declared war on 5 April 1917, pacifism had become tantamount to treason. As evidence of this, *War Brides* – along with all anti-war films – was banned, while Robert Goldstein, producer of *The Spirit of '76*, which recalled the American liberation from the British just as America was about to go to war as Britain's ally, was sentenced to ten years' imprisonment under the Espionage Act.

The climax to the film industry's exhortations to take up arms against the Hun was supplied, not inappropriately, by Cecil B. DeMille, whose *Joan the Woman* and *The Little American* proved powerfully emotive. *Joan the Woman* starred Geraldine Farrar, an established opera-singer who had originally been picked by DeMille to play the leads in *Maria Rosa* and *Carmen*, and who later said, 'I knew when I played Joan of Arc in Mr DeMille's picture that it would be the greatest of pro-Ally propaganda.' DeMille himself described the film as 'an age-old call to a modern crusade', and it did prove a potent stimulator of sentiment in favour of France and the Allies. The film's success led to DeMille's being described in one quarter of the press as 'the Michelangelo of the screen', which was to overpraise what was nevertheless an intelligent and impressive piece of film-making. Employing an ambitious framework which alternated scenes of the war in the trenches with the story of Joan of Arc's victories and martyrdom, the film offered exciting action, eye-catching pageantry and uplifting spiritual emotion, at the same time making the oblique suggestion that the English-speaking nations owed a centuries-old debt to France because of their treatment of the Maid. Wallace Reid, making his debut in the part of an English soldier in both the modern and historical sequences, provided the link between the two.

Joan the Woman was one of many films produced at this time which showed emphatic sympathy for the Allies. The English were romanticized and eulogized in *The Victoria Cross, Whom the Gods Destroy, An Enemy of the King*, and *Heroism of a Spy*; the French in *Hearts of the World, Somewhere in France, Daughter of France, The Belgian*, and *For France* (which, alas, indulged liberally in manifestations of Hun atrocities).

The Little American – like *For France* – used the more familiar propaganda techniques, attempting to outrage every decent American by placing the adored Mary Pickford in peril of not only her life but her honour too ('My men are in need of relaxation,' explains the Prussian colonel played by Walter Long, who, like Erich von Stroheim, was a seasoned player of 'Hun' parts). The plot, concerning the capture by Germans of an American girl suspected of

Arnold Lucy (*right*) in
Douglas Fairbanks's *In Again,
Out Again* (1918).

being a spy, also managed to drag in other hate-rousing features, such as the Prussian rape of Belgium, supposed atrocities against women and children, and the sinking of the Lusitania. It even had a German-American hero (played by Jack Holt) for whom the love of Mary Pickford was stronger than the Fatherland and who consequently rescued his (and America's) sweetheart in the nick of time.

DeMille continued to contribute enthusiastically to the war effort, producing a tract on self-denial (*We Can't Have Everything*) but as often as not exploiting the atrocity and re-crimination angles which characterized American war films of the period. *The Whispering Chorus* (which DeMille himself rated highly), though not actually about war was laced with even more brutality than *The Little American*; while *Till I Come Back to You* urged vengeance on Prussia for its exploitation and maltreatment of the destitute children of war-torn Europe.

Most directors fell in with the blanket view of Germans as barbarians, rapists and vandals: 'these primitive beasts' as they were called. *Bitter Sweet* showed another child suffering at Prussian hands; in *Adele*, the victim was a nurse; and in *The Maid of Belgium*, the heroine

was shocked into amnesia after witnessing enemy atrocities. *Lest We Forget* had Rita Jolivet's beautiful American spy subjected to the firing-squad, while the execution of Edith Cavell was a frequent atrocity theme, as in *The Woman the Germans Shot*, *Why Germany Must Pay*, and *The Martyrdom of Nurse Cavell*.

The main butt of attacks on German fright-fulness was, of course, the Kaiser, who was often depicted symbolically violating the Statue of Liberty, or performing some similar abuse, before being confounded by an heroic 'doughboy'. The most venomous portraits of him appeared in *The Kaiser, Beast of Berlin* and *To Hell With the Kaiser*. In the former, which claimed to give 'an insight into the man guiding the most horrible outrages', the role of the 'enemy of world progress' was played by Rupert Julian, who came to specialize in the impersonation. In the latter, Kaiser Wilhelm (played by another exponent of the part, the Englishman Lawrence Grant) was coaxed by his friend Satan into sinking the Lusitania, releasing poison gas, and bombing Red Cross hospitals. A third Kaiser imitator was Gustav von Seyffertitz, who prudently changed his name to C. Butler Clonebaugh in the rabidly anti-German climate which then prevailed; he

30

Geraldine Farrar as *Joan the Woman* (Cecil B. DeMille, 1917).

also depicted Uncle Sam in patriotic tableaux.

The most successful of the atrocity films was William Nigh's *My Four Years in Germany*, based on a book by US Ambassador James W. Gerard, and purporting to consist of authentic newsreels of German prison camps and courts. In fact, the abuses and atrocities depicted were faked, but this did not stop the film amassing a substantial profit.

A significant development soon after the entry of the US into the war was the setting up of a Division of Films as part of the Committee on Public Information 'to sell the war to America'. Its influence on film content throughout the conflict was considerable, setting the tone itself with the production of four patriotic dramas – *Pershing's Crusaders*, *Under Four Flags*, *America's Answer* (a plodding but popular documentary about the YMCA's war effort), and *The Official War Review* (which showed the benefit of Charles Urban's guiding hand). It ensured, moreover, that the 'news' which reached the public was of the right kind, i.e. confined to Allied victories, even if that meant making most of it up; and it gave approval to the extravagant displays of flag-waving and nationalism which oozed out of such films as *My Own United States*, *American*

Achievements, and *The Settlement of America*. Later on in the war, non-fiction films designed to inform the public improved considerably. Universal came up with a good idea in *The Boys from Your State*, which followed the training of units of men from each state; and documentaries such as *Your Fighting Navy at Work and Play*, *Our Coloured Fighters*, and James Montgomery Flagg's *The Spirit of the Red Cross* all made brave stabs at presenting their themes authentically. Even so, errors of judgment occurred, notably with *When Your Soldier is Hit*, which, far from reassuring audiences about the promptness of medical attention on the battlefield, merely alarmed them with its horrifying realism.

The Division of Films also subsidized independent film-makers and lent them resources, controlled overseas distribution to the advantage of American propaganda films, kept pacifist films off the home screens, and acted generally as a morale-booster and encourager of effort.

With this official prompting, stars, directors and producers began to lend their pull and popularity to the war effort, selling Liberty Bonds by appearing in jokey films or by touring the country making speeches, bolstering

31

recruitment into the Army or into the Red Cross, and entertaining those engaged on war duties. All the great personalities of the day did their bit – Mary Pickford, Douglas Fairbanks, Charlie Chaplin, William S. Hart, Lillian Gish, Marie Dressler, Jack Dempsey, DeMille, Dustin Farnum. 'Fatty' Arbuckle even volunteered to go on a public diet to promote food-conservation.

Movies were an obvious aid to recruiting, which took the form of direct appeals (*Over There, The Spirit of '17, A Call to Arms*) and more devious dramas putting draft-dodgers to shame. Typical of the latter was Christy Cabanne's *The Slacker*, in which a rich reprobate is inspired to join up, partly by his wife's patriotism and partly by a gratuitous historical tableau depicting Abraham Lincoln, the ride of Paul Revere and the surrender of General Lee. *Draft 258*, also by Cabanne, followed a similar line, as did a whole string of imitations, including *The Service Star*, with Madge Kennedy, *Mrs Slacker, The Man Who Was Afraid, The Unbeliever* (directed by Alan Crosland who was able to enlist the help of the US Marines, and *A Man Without a Country*. Children were used to heap even greater humiliation on the slackers, as in an early exercise by King Vidor, *Bud's Recruit*, which had a youngster attempting to enlist in the place of his reluctant elder brother. In *A Little Patriot*, another brat urged her friends to spit on draft-dodging fathers.

The importance of morale on the home front was not forgotten. Women were praised and exalted in *Sweetheart of the Doomed* and *Daughter of Destiny*, and were shown expressing proper anxiety for their men in such romances as Blackton's *Missing*. Men unable to enlist were depicted as making valuable contributions to the war effort none the less, as in *The Gown of Destiny* (in which a physically feeble dress-designer buys ambulances for France) and the feature-length *For Freedom of the World*, a veritable anthology of patriotic themes. And endless emphasis was laid on the idea that out of the war would emerge true democracy, with the removal of class barriers and equality of opportunity for all.

At the same time, an ambivalent American citizenry betrayed some less pleasant characteristics. They displayed an insatiable appetite for scenes showing the carnage and destructiveness of war, and regarded with deep suspicion the many German immigrants in their midst. These unfortunates were warned against disloyalty towards their adopted country in such cautionary tales as Raoul Walsh's *The Prussian Cur*, which shows suspected German-American saboteurs being lynched by hooded vigilantes, and Chester Withey's *The Hun Within*. The government-made *The Immigrant* took a less hysterical approach in demonstrating to these foreign-born citizens where their allegiance lay.

Spying, treachery and sabotage were the most popular themes of all at the height of the United States' participation in the war. Every kind of diabolical conspiracy against America was imagined, including the spreading of polio germs (*The Eagle's Eye*), stealing the plans of secret weapons (*The Kaiser's Shadow*), and the sabotaging of shipyards (*Life's Greatest Problem*), aircraft factories (*Suspicion*), troop trains (*Love and the Law*), tungsten-mines (*Mr Logan, USA* – a Tom Mix Western, no less), even a sugar plantation (*The Marriage Ring*). There was scope here, too, for female emancipation to assert itself in the shape of women agents and lady spy-catchers, among whom could be numbered Florence LaBadie (*War and The Woman*), Billie Burke (*In Pursuit of Polly*), Gail Kane (Henry King's *A Soul in Pawn*), Ethel Barrymore (*The Greatest Power*), Theda Bara (*When Men Desire*), and Marion Davies

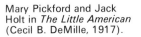

Mary Pickford and Jack Holt in *The Little American* (Cecil B. DeMille, 1917).

(*The Dark Star*). *For the Freedom of the East* could even boast a lady judo expert (the Chinese actress, Tsen Mei).

One of the best of the espionage movies was *Berlin Via America*, in which Francis Ford played a double agent who joins Baron von Richthofen's Flying Circus in order to plot a triumphant Allied raid on Berlin.

Romance was a statutory ingredient of practically all war dramas, but few directors bothered to do more in this respect than have their proudly smiling heroines send their sweethearts off to the front line, and then reunite them at the end of the film. D.W. Griffith was one of the rare exceptions, instilling some welcome character into the two war stories he directed in America in 1918, *The Greatest Thing in Life* and *The Girl Who Stayed at Home*. The first of these starred Lillian Gish (who has always considered it Griffith's best film) and Robert Harron; the second, which was made to encourage enlistment, had Harron, Richard Barthelmess, Clarine Seymour and Carol Dempster. Both movies used some of the mass of footage shot by Griffith for *Hearts of the World*.

As in England, the one treatment to which it was considered the war could not, and should not, lend itself was humour. But as the war progressed and the movies themselves began to reach the areas of greatest stress, namely the front lines and military hospitals, where they were enthusiastically received, so there arose a corresponding demand for comedies to take tense minds off the realities outside the dugout door. There was a similar reaction at home, where melodrama and combat scenes were bound to pall in time, and it was inevitable that sooner or later the war itself would become a subject for fun.

Ridicule of the enemy was, of course, acceptable, with the Kaiser bearing the brunt of it in *Yankee Doodle in Berlin* (with a hilarious impersonation by the boss-eyed Ben Turpin), *The Geezer of Berlin*, and a Mutt and Jeff cartoon, *The Kaiser's New Dentist*. Certain areas such as Home Defence (a kind of Home Guard) and training camps were considered innocuous enough as comic settings, the latter even attracting such stars as Mabel Normand (*Joan of Plattsburg*) and Mary Pickford (*Johanna Enlists*). And parodies – for example, of spy dramas (Sennett's *An International Sneak*, Harold Lloyd's *Kicking the Germ out of Germany*) and propaganda films (*Shades of Shakespeare*) – were permissible. But satire aimed at the war itself was an untried risk.

Untried, that is, until Charlie Chaplin made his brilliant *Shoulder Arms* just as the war was drawing to a close. Chaplin feared that his inventive, ingeniously funny send-up of trench conditions would be offensive, but thanks to his immense popularity and his comic skill, the film was an unqualified success, particularly with soldiers themselves. Putting the tramp

Charlie Chaplin relaxes with the 'Kaiser' and 'John Bull' during the filming of a patriotic propaganda sketch.

figure into ill-fitting uniform hung down with excessive impedimenta (including an egg-beater and a cheese-grater, which turn out to have their uses), and having him shrug off with a gag the desperate hardships of the trenches, made the whole messy affair a little easier to take and at the same time could be recognized as a tacitly humane vote of sympathy for the ordinary soldier. There are, in any case, deliberately poignant scenes such as that in which Charlie, having received no mail from home himself, reads and reacts to a colleague's letter. This kind of brief interlude contrasts most effectively with the hardness of many of the jokes, notably those showing Charlie keeping score as he pots Germans with his rifle, and holding up bottles to be opened by the returning fire. The flooded dugout sequences with Charlie and his buddies trying stoically to sleep while totally submerged in water (and Charlie, with a phonograph trumpet acting as a breathing-tube, succeeding), is a hilarious, farcical exaggeration of wet-weather conditions in the trenches, and is rich with gags – but the hard

Chaplin about to go over the top in *Shoulder Arms* (1918).

core of harsh reality is never entirely lost.

The second half of the film is a dream sequence, with Charlie rescuing a beautiful French girl (Edna Purviance) and capturing the Crown Prince (Jack Wilson) and the Kaiser (Sydney Chaplin), thereby winning the war single-handed.

For some this bold, simple, classic comedy is Chaplin's masterpiece. It is certainly the only war film of lasting magnitude to have emerged from the war itself. It is not, in the pure sense of taking a clear-cut moral stand, an anti-war film; what it does is highlight a set of ridiculous and tragic situations simply by concentrating on the ridiculous rather than the tragic.

Viewed dispassionately, the Great War had an effect on film-making, technically, artistically, socially and emotionally, which was substantial, fundamental and far-reaching.

In specific terms, camera technology and cameramanship were transformed by the war, the cinematographic demands of which had left a rich inheritance of refinements (telephoto lens, hand-held camera, more accurate viewfinders, etc.) and talents (graduates, mainly, of the Army Signal Corps – such future directors as Victor Fleming, George Hill, Ernest Schoedsack, Josef von Sternberg, Alan Crosland, Wesley Ruggles).

In broad terms, the cinema was now recognized as a powerful propaganda weapon, a potential force for good influences as well as bad. Thanks to a four-year absence of European competition, America – more particularly Hollywood – had become the undisputed production centre for films, and the world, in a cinematic sense, was its oyster. And, the most important development of all, the vaguely disreputable medium of the pre-war years had earned respect and gained respectability.

If the Great War could boast anything as noble as a phoenix, perhaps it was the motion picture.

All Quiet...

When the Armistice was signed in 1918, nearly nine million men had been killed and over twenty million more wounded, and the economy of Europe was shattered – and all for reasons which hardly anyone could remember. Not surprisingly, the weary, depleted combatants wanted a respite from war, and one way of achieving this was to remove all manifestations of it from the cinema screens. For England, this was no great hardship since few war movies were being made at this time, anyway; for the American industry, it meant an abrupt, major upheaval as intensive wartime propaganda gave way to palliative peacetime escapism. For a short while after 1918, war films became, with some exceptions, virtually taboo, and the genre remained unpopular until the mid-'twenties.

One of the exceptions came from France, whose position as the world's most progressive film-making nation had been destroyed by the war, but whose contribution to the emergence of film as an art was to be decisive. One of France's most ambitious and talented directors was Abel Gance, and it was his film, *J'Accuse*, which stirred the embers of the late conflict in 1919. This was Gance's first epic, an emphatically pacifist film described by the director himself as a 'modern tragedy . . . a human cry against the bellicose din of armies . . . against the German militarism which destroyed civilized Europe'. It was 'intended to show that if war did not serve some purpose, then it was a terrible waste. . . . To wage war for nothing is totally illogical.' When asked what he meant by the title, Gance explained that he was 'accusing the war, accusing the men, accusing universal stupidity'.

J'Accuse concerns a woman who is raped by German soldiers and consequently has a child. Her husband suspects his best friend, who is in fact in love with the woman. Both men join the Army and go to the front, seeking death. The husband is killed, while his friend, shell-shocked and half-insane, calls up the ghosts of the war dead before dying himself. All this now seems excessively melodramatic, and not entirely impartial, but visually it is an extremely powerful film and it certainly had an impact on contemporary audiences, whose patronage turned it into a considerable success. One commentator wrote that, had it been made in 1913, it might even have prevented the war. The film was remade by Gance in 1937 in an attempt to warn against the impending World War II.

England, alas, had no Gance. Indeed, the indifferent quality of British film-making during the dozen or so years after the war was a fact of life acknowledged even by the contemporary commentators. The best anyone could find to say about it was that it might sometimes rise to 'efficient mediocrity', while the quirky, highly entertaining film periodical 'Close Up' used less equivocal language in describing British production as 'muck' and declaring with measured contempt that the knowledge that a British film was showing in a movie theatre would 'chill the hardiest away from its door'. There was already little inclination to make films about the war, and in this climate there was certainly no chance of anyone producing anything even approaching the stature of *J'Accuse*.

Such fictional war dramas as there were proved fairly unremarkable and showed no advance on previous efforts. Maurice Elvey, just about the only English film-maker of promise at this time (although names like Herbert Wilcox, Michael Balcon, Graham Cutts, Adrian Brunel, Victor Saville, Anthony Asquith, and, of course, Hitchcock, were due to emerge shortly), came up with *Comradeship* (1919), which carried a modicum of disillusion in its story about a pacifist who enlists and is blinded while his friend marries a shopgirl seduced by a German spy. And, in the same year, Martin Thornton made a couple of spy dramas, *The Power of Right* and *The Warrior Strain*, set in Brighton, which dragged in shots of the Prince of Wales, and there was a version of *The Flag Lieutenant*, later remade with some success.

After that, story films about the war numbered a bare half-dozen until the American-inspired revival in the latter half of the 'twenties: an exercise in class snobbery called *General Post*

The Four Horsemen of the Apocalypse (Rex Ingram, 1921).

J'Accuse (Abel Gance, 1919).

Model-work in *Zeebrugge* (H. Bruce Woolfe, 1924).

(1920); a plainly silly semi-documentary melodrama by Percy Nash which purported to tell *How Lord Kitchener Was Betrayed* (1921); an unremarkable adaptation of *The Four Feathers* (1921); *The Reverse of the Medal* (1923), a flying drama with Clive Brook; and George Pearson's partially experimental *Reveille* (1924), about the victory of courage, which starred Betty Balfour and Stewart Rome, and which the director himself described as a 'loosely-built . . . scrapbook of pictures of life caught in the living, no hero, no villain, no plot, no tying up of loose threads, I hoped future audiences would *feel* the things I wanted them to feel.'

The one bright ray of hope in the immediate post-war period was the work done in developing the documentary, reflected in a vogue for scientific, educational and general-interest films, most notable of which were those in the *Secrets of Nature* series. There had been some tentative and largely inefficient attempts to use archive material in 1919 and 1920 – among them Nash's *Women Who Win*, about the women's services, Elvey's *Victory Leaders*, and Fred Paul's crude compilation of War Office actuality film into fifteen two-reel episodes, *The World's Greatest Story*. However, it was one of the industry's mavericks, H. Bruce Woolfe, working for his own company, British Instructional Films, who demonstrated how the war could be effectively presented in factual terms. He did this with a series of six films about World War I battles made and/or produced by him between 1921 and 1927.

The first of these was *The Battle of Jutland* (1921), a decent account of the engagement using a combination of official war film and

38

animated maps and diagrams, which was unexpectedly successful and well received by the critics. Encouraged, Woolfe followed up with *Armageddon* (1923), made with War Office help, a partly re-enacted description of Allenby's campaign in Palestine, and *Zeebrugge* (1924), which included footage of ships being sunk by U-boats, some staged action scenes, and a good deal of ingenious model-work. Woolfe engaged another director, Walter Summers, for his next three productions: *Ypres* (1925), *Mons* (1926) and *The Battles of the Coronel and Falkland Islands* (1927).

Mons was severely criticized in some quarters for being poorly photographed, unrealistic and heavily dependent in its reconstructed scenes on sentimentality. *The Battles of the Coronel and Falkland Islands*, a re-creation of two sea engagements late in 1914, had a far more positive reception, and is normally recognized as being the best of a serious, highly regarded prestige series of 'pre-documentaries'. There were some reservations about the way in which the film romanticized war, but critics were for the most part highly enthusiastic. One called it 'the best naval picture yet made in any country', and even the stern 'Evening Standard' could bring itself to say: 'There has never been a film like *The Falkland Islands*. When the British at last make up their minds to do a thing they do it thoroughly.' With naval co-operation, Woolfe and Summers achieved impressive full-scale reconstructions of the battles, although the difficulty of presenting a modern sea engagement clearly (the ships necessarily being a considerable distance apart) led them to pursue a more personal angle on the drama by introducing actual personalities of the day, portrayed by actors. The public evidently found this ploy acceptable and convincing, and even the movie's severest critic (Bryher in 'Close Up'), while rapping the producers' knuckles for not allowing 'a single suggestion that war was anything other than an elaborate and permissible adventure', conceded that some scenes 'marked a great advance on anything previously seen in an English film'.

An ex-serviceman re-enacting his wartime role in *The Somme* (M.A. Wetherell, 1927).

Roy Travers and fellow German naval officers in *Q Ships* (Geoffrey Barkas, 1928), a dramatized reconstruction of the part played by armed merchantmen in World War I.

wartime footage, and *Q Ships* (1928), a well-made account by Wetherell's producer, Geoffrey Barkas, of the merchant ships used in the war to combat U-boats. But by then the public was beginning to tire of the genre.

Similar to Woolfe's *Battle* films in both style and intention was the best of the French war reconstructions, *Verdun, Visions d'Histoire* (1927), a clever, conscientious dramatization of the epic siege by Léon Poirier. Without avoiding the usual ambivalence of mixing plain heroics with pacifist sermonizing, Poirier's film nevertheless had, in its best moments, a convincing documentary reality. This was achieved by skilful re-creation of action sequences, the blending in of authentic shots of Joffre, Pétain, Foch, the Kaiser, and other notables, and the use of ex-servicemen, rather than professional actors, to play the symbolic character roles of The Old Peasant, The British Tommy, The Youth, etc.

Germany, too, made some good actuality compilations and dramatized documentaries, including *Fighting for the Fatherland* (1926), *Behind the German Lines* (1928), a trilogy called *The Great War*, and *The Emden* (1926). The last of these was an excellent portrait of a cruiser at war, building up genuine tension as the ship moved from engagement to engagement, capturing English ships and their crews and proceeding inexorably to the final bloody battle.

America was due to become, in the mid-'twenties, the source of a massive revival of war films, but in the immediate post-Armistice

There were a couple of attempts by other film-makers to imitate Woolfe's successful technique: *The Somme* (1927), a partial rehash by M.A. Wetherell of the Malins/McDowell

40

period the climate for such offerings was no more conducive in the States than elsewhere. There was a curious hangover of 'vengeance' pictures for a while – like *The Heart of Humanity*, which advocated a lasting formula for peace but at the same time campaigned for revenge for the Germans' invasion of Belgium and their war atrocities; *Why Germany Must Pay*, which demanded retribution for the Nurse Cavell incident; *The Land of the Free* and *Why America Will Win*, two portraits of General Pershing which urged reparations against Germany; *Beware!*, which warned against permitting a revival of German militarism; *Behind the Door*, which showed a US Navy officer flaying a German U-boat commander alive with a razor; and *The Kaiser's Finish*, *America Must Conquer*, *Daughter of Destiny*, and *After the War*, all of which made various unpleasant proposals concerning the Kaiser and his family and military entourage (including public hanging, extermination and sterilization).

The mood passed, however, and even directors lumbered with expensive, unfinished pre-Armistice productions (like Marshall Neilan with *The Unpardonable Sin*) tried to make them conform to the advocacy of the trade press to 'use after-the-war characters . . . avoid harrowing scenes of human destruction . . . carry our thoughts brightly and encouragingly forward'. The few exceptions included a number of comedies, like the Hoot Gibson Western-derived vehicles *Shootin' for Love* and *The Gentleman from America*; occasional star-vehicle melodramas such as *Honour Bright*, with John Gilbert, and *The Love Light*, with Mary Pickford; and several films dealing with the problems of returned soldiers, typified by Herbert Brenon's *The Side Show of Life*, about a clown, a general during the war, unable to readjust to being laughed at, and Frank Borzage's *Humoresque*, concerning the similar predicament of a concert violinist.

There was one major war-oriented production in this doldrum period: *The Four Horsemen of the Apocalypse* (1921), a phenomenally successful epic which made several Hollywood reputations. It turned Metro into a leading studio, brought fame to its director, ex-aviator Rex Ingram, and recognition to its pioneering editor, June Mathis, and created an instant star out of its leading actor, Rudolph Valentino, the moment he appeared in Latin-American fancy-dress and danced the tango with Helena Domingues. Valentino represented a new kind of hero, sexy and experienced, whose seduction technique was made devastating by a fatal combination of chivalry and male chauvinism.

The intention behind *Four Horsemen* was probably to make an anti-war film, but its blindly bigoted attitude towards the Germans (depicting them as blood-lusting savages), the relish and realism of its spectacular battle scenes, and the visual splendour of its symbolism (notably the Four Horsemen themselves – War, Pestilence, Famine and Death – galloping through clouds) created the opposite effect. The

story, too, has nationalistic and patriotic overtones, describing the awakening of a young, high-living Franco-Argentinian to his duty to France when the husband of the woman he loves (Alice Terry) returns blinded from the trenches. Technically and pictorially, however, its virtues are considerable – certainly more so than the ambitious 1961 remake by Vincente Minnelli (with Glenn Ford on a certain loser in the Valentino role) which updated the plot to World War II and lost as much money as its predecessor had earned.

It can be argued that Ingram's *Four Horsemen* owed its success more to its exoticism and glamour and its reactionary emphasis on sentiments of vengeance than to its pretensions to being a true anti-war statement. Nevertheless, it anticipated the big pacifist movies and dramas of disillusionment which were to hold sway during the decade from 1925 until the beginnings of a new awareness of threats to international peace in the mid-'thirties.

A white bandage testifies to the hazards of filming machine-gun fire for the French dramatized documentary, *Verdun, Visions d'Histoire* (Léon Poirier, 1927).

On the set of *The Four Horsemen of the Apocalypse*, with Curt Rehfeld (*second from left*), Rudolph Valentino (*third from left*), John Sainpolis (*in wheelchair*), Alice Terry (*in nurse's uniform*) and director Rex Ingram (*seated in front*).

Back to the Front

The first big revival of the war film (at least as far as World War I was concerned) came in 1925 with as positive a demonstration of its renewed box-office potential as exponents of the genre could have wished for. It came in the shape of King Vidor's *The Big Parade*, which remains one of the most accurate renderings in fiction of the real experience of having fought in, and survived, the Great War. Its sincerity and stature mocked and helped to suppress for a while the absurd, routine heroics, the chauvinism, and the tasteless rookie humour which had always been the statutory ingredients of the standard war film. It also brought fame and recognition to its humanistic director, King Vidor, although artistically the film has been overpraised and was, in Lewis Jacobs's words, 'based in sentimentality' and 'cheapened by "girl-meets-boy" clichés'. Vidor himself admits to some deliberate tear-jerking.

Taken from a story by Laurence Stallings, *The Big Parade* tells simply of an American playboy (John Gilbert, who became one of the top silent-screen stars on the strength of Vidor's film) who befriends two fellow draftees (Tom O'Brien and Karl Dane), falls in love with a French peasant girl (Renée Adorée), and is subjected to the horrors of combat in the trenches. The strength of the film lies in its objectivity, not always maintained but sincerely aimed at. Vidor has described it as an attempt to convey the emotional responses of a man who 'walks through the war and looks at it, neither a pacifist nor a soldier ... simply goes through and has a look and is pulled into these experiences.... He is not overly in favour of the war, nor abnormally belligerent against it ... he goes along for the ride and tries to make the most of each situation as it happens.' He has also declared: 'I am certainly not in favour of wars but I did not want to preach against them.'

The 'Close Up' critic of the day saw the film's greatness 'in the early opening scenes, the sweeping of everyone into something that they did not clearly understand, the enlistment through sheer mass hypnotism, the unthinking but definite cruelty of many women seeing war as romance instead of reality'. She was also appreciative of the courage required to inject into a commercial undertaking 'so much scorn of war, so much stripping of what people in general like to regard as heroism ... the reckless unthinking plunge into an army, the actual dirt and horror and tyranny behind all warfare'.

Vidor's outstanding achievement, however, was his filming of the battle scenes and their build-up. He wanted to convey infantry combat as authentically as possible. After intensive viewing of wartime newsreels and Signal Corps footage, he observed that each aspect of the fighting had its own tempo, and this he imitated brilliantly in the urgency of troops and lorries moving up to the front, followed by the slower, more rhythmic pace of the soldiers' advance through Belleau Wood while machine-gun fire reduces their number. Vidor called his technique 'the transformation of parallel units of action into a kind of musical counterpoint'. 'Close Up' expressed its effect more simply and vividly: 'It was amazing how much fear could be suggested in the mere continuous pace of movement.'

For all its faults (among them a failure *not* to romanticize the war), *The Big Parade* formed a blueprint for that brand of intelligently committed war film which has attempted periodically to describe the predicament of the ordinary citizen caught up in the web of politically motivated warfare.

The Belleau Wood attack is also re-created to good effect in another box-office hit, Raoul Walsh's *What Price Glory?* (1926), an adaptation of the Laurence Stallings/Maxwell Anderson play, famous for its dressing-station scene in which Leslie Fenton cries out with great meaning: 'Stop the blood! Stop the blood!' In other respects, however, the resemblance to *The Big Parade* is slender – indeed, Walsh's film loses much of the sharp, anti-war sentiment of the original play (along with its notorious bad language) by concentrating heavily on the ponderously humorous sexual rivalry of its leading characters, Captain Flagg (Victor McLaglen) and Sergeant Quirt (Edmund Lowe). But cinemagoers didn't seem to

The Blue Max
(John Guillermin, 1966).

43

Scenes from *The Big Parade* (King Vidor, 1925) with John Gilbert (*above*).

mind, and the antics of Flagg and Quirt were continued in *Women of All Nations* and *The Cockeyed World* (1929), which was even bawdier, even more popular than *What Price Glory?* Walsh's film was remade (without distinction) by John Ford in 1952, with James Cagney and Dan Dailey as Flagg and Quirt.

Shortly before *The Big Parade* and *What Price Glory?* had made their sensational appearance, D.W. Griffith had quietly brought out his last important film, *Isn't Life Wonderful?*, a compassionate study of inflation, unemployment and hunger inside post-war Germany (where it was shot). Although superior to Vidor's film on both artistic and humanitarian levels, it flopped at the box-office and contributed to Griffith's subsequent decline. It was a particularly courageous film in that its story of impoverished Polish refugees settling in Germany advocated sympathy for the defeated enemy, whose internal sufferings were proving punishment enough for his crime of aggression. Such sentiments were not popular in the United States of 1924.

Not many films followed Griffith's example in giving the Germans a human face. Those which did included John Ford's *Four Sons* (1928), the story of a German mother who loses three of her sons in the war; Fred Niblo's *The Enemy* (1928), the tragedy of a young Austrian bride, played by Lillian Gish; and *Barbed Wire*, which has Pola Negri, as a French peasant girl, falling in love with a German prisoner of war (Clive Brook).

More common were the myriad comedies, action dramas, romances and spy melodramas spawned by the success of the Vidor and Walsh films, many of which failed even to keep the pot boiling.

Training-camp and front-line farces were rife, and, for the most part, tasteless and unfunny. A typical parade-ground caper was *Rookies* (1927), which had Karl Dane and George K. Arthur falling foul of the Army brass. Funnier – though oddly disturbing – were the opening scenes of *The Strong Man* (1927), in which Harry Langdon, his baby face set in an impish grin, playfully picked off Germans with a machine-gun. Other established comedians – Buster Keaton, Larry Semon, Wheeler and Woolsey – tried their hands at service comedies, but none could

match Laurel and Hardy's *Pack Up Your Troubles* (1932), which had trench gags as good as those in *Shoulder Arms*, plus a not dissimilar climax in which the pair captures a whole German regiment with the aid of a runaway tank.

A minor comment on differing national attitudes to humour was provided incidentally by the American version of *The Better 'Ole* (1926), in which Sydney Chaplin got good comic mileage out of a pantomime horse. This was evidently far more acceptable to American audiences than George Pearson's English-made original of 1918, in spite of (or perhaps because of) the indigenous nature of the humour.

The sudden demand for serious war dramas was satisfied by a plethora of indifferent movies with repetitive plots padded out with chunks of old newsreels. Some stars found themselves commuting to and from the front on a fairly regular basis. Among them was Richard Barthelmess, who came off best in *The Patent Leather Kid* (1927), about a boxer who discovers he is a coward in the trenches, but who is regenerated by a sense of duty and his love for Molly O'Day; and *Out of the Ruins* (1928), in which he deserts to save a girl's honour and survives a firing-squad. Even the cowboy stars found themselves transferred occasionally from the West to the Western Front – Gary Cooper, for example, in *A Man from Wyoming* (1930), and Buck Jones in *The War Horse* (1927).

One or two of the battlefield pictures managed to rise above mere routine. Rowland Lee's *Havoc* (1925), though saddled with a number of unsympathetic characters (George O'Brien, Madge Bellamy and Margaret Livingston were leading players), was praised for its depiction

Victor McLaglen (*left*) as Captain Flagg and Edmund Lowe as Sergeant Quirt in *What Price Glory?* (Raoul Walsh, 1926), with Dolores del Rio.

Bread queue in *Isn't Life Wonderful?* (1924), D.W. Griffith's poignant portrayal of hardship in post-war Germany.

of 'the stark brutality of war, with its horrors of mud, discomfort, privation and death', and vivid action scenes were also a strong feature of *Beyond Victory* (1931), whose cast included William Boyd, James Gleason, Zasu Pitts and Lew Cody. Remembered more than most is Renaud Hoffmann's *The Unknown Soldier* (1926), by all accounts a highly sentimental but affecting story of the return of a soldier from three years at the front to a wife who has never given up hope. A more ambitious affair was Michael Curtiz's somewhat bizarre *Noah's Ark* (1929), which paralleled a modern war story with the Old Testament deluge (during the shooting of which, evidently, several extras were drowned); Dolores Costello, George O'Brien and Myrna Loy were among the time-travellers.

Spy dramas came into fashion once again. The most celebrated of these was Rupert Julian's *Three Faces East* (1926), in which an English girl (Jetta Goudal) outwitted the German secret service. Clive Brook was cast as one of the enemy, and the director himself, pastmaster at Kaiser impersonations, did his usual portrayal of Wilhelm II. A rich crop of exotic lady spies sprang up over the next few years. Pola Negri conducted intrigues on the Austro-Russian frontier in *Hotel Imperial* (1927 – remade in 1939 with Isa Miranda and Ray Milland), while the inscrutable Greta Garbo (described with some perceptiveness in a contemporary edition of the 'Bioscope' as 'one of those enigmatical personalities arousing intense admiration in some, and a feeling akin to antipathy in others') took to espionage twice, in Niblo's *The Mysterious Lady* (1928), with Conrad Nagel, and George Fitzmaurice's celebrated *Mata Hari* (1932), which also boasted Ramon Novarro, Lionel Barrymore and Lewis Stone in a distinguished cast. The latter was also remade, in 1964, with Jeanne Moreau in the name-part; she was fine, contributing nicely to the parody overtones, but the film was otherwise unremarkable.

Spying also crept into naval dramas, such as *Convoy* (1928), directed by Lothar Mendes, and *Mare Nostrum* (1926), Rex Ingram's powerful, melancholic tale of a Spanish merchant captain seeking revenge for some frightfulness committed by a U-boat. More conventionally exciting were *The Seas Beneath* (1931), directed by John Ford and full of his special brand of war bonhomie, though not too convincing, and Jack Conway's technically accomplished *Hell Below* (1933), the story of an American submarine in action, with Robert Montgomery, Walter Huston, Jimmy Durante and Madge Evans.

Tear-jerkers with a war theme were also popular, if somewhat exploitative. *Corporal Kate*, for instance, copied *The Big Parade*, but perversely sent its *heroine* off to the front to lose a limb (an arm, as opposed to John Gilbert's leg). Robert E. Sherwood's play, *Waterloo Bridge*, a weepie about a London chorus girl's hopeless love for a Canadian soldier, enjoyed

Above: Alice Terry and Antonio Moreno in *Mare Nostrum* (Rex Ingram, 1926).

William Wellman's *Wings* (1927), with (*above*) Charles 'Buddy' Rogers after he has shot down best friend Richard Arlen, and (*below*) Rogers, Arlen and Gary Cooper.

its first screen adaptation in James Whale's 1931 version with Mae Clark and Kent Douglass (to be remade in 1940 by Mervyn LeRoy, who found Vivien Leigh and Robert Taylor in good acting form). The ultimate in war romances, however, was Frank Borzage's *Seventh Heaven* (1927), which paired Janet Gaynor and Charles Farrell ('the ideal couple') for the first time, in an emotional love story set in Paris which ended with the hero returning blinded from the war to the arms of his sweetheart. It was a great success in the States, acquired a cult following abroad, and captured three Oscars, including one each for Borzage and Gaynor. In 1937, the film was pleasantly remade by Henry King, with Simone Simon and James Stewart.

A more significant Oscar-winner – the first film, in fact, to gain an Academy Award – made its appearance in 1927: William Wellman's monumental *Wings*. This was the first film to deal importantly with aerial combat and to provide the relatively unexploited theme of aviation with the broad canvas it required. It was also the last of the great silent spectaculars, yet at the same time it sparked off a whole frenetic series of aviation movies, many of which fed hungrily off the parent pictures and each other in order to fatten up their aerial scenes. None of them, however, came near to matching the artistry, technique or epic quality of *Wings*.

The appeal of the flying film was obvious: the air aces of World War I were the last of the chivalrous knights, colourful, dashing, courageous, fatalistic, engaged in an esoteric struggle that had nothing to do with the political issues which governed what happened on the ground. This was deadly jousting for personal honour, spiced with the chilling

Wings

statistic that the average life of a combat pilot in the air was a mere forty-eight hours. The reasons Hollywood took so long to realize the possibilities of aerial conflict were also easy to deduce: the hazards, the technical and climatic problems, and a reluctance to launch such a costly project without evidence (eventually supplied by the box-office returns from *The Big Parade*) that the public was ready to accept a war subject on the grand scale.

William Wellman, relatively raw apart from an unexpected success with *You Never Know Women*, was the young director selected to surmount the attendant obstacles (with generous War Department help) – on the grounds that he was the only available director who had seen active duty as a pilot (with the Lafayette Flying Corps, an offshoot of the legendary Lafayette Escadrille). He proved an inspired choice: courageous, far-sighted, demanding, uncompromising, and instantly alive to the complexities of photographing aircraft in flight. He and cameraman Harry Perry quickly learned, for example, that you needed a combination of sun *and* cloud to form a backdrop which would give scale, speed and perspective to the flying scenes. 'We waited,' said Perry, 'for the right kind of clouds. . . . Against the clouds we could see the planes dart at each other. . . . We could sense the plummet-like drop of a disabled plane. . . . Always we had to contend with the immobility of the sky as a background. We found long shots were more spectacular and effective than close-ups.' Wellman put it more bluntly – 'Against a blue sky, it's like a lot of goddam flies!' – and had no qualms about holding up shooting for a month if necessary to get exactly the right conditions.

Wellman was also an innovator, making exciting use of camera movement. He practically invented the big boom shot when he sailed his cameras over the table-tops in the famous French café scene – though he became disparaging about it when every other director in Hollywood started adopting the same techniques.

All this virtuosity applied, of course, mainly to the actual filming, the aerial sequences in particular. The script is strictly routine – telling the conventional, contrived story of two friends (Buddy Rogers and Richard Arlen), both in love with refined Jobyna Ralston, who join the Air Service when war is declared. Clara Bow, the girl next door, has a crush on Buddy Rogers. In France, after training, the boys experience aerial combat – and a little relaxation in Paris, where Clara, now in the Red Cross, coincidentally finds Rogers dead drunk. Eventually the friends fall out over Jobyna prior to going off on patrol. Arlen is shot down, but succeeds in commandeering a German Fokker which he proceeds to fly back to the Allied base. Rogers unwittingly shoots him down, learning only subsequently that it is his friend he has killed. Later, he becomes aware of his love for Clara. Some of this is long and wearisome, and there are a number of unbearably maudlin moments with the resistible Richard Arlen, such as those when he bids farewell to his family. But there are compensations, too – notably a riveting four-minute appearance by Gary Cooper, which must have had a dozen producers reaching for their long-term contracts.

The *raison d'être* for *Wings*, however, is what goes on in the air. Army officers, cadets and stunt-pilots, led by the intrepid Dick Grace, did the flying, producing such highlights as the encounter with Captain Kellermann's Flying Circus; an attack on a German Gotha bomber; the strafing of enemy observation balloons; and the massing of scores of aircraft for the reconstruction of the St Mihiel Battle. It is difficult to go all the way with Kevin Brownlow's eulogistic opinion that 'death and destruction have seldom been more lyrically and sweepingly portrayed', but *Wings* is nevertheless a stunning achievement.

The first inferior imitations of Wellman's record-breaking blockbuster appeared in 1927 and 1928 and included *Hard Boiled Haggarty*, with Milton Sills; a Rin-Tin-Tin adventure, *Dog of the Regiment*; and a couple of low-budget affairs called *The Lone Eagle* and *Captain Swagger*. George Fitzmaurice's *Lilac Time* (1928), starring Colleen Moore and the now highly regarded Gary Cooper, was better. It carried some well-handled and original aerial footage to sharpen up the sentimental story of pilot Cooper's love for a French girl, Miss Moore, who mistakenly believes he has died after crashing conveniently near to her back garden.

Wellman's next aerial venture was *The Legion of the Condemned* (1928), with Gary Cooper (again) as one of 'a group of valiant young men whose last illusions and first women were dim memories, and who had tried everything in life but death'. Unused shots from *Wings* were incorporated to equally good effect. Wellman did the exercise yet again in *Young Eagles* (1930), complete with Buddy Rogers and old *Wings* material, but even he disliked it.

The first air drama capable of competing with *Wings* in scope and spectacle took off in 1930. *Hell's Angels* was a project dreamed up by Howard Hughes to 'glorify and perpetuate the exploits of the Allied and German airmen of the World War', a sentiment which might have been expanded at the end of the filming to take in the three men killed during shooting of the flying sequences.

Silent at first, the film was eventually refurbished with dialogue and a new leading lady (Jean Harlow) to replace the thickly accented Greta Nissen. Hughes himself took over the direction from Luther Reed, and called in James Whale to oversee the dialogue scenes. He also added two-colour Technicolor to one of the sequences, and all in all managed to plough a phenomenal $4,000,000 into the entire project.

The time, effort and money were well spent, however, for although the public dismissed the plot as absurd, they were bowled over by the aerial scenes. These included a Zeppelin raid on London, followed by an attack on the Zeppelin by four planes, three of which were shot down, the fourth destroying the airship by kami-kaze methods; and a mission against a munitions depot, which led to an epic dogfight

Howard Hughes's *Sky Devils* (A. Edward Sutherland, 1932), which starred Spencer Tracey, William Boyd and Ann Dvorak, and borrowed its aerial scenes from *Hell's Angels*.

involving no fewer than thirty-one aircraft.

Ben Lyon and James Hall were the stars of the film, barely emerging unscathed from a story which cast them as brothers, rivals for the seductive charms of the amoral Miss Harlow ('Would you be shocked,' she asks Ben Lyon, 'if I got into something more comfortable?'), one of whom kills the other when he threatens treachery. The scenes of spectacle, however, were compensation enough for the triteness of the screenplay.

The Sky Hawk appeared at about the same time as *Hell's Angels*, but was no better than routine. The opposite is true of another 1930 production, *The Dawn Patrol*, a Richard Barthelmess vehicle directed by Howard Hawks which was made and released with a minimum of publicity and fuss, despite its subject-matter. Accurately described by Georges Sadoul as a 'virile and violent film', *Dawn Patrol* really belongs among the small but powerful group of fervently pacifist movies which emerged in the early 'thirties, although its dazzling special effects, and stylish, exciting air sequences prevent it from being as positive a statement as, say, *All Quiet on the Western Front*.

The grim story tells of a squadron of Britain's Royal Flying Corps which is rapidly being decimated by the Germans. When Barthelmess becomes squadron leader, the strain and anguish of command lead him first to crack up and then to undertake a suicide mission, bequeathing his leadership to his friend, played by Douglas Fairbanks Jr. There is an authentic

undertow of fear and futility in the dialogue and characterizations, and the senselessness of war is well conveyed.

Edmund Goulding directed a decent remake of *Dawn Patrol* in 1938, with Errol Flynn and David Niven effectively matched in the

Douglas Fairbanks Jr, Richard Barthelmess and Neil Hamilton in *The Dawn Patrol* (Howard Hawks, 1930).

Basil Rathbone, David
Niven and Errol Flynn in
Edmund Goulding's worthy
remake of *The Dawn Patrol*
(1938).

Fredric March in *The Eagle
and the Hawk* (Stuart
Walker and Mitchell Leisen,
1933).

Bartholomess and Fairbanks roles. The script was virtually the same and all the flying sequences were lifted from the original version, but there was a slight shift in emphasis towards a pro-war sentiment more in line with the times.

Another aviation movie which emphasized human suffering was the mature, anti-glamorous *The Eagle and the Hawk* (1933) whose action sequences were largely from other films. Fredric March played a neurotic pilot who commits suicide after making an impassioned speech about the wastefulness of war. Cary Grant played his cool buddy, and Carole Lombard an understanding and amorous acquaintance.

The air combat of World War I has been virtually ignored on film since the remake of *Dawn Patrol*, apart from reminders in odd movies like the Astaire/Rogers biopic *The Story of Vernon and Irene Castle* (1939), *Men with Wings* (1938), a history of aviation with Fred MacMurray and Ray Milland, and William Wellman's sadly inept last fling, *Lafayette Escadrille* (1958).

Two more recent productions have pointed to a possible revival – *The Blue Max* (1966) and *Von Richthofen and Brown* (1971, *The Red Baron* in Britain). The former, directed by John Guillermin, is long and ambitious and has some fine, carefully handled flying sequences, but, complained the 'Monthly Film Bulletin', it is 'padded out with tedious chunks of indoor chat . . . leaving the audiences with little more to do than speculate about improvements in the disrobing technique of Ursula Andress'. *Von Richthofen and Brown*, with John Phillip Law and Don Stroud in the name-parts, is Roger Corman's version of the personal conflict between the romantic, dashing, irresponsible German ace and the cold, professional tactician of the new school out to destroy him. Efficient, glossy, and intelligently scripted, it nevertheless lacks warmth and is memorable only for Don Stroud's portrayal of Brown.

There was no equivalent among British film offerings of the mid-'twenties to the Hollywood aviation spectacular, but as in the USA, war films in general enjoyed a substantial revival in Britain after the success of *The Big Parade*. Films with solemn war themes commonly won lead reviews in newspapers and the trade press, and they were frequently regarded as the industry's major prestige productions. Even the fearsome and disdainful 'Close Up' deigned to comment on them occasionally, though usually as an excuse to deliver a blistering broadside at British film-making standards.

One dissenting voice was that of 'Picturegoer' which, in a 1926 article entitled 'Featuring Mars', deplored the way in which filmmakers on both sides of the Atlantic were turning 'one of the illest winds that ever blew across the universe' to profitable account, and went on to point out, presumably without too much exaggeration, that 'a picture presenting a member of any of the Allied armies killing a German, will still rouse a burst of hysterical cheering from the major portion of an audience'.

However, such expressions of pacifism from
popular quarters, though they became common enough a few years later, were rare at this
time, and the war film flourished. For four years
or so, a familiar blend of battle scenes and trite
love plots was regurgitated in dozens of unlikely dramas about the war: *Every Mother's
Son*, with Rex Davis; *Second to None*; Herbert
Wilcox's *Mumsie*; two more Rex Davis vehicles,
Remembrance and *Motherland*; *Land of Hope
and Glory*, with Ellaline Terriss, *The Luck of
the Navy*, with Evelyn Laye, and *Carry On!*,
with Moore Marriott, all of which had espionage complications; M.A. Wetherell's somewhat
naïve *Victory*; Sinclair Hill's ambitious and
well-liked *The Guns of Loos*, which boasted
Madeleine Carroll, Bobby Howes and Her-
mione Baddeley among a distinguished cast;
the imperialistic *Tommy Atkins*; an early version of *The Lost Patrol*; Arthur Maude's *Poppies
of Flanders*, adapted from a 'Sapper' story;
George J. Banfield's tragedy set in occupied
Belgium, *The Burgomaster of Stilemonde*, with
Sir John Martin Harvey; the self-explanatory
Cockney Spirit in the War series, with Donald
Calthrop (episodes included *All Riot on the
Western Front*); and a Victor Saville warm-up,
The W Plan, a richly cast (Brian Aherne,
Madeleine Carroll, Gordon Harker, etc.) im-
probable spy adventure (the Germans, said one
reviewer, were shown as 'a race endowed with
abnormal simplicity').

In addition to these largely indifferent offerings there was a handful of war pictures which
managed to rise above the general mediocrity
as well as prove successful at the box-office. A
characteristic example was Adrian Brunel's
Blighty, which mixed extensive actuality footage into an Ivor Montagu story of extreme
sentimentality, and brought together a fine
cast which included Ellaline Terriss, Lillian
Hall-Davis, Jameson Thomas, Seymour Hicks,

John Hamilton and Alexander Field in the series, *The Cockney Spirit in the War* (Castleton Knight, 1930).

Henry Edwards (*centre, with revolver*) and Fred Raynham (*with moustache*) in *Further Adventures of the Flag Lieutenant* (Maurice Elvey, 1927).

Performance. It starred a highly praised Henry Edwards as a lieutenant unjustly branded as a coward in spite of saving a beleaguered fort, and 'Bioscope' said it 'should be shown everywhere'. The film's success inspired a sequel, the less satisfactory *Further Adventures of the Flag Lieutenant*, and was remade in the early 'thirties.

Elvey's other hit of 1926 was *Mademoiselle from Armentières*, a Victor Saville story describing how the French heroine of the famous song (played by Elvey's popular discovery, Estelle Brody) helps captured English troops by using her influence with the enemy. (This also led to a sequel, the non-war *Mademoiselle Parley Voo*.) This he followed in 1927 with *Roses of Picardy*, which starred John Stuart and which was praised for its convincing battle scenes and for being 'sincere, efficient, restrained'. Elvey's success with these films was a demonstration of his shrewdness, practicality, technical skill and ability to assess (and milk) public taste at any given time.

One of the most celebrated films of this brief period was Herbert Wilcox's 1928 production, *Dawn*, attitudes to which hinted at a change in the mood that had made war films such a healthy box-office commodity. *Dawn* told the story of Edith Cavell, the nurse who helped Englishmen to escape from Belgium in 1914

a young Godfrey Winn, and Wally Patch.

By far the best and most consistently successful director of war films at this juncture was Maurice Elvey, who reeled off three popular titles in quick succession. He was particularly adept at handling crowd and battle scenes, as he demonstrated in *The Flag Lieutenant*, a major production which received Admiralty backing, and was given a Royal Command

until she was captured and executed by the Germans. The name-part was impressively played by Sybil Thorndike and the story honestly enough told, but the film aroused bitter controversy at government level and sparked off an unpleasant censorship case. Although not especially hostile towards Britain's one-time enemy, it was proclaimed that 'exhibition of the film would be undesirable on the grounds of international comity' – or, as George Bernard Shaw put it more bluntly, the film was 'suppressed on the ridiculous pretext that it might offend Germany'.

The Foreign Secretary and the German Ambassador both objected strongly to the film, the former describing it as an 'outrage on a noble woman's memory'; the press fanned the flames, questions were asked in Parliament, and sufficient pressure was put on the Board of Film Censors for it to deny *Dawn* a certificate. Most local authorities, however, including London, passed the film for exhibition, and it entered England's cinemas in a blaze of useful publicity.

The film itself marked an advance in Wilcox's skills, a maturing of technique and a growing preference for simpler narratives. It even impressed the strong-hearted 'Close-Up', whose critic, while not going so far as to acclaim it as an important piece of cinema, found it 'an

Sybil Thorndike as Edith Cavell in *Dawn* (Herbert Wilcox, 1928).

invigorating influence' and described it as 'an interesting work because it tells a straightforward story straightforwardly, is beautifully acted by Sybil Thorndike, and, dealing with a theme still full of dynamite, it was thoroughly impartial and honourable in its treatment'.

More significantly, *Dawn* carried a vein of humanity and demonstrated an antipathy to war which anticipated the great pacifist films of the early 'thirties.

Maurice Elvey's *Mademoiselle from Armentières* (1926).

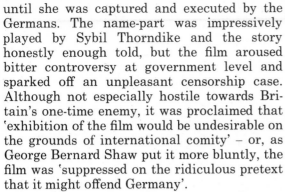

55

Peace Offerings

The continuing popularity of post-World War I war films overlapped with the beginnings of sound and brought to the screen the first, and some of the greatest, major pacifist statements to be expressed in motion-picture form (*pace* certain noble precursors such as *J'Accuse*). This new, mature, and largely unequivocal attitude towards the futility of war continued to prevail until the mid-'thirties, when the growing instability of world peace caused film-makers to revert to expressions of patriotism and aggression in preparation for the inevitable conflict to come. One irony of the anti-war films of this period was that their effectiveness tended to cloud any awareness of what was happening in the fascist countries and helped to delay both Britain's preparedness for and America's entry into the desperate fray of World War II.

Hatred of war was clearly expressed, in Britain, by Maurice Elvey's *High Treason* (1929), Gaumont's first all-talking sound feature. This futuristic fantasy, set in 1940 and starring Benita Hume and Jameson Thomas, imagines a confrontation between two world super-powers provoked by vested interests. In the nick of time, women unite to prevent war. Although bearing faint traces of *Battleship Potemkin*, the film is fairly naïve and hardly merits the 'Bioscope' critic's excited eulogy: 'A production . . . which confirms the impression that the talking picture is the medium in which Britain is qualified to lead the world. Comparisons with the great German film *Metropolis* will naturally arise, but as popular entertainment such comparisons must be in favour of the British film.' (Curiously, the reviewer then went on to criticize the sound as being the film's weak point.) Its sentiments were sincere, however, and its standard of prophecy high (though in depicting a completed Channel tunnel it turned out to be somewhat premature).

The new mood was confirmed in the vignette, *Memories*, in which a group of club members (Jameson Thomas, John Stuart, John Longden, Jack Raine) recall the 1914–18 War and express a fervent hope for the maintenance of peace. And it was continued in *Two Worlds* (1930), a rather pretentious drama of divided loyalties.

However, these were only very hesitant pleas for peace compared with the sudden and uncompromising rejection of war which, in 1930, found expression in three of the cinema's most significant comments on World War I: Lewis Milestone's *All Quiet on the Western Front*, G.W. Pabst's *Westfront 1918*, and Anthony Asquith's *Tell England*. It is not unimportant to note that the directors of these three films were, respectively, an American (albeit of Russian birth), a German, and an Englishman, and that between them they represented a neat triangle of attitudes and methods. *All Quiet . . .* tends to work through poetic means, *Westfront 1918* favours stark realism, and *Tell England* (restricted as it is by a built-in chauvinism) stands somewhere between the two.

Milestone's film – a faithful but wholly cinematic distillation of Erich Maria Remarque's novel about the gradual decimation of a German unit in World War I – has become, if not the most praised, then certainly the most reappraised of all war films. It falls occasionally into the common traps of romanticizing aspects of the very thing it is condemning (e.g. the camaraderie generated by war) and of carrying an excess of symbolism and sentimentality. But despite such weaknesses, the film is a potent indictment of what Robert Hughes calls 'the basic . . . contradiction of war: men fight other men who are like themselves'. When the young hero (Lew Ayres) reaches his moment of deepest disillusionment and despair, the message comes across, clearly and unequivocally: 'When it comes to dying for your country, it's better not to die at all.' And it is this total commitment to non-partisan non-violence (emphasized by the fact that the film's viewpoint is German, not American) which is the great strength of *All Quiet. . . .*

The film is about the brutality of warfare, dramatized by following the brief lives of a detachment of young recruits on the French front in 1916. They are initiated by a veteran (Louis Wolheim) and tyrannized by a fierce NCO (John Wray). Enthusiastic and patriotic at first, they rapidly become disillusioned and

Lewis Milestone's *All Quiet on the Western Front* (1930).

57

High Treason (Maurice Elvey, 1929).

played by Raymond Griffith, an accomplished silent comedian forced to retire when talkies arrived because of a voice affliction, but able to make this one final appearance since the part did not require him to speak); Ayres carrying the wounded Wolheim on his back and chatting cheerfully to him, not knowing he has been killed by a shell splinter; and, of course, the closing scene of the hand reaching out from the trenches to clutch at a butterfly only to fall limply back as a sniper's bullet thuds home. The butterfly ending was, according to Bryan Forbes, apparently suggested to Milestone by the swishing of the windscreen-wipers on his car, and the whole scene shot on impulse, in the rain, using some swiftly acquired butterflies (Hollywood being able to supply such exotica at short notice), car headlamps to light the camera, and Milestone's own hand and arm to carry out the poignant last act.

All Quiet . . . was well received in America, but banned in France (staying banned until 1962) and forced off the screen in Germany by demonstrating Nazis (who allegedly wrecked the Berlin première by letting white mice loose in the audience). *Westfront 1918*, Pabst's parallel exercise to *All Quiet . . .*, met with a similarly hostile reaction in its own country, but was acclaimed elsewhere and is considered by many to be superior to Milestone's film.

The chief purpose of *Westfront*, brilliantly realized, was to arrive at an objective, truthful, naturalistic depiction of trench warfare: its desolation and deadliness, its monotony and muddy chaos. Pabst achieves this with long tracking shots, taking in barren stretches of land strewn with bodies and smoke-straddled barbed wire, and, in the action sequences, by giving an impression of the actual experience of battle rather than a careful staging of it. Dialogue is kept to a minimum and there is effective use of natural sounds.

The film follows the existence of four ordinary soldiers fighting on the French front during the last months of the war. Between them, they experience love, infidelity, insanity, and, ultimately, death. They are the innocent and helpless victims of a grotesque stupidity, and the poignancy of their predicament is emphasized rather than diminished by Pabst's austere approach and the film's pervading atmosphere of pessimism. *Westfront* is, as the French film historians, Bardèche and Brasillach have described it, a 'sombre and hopeless picture of war'.

Pabst followed *Westfront 1918* with *Kameradschaft*, which is not strictly speaking a war film, but which makes a strong, persuasive plea for international brotherhood and lasting peace between nations. It reconstructs an actual mining disaster in which German miners go to the aid of their stricken French comrades, ignoring old animosities and national frontiers. After the rescue, the workers pledge unity against war, and a Frenchman says, 'Why don't we stick together when we need each other? Why not always?' But after a while officials come back and replace the frontier barriers

are progressively wiped out, only to be replaced at the end by another set of eager youngsters. Lewis Jacobs described the theme as 'a critical recapitulation of the slaughter of innocents', and praised its sincerity and integrity above all else. The film itself asserts, in a preface, that it is 'to be neither an accusation nor a confession, and least of all an adventure, for death is not an adventure to those who stand face to face with it. It will try simply to tell of a generation of men who, even though they may have escaped its shells, were destroyed by the war.'

It was also, for its time, a remarkable film technically. Milestone planned it as a sound film, but it kept many 'silent' values; thus while acting and speech appear a little stiff, the camerawork, cutting (Milestone was considered a brilliant, innovatory editor) and pictorial values are fluid, rhythmic and imaginative, uninhibited by early talkie conventions. The scenes at the front have an authentic feeling of waste, desolation and menace, and the relentlessly grey, chaotic, drawn-out panoramas of trench warfare are justly celebrated.

The film contains many famous sequences and set-pieces which still retain their power: the much-coveted soft-leather boots being continually taken over as successive owners are killed; Lew Ayres rambling impotently on about the brotherhood of man and the futility of killing as he watches his French foe die beside him in a shell crater (the latter was between the French and German mines.

In many ways, *Tell England* is the antithesis of Pabst's films. Where the German director is sober, restrained and concerned with classless comradeship, Asquith is theatrical, emotional and steeped in upper-crust nostalgia. But their aims were the same, and when, in the latter half of the film, Asquith allows his instinctive talents full rein, *Tell England* emerges as a genuine and valid anti-war statement as well as one of the most accomplished of English films.

The enterprising producer Bruce Woolfe had for some while been planning an epic about the Gallipoli campaign along the lines of his earlier *Zeebrugge*, *Mons*, and other battle reconstructions, with the bright young Asquith as director and Geoffrey Barkas (who had made *The Somme* and *Q Ships*) as co-director. The decision to adapt Ernest Raymond's acutely class-bound novel proved a major drawback, but once the film escaped from its reactionary literary bonds into the bitter campaign scenes (splendidly re-created by Asquith in Malta) it took on a grim reality which has rarely been matched.

The story of *Tell England* echoes *All Quiet* in that it concerns two friends, public school-boys (called, symbolically, Edgar Doe and Rupert Ray) who have been instilled with an irrepressible romanticism and enthusiasm for the war with Germany. They enlist, become officers, are sent to Gallipoli, and experience a gradual erosion of their illusions and jingoistic high spirits. One of them cracks up, but

Lew Ayres (*left*) and Ben Alexander in *All Quiet on the Western Front*.

French and German veterans of World War I — seen here relaxing together between takes — engaged to recreate the fighting in *Westfront 1918* (G.W. Pabst, 1930).

From public school . . .

recovers in time to lead a heroic raid on the Turkish trenches which leaves him mortally wounded. Finally, the British withdraw, tacitly acknowledging that a sizeable military blunder has been perpetrated, and leaving behind them a mass of English graves to commemorate another tragic and futile campaign.

Jeffrey Richards, in his very entertaining study of cinema ideologies, 'Visions of Yesterday', views the imperialistic stance and boarding school ethics of *Tell England* with unmerciful contempt – a little unfairly at this distance, when social attitudes have softened. It is true, though, that Asquith's film does establish a number of the common characteristics of the British fictional war film: the emphasis on the officers (well bred, well educated, intelligent, heroic) rather than the other ranks (comic, patronized, salt-of-the-earth, dependable, stupid) who serve principally as cooks and cannon-fodder; the commanding officer as father-figure (or headmaster); the stiff-upper-lippery at moments of stress and the general attitude that war is a game; the Old Boy camaraderie and repressed emotionalism of the relationships; the redemption, by a recklessly (and usually fatal) heroic deed, by a coward (or drunkard, or otherwise less-than-perfect personality); and the insular nationalism and utter rightness of the British cause ('Tell England,' says the epitaph on Edgar Doe's grave, 'ye who pass this monument, we died for her and rest content').

Another study of disillusionment in the

. . . to Gallipoli. Tony Bruce and Carl Harbord in *Tell England* (Anthony Asquith, 1930), with Fay Compton (*above*) and (*right*) C.M. Hallard and Dennis Hoey.

trenches, James Whale's *Journey's End*, a faithful adaptation of R.C. Sheriff's remarkably successful play, was produced (in America) in 1930. In this, the conventions and characteristics described above are, if anything, even more distilled, and Sheriff's play has been called 'the most effective propaganda for the English upper classes written in our time'. Nevertheless, it is a compelling piece of work and still effective as a film in spite of its single set, static camerawork and overwrought performance from Colin Clive as the sensitive, drink-sodden Stanhope.

Few of the war films produced after the vintage year of 1930 were able to match the power or significance of *All Quiet . . .* or *Westfront 1918*, but some succeeded in making interesting statements none the less.

In 1931, Viktor Trivas, a pupil of Pabst's, made one of the most progressive films of pre-Hitler Germany, *Hell on Earth* (also known as *No Man's Land*). An intensely pacifist film which tried to emulate *Westfront 1918*, it is a fantasy about five soldiers of differing nationalities (a Frenchman, an American Negro, a German, a Briton, and a Jew) who get lost in the front lines in 1918 and fetch up together in an abandoned trench. As the war rages on, they learn to tolerate, understand and respect each other. Although not as accomplished nor as effective as Pabst's film, it is an original idea, well executed and sincerely conveyed.

It was unusual at this period to use satire as a means of denouncing war and international intrigue, but there were one or two brave exponents, the most famous of whom were the Marx Brothers. Their deliciously funny *Duck Soup* (1933) is a merciless send-up of pomp, diplomacy, fascism, militarism, and war itself, with Groucho as an anarchic president ('There must be a war,' he says, 'I've paid a month's rent on the battlefield'), and Harpo and Chico as peanut-vending revolutionaries. A chaotic, climactic battle incorporates such classic gags as Groucho pulling down the blinds of a house to stop the shells coming in.

Belgian director Henri Storck's brief, savage attack on political chicanery, *L'Histoire du Soldat Inconnu*, uses satire more polemically. A compilation of actuality material, taking in military parades, riots, unemployment and warfare, it is a denunciation of capitalism and the middle classes who finance militarism. Norman McLaren's early montage exercise, *Hell Unlimited* (1936), has a similar theme.

One of the more thoughtful dramas to come out of Hollywood in the early 'thirties was Ernst Lubitsch's scarcely remembered but much admired *The Man I Killed* (also known as *Broken Lullaby*, 1932), a study of the emotional damage suffered by a sensitive French soldier (Phillips Holmes) after he has killed a German in the war. Guilt-ridden, he anonymously seeks out the dead man's family after the Armistice and is accepted by them as a friend before finally facing up to the cause of his torment. Although marred by an over-hysterical performance from the

"How can I eat when Osborne's lying out there?"

David Manners and Colin Clive in *Journey's End* (James Whale, 1930).

61

Chico and Harpo undermine Louis Calhern's dignity in the Marx Brothers comedy *Duck Soup* (Leo McCarey, 1933).

inadequate Phillips Holmes, Lubitsch's style and sincerity made this a moving and unjustly ignored film.

Also unusual is Edward Ludwig's violent tirade against the munitions industry, *The Man Who Reclaimed His Head* (1933), in which Claude Rains is a pacifist journalist in contention with an ambitious newspaper-proprietor (Lionel Atwill) who has sold out to a powerful group of armament-manufacturers. Somewhat

simplistic and prone to heavy symbolism (the juxtaposition of bayonet and crucifix, for example), this is nevertheless one of the bitterest anti-war statements to come out of Hollywood.

An American director credited with great social awareness in the 'thirties was Frank Borzage, who was often engaged to direct anti-war films, the best known being his version of Ernest Hemingway's tragic love story, *A*

Symbolism from *The Man I Killed* (Ernst Lubitsch, 1932).

Farewell to Arms (1933). Set on the Italian front in World War I, this has Gary Cooper as an American officer who falls in love with an English nurse (Helen Hayes). They are separated and he deserts, only to discover her desperately ill; finally, as the bells of the Armistice ring out, she dies in his arms. Borzage's restrained, sympathetic direction and the effective war scenes (in particular, second-unit director Charles Vidor's impressive handling of the Italian withdrawal at Caporetto) justify the adjectives of one contemporary review, which found the film 'vivid, thrilling and poignant'. It is certainly superior to the 1958 remake, in which the casting of Rock Hudson and Jennifer Jones in the Cooper/Hayes roles proved less than ideal.

Borzage brought two more important pacifist novels to the screen: *No Greater Glory* (1934, from Ferenc Molnar's 'The Paul Street Boys') and Remarque's *Three Comrades* (1938). The first of these is an anti-militaristic allegory, set in Hungary in 1914, in which rival gangs of schoolboys wage organized war over possession of a playground in exact imitation of their elders, until one of the young combatants becomes seriously ill and dies as a result of his enthusiasm for the 'game'. Undue emphasis on the heroism and glamour of warfare obscures the film's anti-war sentiments to some extent, but it stands as an effective comment on the folly of jingoism. *Three Comrades*, about a trio of ex-soldiers (Robert Taylor, Franchot Tone, Robert Young) struggling to survive in a depressed post-war Germany, wavers between sensitivity and sentimentality, but shows genuine sympathy for the defeated enemy.

Similar to *Three Comrades* in theme (and yet another Remarque adaptation) is James Whale's *The Road Back* (1937), a continuation of *All Quiet . . .* into the post-war years which

Gary Cooper in *A Farewell to Arms* (Frank Borzage, 1933).

highlights the despair and disillusionment of a defeated nation and the problems of readjustment to civilian life after the hell of the trenches. Whale made effective use of *All Quiet . . .* sets, and borrowed Slim Summerville from the original cast, but weakened the power of his message (that war makes murderers of us all) with inappropriate injections of comedy and sentimentality.

There are ambiguities also in Hawks's glossy

'The Paul Street Boys' of Frank Borzage's *No Greater Glory* (1934).

Great War melodrama, *The Road to Glory* (1936), which mixes repellently horrific aspects of war with unashamed nationalism, a hint that Hollywood was beginning to revise its pacifist stance as threats of another war were looming. However, skilful direction and decent playing by Fredric March, Warner Baxter and Lionel Barrymore (as a symbolic veteran of the Franco-Prussian War) help to alleviate the chauvinism. Hawks's film was a remake of Raymond Bernard's *Les Croix de Bois* (1932), a film produced and acted entirely by French ex-participants of the war. Its enduring potency to evoke the realities of the Great War was movingly demonstrated in 1962 when, following a revival of the film on television, a veteran of the trenches tried to kill himself.

Readjustment was a well-worked theme in American films, a principal concern being the criminal susceptibilities of ex-soldiers disoriented and brutalized by the war. In *They Gave Him a Gun* (1937) W.S. Van Dyke attempted to show how war breeds gangsters in a story about a decent man, trained to kill in the war, who becomes a professional murderer in peacetime. The Depression and its effect on veterans was also a matter for occasional concern, cropping up, rather bizarrely, as a lavish production number in the magical Mervyn LeRoy/Busby Berkeley musical, *Gold Diggers of 1933*, in which Joan Blondell, to a backing of marching doughboys, sings out a plea to 'Remember My Forgotten Man'.

Forgotten Men happened also to be the title given to a brace of disturbing documentaries made simultaneously in America and England in 1934. Their joint aims were to present the Great War 'as it was', to ensure that those who died did not become forgotten men, and to make youth aware of the horrors of modern warfare and thus prevent its reoccurrence. They were quite separate productions (the American version was compiled by Samuel Cummins, the English one was the work of Norman Lee), but they employed the same format – ex-servicemen describing their wartime experiences alternated with official war film from all sources – and shared 75 per cent of the newsreel footage.

The English version is, if anything, better edited and more informative, but the impact of both is in the similar tabloid presentation of their actuality material. This is raw, compelling, horrific, sensational, and obviously intended to shock, though often leading to a conflict between glorification and condemnation of war – a kind of indignant voyeurism. Allied merchantmen are sunk by (and photographed from) German U-boats; men going over the top are shot dead before they have had time to leave their trench; two men, photographed in long shot, are felled by a shell while crossing a field. And to ensure that no horror is missed, bald captions intermittently underline the visuals with such wording as 'Notice human bodies blown up into the air' and 'Watch this man being killed'. One shot of soldiers advancing amidst exploding shells ends abruptly and a caption explains: 'The sudden termination of this battle scene is due to the death of the cameraman filming it.'

Modern audiences accustomed to wartime newsreel compilations on television have become inured to this kind of footage, but in the 'thirties it was strong stuff and appeared to

Newsreel shot from the British version of *Forgotten Men* (Norman Lee, 1934).

many, not without reason, to be more than a little gratuitous. The 'Bulletin' voiced a generally held reservation in its review of the English version: 'An astonishing production . . . (but) it has no constructive suggestion to offer – not even so non-committal a statement as that friendships and co-operation between the peoples are the only ways to avoid a repetition of such ghastly, futile havoc as we are here shown the last war to have been.'

All the same, whatever their shortcomings, the two *Forgotten Men* of 1934 began the invaluable process, now commonplace, of knitting together unique records of past events, and both anticipated and advanced (in the words of Bardèche and Brasillach, speaking of the French newsreel archives in 1935) 'the time when some future poet of the screen (would) delve into this living record and recompose a visual symphony of the past'. The only comparable exercise at this time was a biased but reasonably cool and admonitory commercial compilation, *The First World War*, produced by Fox and edited and scripted, significantly, by Laurence Stallings.

As exemplified by Norman Lee's *Forgotten Men*, British pacifism in the 'thirties was expressed mainly through newsreels, documentaries, and direct propaganda films, and as such it was extensive and a subject of continuing controversy. British Movietone News, for example, produced a number of current affairs shorts in which contemporary intellectuals like Beverley Nichols, C.E.M. Joad, and Vernon Bartlett asserted their anti-war opinions; Paul Rotha made what he chose to call quite simply *The Peace Film* (1936); and

independent groups like the Peace Pledge Union got themselves onto film. One of the most forceful manifestoes was Hans Nieter's *Thunder in the Air* (1935), an experimental blend of dramatization and actuality material assembled into an attack on the armaments racket, with Ralph Richardson and Hilary Eaves taking care of the histrionics. This showed plainly the influence of the documentary movement on British pacifist films of the 'thirties.

On the fiction front, however, British films indulged only very rarely in war subjects until the approach of renewed hostilities at the end of the decade. Even Frank Lloyd's *Cavalcade* (1933) – an ingenious adaptation of Noël Coward's family saga extolling English nationalism through thirty years of British history – was made in America (though the cast, including Clive Brook and Diana Wynyard, was entirely British, and the settings and atmosphere a convincing imitation).

Cavalcade was, in fact, a good example of what, in propaganda terms, the British cinema of the 'thirties was more concerned with than anything else – a reassertion of Britain's imperial traditions and her place in the world. The most effective expression of this was Tim Whelan's *Farewell Again* (1937), an upbeat, optimistic tribute to the British Army and its built-in values – loyalty, duty, discipline and service.

Such British war films as were produced at this time were otherwise largely unremarkable and becoming increasingly concerned with espionage. *On Secret Service* (1933), with Greta Nissen, *The Battle* (1934), with Charles Boyer,

Jeffrey Hunter in *Singlehanded* (1953), Roy Boulting's remake of *Brown on Resolution* (1935), adapted from the C.S. Forester story.

Madeleine Carroll in *I Was a Spy* (Victor Saville, 1933).

Merle Oberon and John Loder in a 1904 Japanese setting, and Asquith's *Moscow Nights* (1935), with Harry Baur, Laurence Olivier and Penelope Dudley Ward in a 1916 Russian setting, were all about spies. Walter Forde, meanwhile, directed the first version of C.S. Forester's classic story of World War I heroism, *Brown on Resolution* (1935), in which John Mills earned a posthumous VC by laying siege to a German cruiser single-handed with only a rifle (remade by Roy Boulting in 1953 as *Singlehanded*, with Jeffrey Hunter).

The one film which stood out from these mediocre melodramas was Victor Saville's *I Was a Spy* (1933), an intelligent, well-made, austerely good-looking suspense drama based on the experiences of Marthe Knockaert (beautifully played by Madeleine Carroll), a Belgian nurse who revealed to the Allies the German intention to use poison gas. C.A. Lejeune, in 'The Observer', called it 'a war film without vituperation . . . moving and pitiful', and noted its refreshing lack of sentimentality and hysteria. It is also uncommonly free of chauvinism; indeed, the most memorable characterization is Conrad Veidt's German commandant whose emotional predicament invites sympathy despite his odious status as invader. The acting generally (Herbert Marshall, Sir Gerald du Maurier, Edmund Gwenn, Nigel Bruce, Martita Hunt) is of a high standard; the sets and atmosphere are authentic; and Saville's direction is admirably lucid and restrained. In short, it is an unusually accomplished piece of British cinema, and it is remarkable that it has taken nearly forty years for it to be revived and reappraised.

Vivien Leigh in *Dark Journey* (Victor Saville, 1937), with Austin Trevor (*right*).

Veidt, an actor prominent in the German Expressionist cinema of the 'twenties, found himself in the later part of his career (he died in 1943) typecast as cruel Nazi or charming German officer in a number of British and American films. He joined Victor Saville again in 1937 for *Dark Journey*, an espionage story set in neutral Sweden in 1915 in which he is a German Intelligence chief who falls in love with a French spy (Vivien Leigh); and in 1939 he made *The Spy in Black* for Michael Powell, playing a German U-boat commander whose plans to torpedo British destroyers are foiled by counter-spies Valerie Hobson and Sebastian Shaw.

A setting not often exploited in films about World War I was the prisoner-of-war camp. Roy Del Ruth used it effectively in *Captured* (1933), an exciting but rather absurd escape story centred on a triangle love situation (conducted with impeccable decency by the rival officers involved, played by Leslie Howard and Douglas Fairbanks Jr) and featuring an Oxford-educated camp commandant (Paul Lukas). And the same plot was employed, with variations, by Maurice Elvey in *Who Goes Next?* (1938), in which Jack Hawkins made an early appearance in uniform.

A prisoner-of-war camp did, however, serve as the background and catalyst for one of the most memorable of all war films, a last eloquent plea for peace before it was shattered in 1939, and a film which has at times been placed critically among the greatest ever made: Jean Renoir's *La Grande Illusion* (1936). Unlike many of the other great pacifist statements, this film is not about the horrors of war – in

Conrad Veidt in *I Was a Spy*, one of several appearances by this *émigré* actor as a German officer and gentleman.

fact it is not so much a direct memory of World War I as (in the words of David Robinson) 'a reflection in retrospect . . . by a new generation'. It is, rather, about the absurdities of war, the meaninglessness of national boundaries and their preservation by means of human conflict, and the futility of impersonal, large-scale warfare in which no individual animosities exist.

The basic story is of three French officers held as prisoners of war – an aristocrat, Boieldieu (Pierre Fresnay), a mechanic, Maréchal (Jean Gabin), and a Jewish banker, Rosenthal (Marcel Dalio). They differ in social class, but unite in making escape plans. A curious friendship develops between Boieldieu and the Camp Commandant, Von Rauffenstein (Erich von Stroheim, complete with neck-brace) who, as gentlemen career officers, discuss the role of their class after the war. Boieldieu nevertheless helps his companions to escape, compelling Von Rauffenstein to shoot him. With the help of a sympathetic German peasant woman (Dita Parlo) with whom Maréchal falls in love, and despite a long and arduous journey marked by bitter quarrelling, Maréchal and Rosenthal finally cross the Swiss border to safety.

Although not entirely realistic (the stress of war would surely prevent the amount of easy

Marcel Dalio, Jean Gabin and fellow prisoners of war in Jean Renoir's *La Grande Illusion* (1936).

empathy between combatants that is apparent here) Renoir described his film as 'a kind of reconstructed documentary, a documentary on the condition of society at a given moment'. It is a complex study of relationships, objectively but compassionately observed by Renoir and instilled with his indefatigably optimistic opinion of human nature. 'The Frenchmen in this film,' he explained simply, 'are good Frenchmen, and the Germans good Germans . . . I found it impossible to take sides with any of the characters.'

Goebbels and Mussolini recognized the film's pacifist intent, and it was banned in Germany and Italy. In response Renoir declared his philosophy: 'I hear Hitler yelling on the radio, demanding the partition of Czechoslovakia. We are on the brink of another "Grand Illusion". I made this film because I am a pacifist. To me a true pacifist is a Frenchman, a German, an American. The day will come when men of good faith will find a common meeting ground.'

Years later he gave a more cryptic reply to a question put to him by Robert Hughes (and quoted in Hughes's book 'Films of Peace and War'): 'In 1936 I made a picture named *La Grande Illusion* in which I tried to express all my deep feelings for the cause of peace. This film was very successful. Three years later the war broke out.'

Camp Commandant Erich von Stroheim comforts the dying officer he has just shot (Pierre Fresnay) in *La Grande Illusion*.

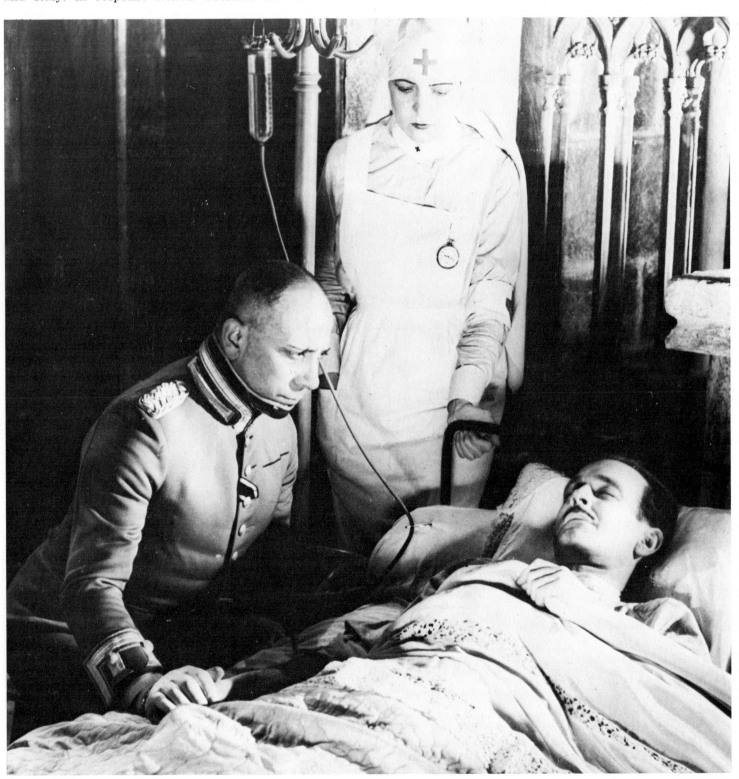

New Régimes

While the British and American war films of the 'twenties and 'thirties continued steadfastly, whatever their point of view, to concern themselves with aspects of World War I, new and uniquely powerful expressions of conflict and aggression were emerging from the cinema born out of the cataclysmic domestic upheavals in Russia and Germany. In Russia, these formed part of the monumental and (at least as far as the silent period is concerned) inestimably influential body of cinematic achievement inspired by the Revolution; in Germany, they made up the substantial group of potent propaganda films which extolled the glories of Nazism, sometimes harking back to the Great War but frequently hinting at hostilities to come.

Immediately following the October Revolution in 1917, the Red Russian leaders laid emphasis on the role films were to play in the new Soviet Union's cultural revolution. 'The cinema,' said Lenin, 'is for us the most important of the arts', and Stalin echoed his words by declaring that 'the cinema is the greatest means of mass propaganda. We must take it in our hands.' The film industry was nationalized, 'agit-trains' (mobile, self-contained propaganda centres equipped to show and produce films) were sent round the country, film schools were established, and it was made clear that film had 'to become an effective expression and weapon of the new society'. The end result was (in the words of Furhammar and Isaksson's admirable book, 'Politics and Film') the creation of 'the only artistically significant style ever to emerge in films with unequivocally propagandist intentions'.

One of the first successful revolutionary films was Perestiani's *Little Red Devils*, about a group of children caught up with Red guerrilla fighters. This was followed by Len Kuleshov's political satire, *The Strange Adventures of Mr West in the Land of the Bolsheviks* (1924), which mocked the nervous reactions of the West to the new régime in Russia. But the first authentic classic of the revolutionary cinema was Sergei Eisenstein's *Strike* (1924), an attack on industrial oppression in 1912 which put forward the working classes *en masse* as hero, and, with its dynamic editing, heralded a whole new cinematic style.

This style was perfected by Eisenstein in his next film, *Battleship Potemkin* (1925), which began its cinematic life as a single sequence designed as part of a larger project to celebrate the twentieth anniversary of the 1905 Revolution, and grew into a vivid reconstruction of the attempted Potemkin mutiny of 1905 in Odessa. Twice voted by critics and historians the greatest film ever made, *Potemkin* is most famous for its horrendous and superbly edited Odessa Steps sequence in which soldiers fire on a crowd, killing adults and children alike, and then march over the dead bodies. *Potemkin* was the first Soviet film to attain international recognition (Russian acclamation, by contrast, was slow in coming) and became the inspiration for a brief but brilliant period of Soviet silent film-making.

In 1926, Vsevolod Pudovkin, who specialized in the theme of individuals being converted to the communist cause, made his first and best feature, an adaptation of Gorki's *Mother*. This simple tale of a woman's radicalization through her son's revolutionary activities in 1905, to the point where she dies clutching the Red Flag before a Tsarist cavalry charge, is characterized by Pudovkin's instinctive lyricism and emotiveness, and heightened by some remarkable acting, particularly from Vera Baranovskaya as the mother and Nikolai Batalov as the son. The film's climactic sequence, which includes symbolic shots of ice breaking up on a spring-thawed river, is almost as celebrated as the massacre on the Odessa Steps, and indeed, *Mother* can, in many ways, claim as strong an influence as *Potemkin* on subsequent film-making everywhere.

Pudovkin rapidly completed two more important films about the Revolution. The first of these, *The End of St Petersburg*, was one of a flurry of films brought out in 1927 to commemorate the tenth anniversary of the Revolution: an energetic reconstruction, through the eyes of a young peasant, of events in St Petersburg which culminated in the 1917 Revolution

Morgenrot (Gustav Ucicky, 1933).

71

The Odessa Steps sequence from *Battleship Potemkin* (Sergei Eisenstein, 1925).

and the replacing of the old city by the new Leningrad. It is one of the masterpieces of the period, poetic, symbolistic and visually breathtaking: a 'film of images', as one contemporary critic aptly described it. One of its strengths was Pudovkin's use, where possible, of untrained actors: the peasant boy, for example, really was a peasant, and the stockbrokers were all re-creating their former real-life occupation.

Storm Over Asia (1928) – originally called *The Heir to Genghis Khan* – is a continuation of Pudovkin's 'conversion' theme: a young Mongolian trapper becomes involved in the war between Red partisans and White and interventionist troops in Central Asia in 1920; he is captured and used as a puppet leader by his imperialistic oppressors, but escapes and rallies the partisans for a final liberating attack. Exotic, prophetic, and shot on location with documentary authenticity, Pudovkin's third film is a blossoming of his techniques of 'emotive' editing (in contrast to Eisenstein's ideas of 'intellectual montage' which in practice often passed well over the heads of his audiences): Jay Leyda called it 'a glittering flow of polished, glossy images that could leave breathless a spectator accustomed to the "normal" film'. An interesting element in the film for English audiences is the satirical depiction of bloated British imperialists.

The most spectacular of the films made to commemorate the events of 1917 is Eisenstein's epic portrayal of the Revolution, *October* (also called, in a cut-down export version, *Ten Days that Shook the World*). Intelligent, resourceful, exciting, and made with apparent objectivity and authenticity (Eisenstein had the run of Leningrad – including the Winter Palace – and made effective use of non-professionals in all the parts), the film nevertheless ran into trouble with the politicians. Audiences failed to grasp Eisenstein's 'intellectual dynamism' – the juxtaposition of seemingly unrelated images, such as the intercutting of shots showing a bust of Napoleon with close-ups of Kerensky to denote the latter's character and ambitions, and the 'stretching' of time in the bridge-raising sequence – and references to the suddenly disaffected Trotsky had to be cut out. Eisenstein was accused of 'formalism' and the cramping imposition of State ideology on the film-makers' art began to be felt. The hardening dogma of social realism was experienced again in establishment attitudes to Eisenstein's next film (and his last for nearly a decade), *The General Line* (1929 – revamped as *Old and New*), and Alexander Dovzhenko's masterpiece, *Earth*

Russian caricature of British imperialism in *Storm Over Asia* (Vsevolod Pudovkin, 1928).

October (Sergei Eisenstein, 1927).

(1930) – a double celebration of the collectivization of agriculture – the latter being put down as 'defeatist', 'counter-revolutionary' and 'too realistic'(!).

Another remarkable achievement of 1927 (completed in 1928) was Esther Shub's pioneering trilogy of creative historical compilations, *The Fall of the Romanov Dynasty*, *The Great Road* and *The Russia of Nikolai II and Lev Tolstoy*, important exercises in the use of archive material and especially interesting for the way in which they purposefully trigger off preconceived emotions by juggling newsreel fragments into an artistic whole. Shub was not the only woman director of this period; Olga Preobrazhenskaya, a star of pre-revolutionary

films, also contributed to the rich creativity of 1927 with her *Peasant Women of Ryazan*, a fresh, simple study of life in a small Russian village at the outbreak of World War I. To round off an extraordinary year, Yakov Protazanov made *The Forty-First*, the story of a Red Army girl who falls in love with a White Guard officer but confirms her commitment to communism by shooting him.

A relative late-comer to the cinema, Dovzhenko brought together, in his best work, all the theories of montage, metaphor and imagery of the great Soviet film-makers. He had demonstrated his unusual talent prior to *Earth* with the astonishing *Zvenigora* (1928), a wildly experimental anthology of folkloric legends

Yelena Kuzmina in *The New Babylon* (Leonid Trauberg and Grigori Kozintsev, 1929).

73

Arsenal (Alexander Dovzhenko, 1929).

which alarmed the cultural authorities but led Eisenstein and Pudovkin to proclaim the arrival of a 'remarkable man' in film art. The following year he made *Arsenal*, a romantic epic poem about the Ukraine, the war, revolutionary stirrings, and the bloody repression of a workers' rebellion in a Kiev munitions factory in 1918. An intense, fabulous, lyrical film, justly famous for its climax in which the hero, his chest bared, is shot down by the Whites, it was acclaimed by Eisenstein for its 'liberation of the whole action from the definitions of time and space'.

There were two other important films from the silent period (both made in 1929) which reflected on war and revolution. Friedrich Ermler's *Fragment of an Empire* is the story of a soldier who has lost his memory in World War I and regains it ten years later, unaware of the changes brought about by the social upheaval: a sharply observed, satirical, and not uncritical study of the old and the new Russia. *The New Babylon*, directed by Leonid Trauberg and Grigori Kozintsev, is a period piece set during the heroic rise and tragic fall of the Paris

Fragment of an Empire (Friedrich Ermler, 1929).

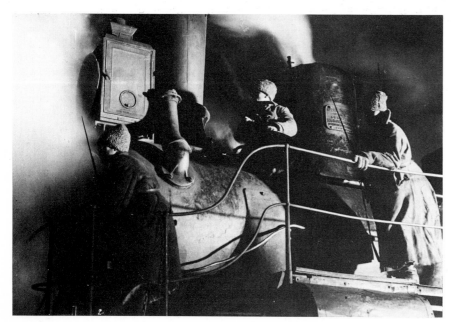

Commune in the Prussian War of 1870–71, focusing on the life and death of a shop-assistant, the model for all subsequent heroines of the Russian Revolution.

As Soviet cinema moved, slowly and deliberately, from silence to sound, the grip of social realism tightened. Ideas and style became standardized to conform with the official Party directive that all films should be addressed, without equivocation or experiment, to the masses. The vitality and imagination which had fired the film-makers of the 'twenties were thus, for the most part, lacking in their successors of the 'thirties.

The first successful Russian sound film was Nikolai Ekk's *The Road to Life* (1931) – a moving, humane study of the abandoned children of the Revolution, victims of war and famine – which actually owed more to the techniques of silent film-making than to the new medium. Also highly regarded is Boris Barnet's *Okraina* (*Patriots*), made two years later, a World War I story of a provincial Russian girl and her love-affairs with a student and a German prisoner – 'a sort of proletarian *Cavalcade*', as it has been called, notable for its charm, humour, and powerful war scenes.

The Vasilievs, Sergei and Georgi, also managed to escape temporarily from the strait-jacket of social realism with *Chapayev* (1934), and in so doing started a vogue for biographies of revolutionary heroes. Chapayev (played by Boris Babochkin) – an individualistic Red Army commander who fought in the Civil War of 1919 – and his compatriots are shown to be human as well as heroic, fallible as well as clever, arousing sympathy and the kind of popular emotions which a more idealized hero would have failed to do.

Even more likeable is the portrait of Bolshevik scientist K.A. Timiriazev by Alexander Zharki and Josef Heifitz in *Baltic Deputy* (1937), a passive, whimsical account of how the old professor offended a group of starving people in 1917, but came to realize his place was with them and the Revolution and was eventually elected to the Soviet by the sailors of the Baltic fleet. The film's sense of intimacy and lack of pretension are due in large measure to the outstanding performance, in the title-role, of the great actor, Nikolai Cherkassov, who later portrayed Alexander Nevsky and Ivan the Terrible in Eisenstein's last epics.

'Synthetic' revolutionary heroes were also popular, the most celebrated being Kozintsev and Trauberg's Maxim, whose adventures are depicted in an epic trilogy composed of *The Youth of Maxim* (1935), *The Return of Maxim* (1937) and *The Vyborg Side* (1939). The last of these has among its characters a re-creation of Lenin by the actor Maxim Straukh, one of a series of generally rather endearing portraits which make up a veritable genre, beginning with *October* and Dziga Vertov's *Three Songs of Lenin* (1934). Straukh also played him as 'the most human of men' in Sergei Yutkevich's *The Man with the Gun* (1938) and *Yakov Sverdlov* (1940), and again years later in the same director's *Stories About Lenin* (1958) and *Lenin in Poland* (1965). Lenin was first portrayed dramatically, however, in 1937, by Boris Shchukin in Mikhail Romm's *Lenin in October*, an impersonation repeated in 1939 in Romm's *Lenin in 1918*, soon after which Shchukin died. Stalin approved of these reincarnations, basking in Lenin's unquestionable popularity by having himself frequently portrayed as the great man's fraternal sidekick, usually by Mikhail Gelovani, who appeared in the role in twenty films.

One of the more impressive biographies of less elevated heroes is Dovzhenko's *Shchors* (1939), an improbable, idealized portrait of the Ukrainian partisan leader designed to reflect Stalin (whose suggestion it had been to 'give us a Ukrainian *Chapayev*'), but retrieved by its many epic images. Less personal recollections of the Revolution included Yefim Dzigan's *We From Kronstadt* (1936), an account of the defence of Petrograd against the Whites in 1919, famous for its execution scene in which sailors are thrown into the Baltic from a high cliff; and Yuli Raizman's *The Last Night* (1937), a 'Romeo and Juliet' love story set in October 1917, which contains an even more celebrated sequence – that in which a troop train steams slowly into a station and nobody among those waiting for it knows whether it contains friends or enemies.

As the murky international diplomacy of the 'thirties began to push aside memories of the Revolution, so Russian films, like those of other countries, began to reveal nationalist tendencies and an awareness of potential threats from outside its borders. This feeling had found early expression in Dovzhenko's *Aerograd* (1935), a visually magnificent espionage drama set in Siberia, where frontier guards combat sabotage, Japanese infiltration, and treachery from within during the construction of an airport. The mainstream of attack, however, was against fascism, anticipated even earlier by Pudovkin's first sound film, *Deserter* (1935), the story of a German worker who escapes to Russia but gradually comes to realize that he must return to his country to fight Nazism and help bring about the proletarian revolution.

The year of girding the loins, however, was 1938, when a spate of anti-German films reached the Russian cinemas, including Alexander Macheret's *Swamp Soldiers*, set in the Nazi concentration camps, and, more notably, Adolf Minkin and Herbert Rappoport's powerful indictment of anti-Semitism, *Professor Mamlock*. The most vivid warning to Germany was issued by Eisenstein in his marvellously operatic return to film-making, *Alexander Nevsky*. Set in the thirteenth century, this reconstruction of the invasion of Russia by the Knights of the Teutonic Order and their spectacular defeat in the Battle on the Ice drew transparent parallels with the new German threat. 'This,' wrote Eisenstein, 'is the fate in store for all who may dare attack our Country,' and the insignia and sinister helmets with which he adorned the disciplined, iron-clad Teutonic

Nikolai Cherkassov (*right*) as the *Baltic Deputy* (Alexander Zharki and Josef Heifitz, 1937).

Cherkassov (as Maxim Gorky) and Boris Shchukin (as Lenin) in *Lenin in 1918* (Mikhail Romm, 1939).

Below: Yevgeni Samoilov as the Ukrainian partisan hero, *Shchors* (Alexander Dovzhenko, 1939).

Knights made it quite clear whom he meant.

In 1939, the USSR reluctantly signed a non-aggression pact with Germany and shelved her cycle of anti-Nazi films. In 1941, Hitler violated the agreement by invading Russia, and the films began to be released once again, along with a series of morale-boosting short propaganda films. In the war years, however, the documentary was to come into its own and achieve a dominance over feature films rare in the Soviet cinema.

Hitler and Goebbels were no less appreciative than Lenin and Stalin of the power of propaganda in the cinema. 'We are convinced,' said Goebbels, who had a particular fondness for movies, 'that films constitute one of the most modern and scientific means of influencing the mass. Therefore a government must not neglect them.' Whereupon, after its rise to power in 1933, on a fortuitous wave of depression, famine and unemployment, the Nazi régime proceeded to exercise strict bureaucratic control over the ideological content of every film made in Germany.

The rapidity with which the German cinema had reached this sorry pass was startling. During the 'twenties, under the Weimar Republic, it had experienced its own Golden Age,

practically inventing new genres such as Expressionism and Kammerspiel, and cultivating a hot-house of talent which included directors like Lubitsch, Murnau, Lang, Dieterle, Oswald, Siodmak, Sirk and, later, Billy Wilder and Fred Zinnemann, and stars of the calibre of Marlene Dietrich, Conrad Veidt, Elizabeth Bergner, Peter Lorre, Fritz Kortner, Anton Walbrook, and Richard Tauber. A few of these were lured away by Hollywood, but as the Nazi grip on the country – and its culture – tightened, and the Party policy of *Gleichschaltung* (the remoulding of all aspects of German life to conform with Nazi philosophy) combined with total repression of liberty began to hold sway, most of them simply fled. German cinema in the 'thirties and early 'forties was thus artistically and creatively emasculated, and films made under the Nazis were at best (and with few exceptions) no more than efficient, insidiously skilful idealizations of the New Germany.

Goebbels was shrewd enough to realize that the way to keep cinemas well attended was to lay emphasis on escapism rather than propaganda. He therefore restricted direct propaganda in feature films to a few prestige productions (their effectiveness to be enhanced by their scarcity) while ensuring that all cinema programmes were supplemented with

Sergei Mezhinsky as *Professor Mamlock* (Adolf Minkin and Herbert Rappoport, 1938).

a regular compulsory quota of propaganda newsreels and shorts. At the same time he banned the exhibition of 'subversive' or 'liberal' films like *Westfront 1918*; *Kameradschaft*; Richard Oswald's satire on militarism, *The Captain of Köpenick* (1931); Leontine Sagan's indictment of authoritarianism, *Girls in Uniform* (1931); and *The Last Will of Dr Mabuse* (1932), Fritz Lang's resurrection of his criminally insane megalomaniac, whom he later claimed to be a thinly disguised portrait of Hitler.

The Nazi propaganda features were simple, unequivocal and mindful always of Hitler's premise that 'the teachability of the great masses is very limited, their understanding small and their memory short'. They kept, for the most part, to a restricted number of ideological themes – anti-Semitism, Aryan superiority, war heroism, Germany's glorious past, 'Strength through Joy', loyalty to the Fatherland, Fuehrer-worship – and, in the sense that they all promoted militarism and the idea of one race having a natural right to dominate others, they were all films of war.

At first, the Party favoured documentaries. Goebbels had one of his own speeches filmed; *Hitler's Flight Over Germany* chronicled the Leader's election campaign of 1932; *Germany Awakes* (1933) celebrated the rise of National Socialism; and *Our Fuehrer* attempted to persuade voters to support Hitler's assumption of the dictatorship in 1934. More importantly, Leni Riefenstahl – the one remaining directorial talent in Germany – conducted a rehearsal of her monumental *Triumph of the Will* (1934) with *Victory of Faith*, a record of the 1933 Nazi Rally, suppressed after the purge of the SA (in the notorious 'Night of the Long Knives') who were prominently represented at the rally. In the same year, Rolf von Sonjewski-Jamrowski propounded a pet Nazi doctrine with his *Blut und Boden* (*Blood and Soil*), about the improved lot of the German farmer with the advent of National Socialism.

The major propaganda productions of 1933, however, were all features extolling the Party and its loyal members. The first of these was Franz Seitz's *SA-Mann Brandt*, about the struggles of a devoted Nazi and his Hitler Youth protégé against the brutal communists in pre-Hitler Germany. Far superior, and a better representation of the Nazi archetype, is *Hans Westmar* (directed by Franz Wenzler), which began as a biography of Horst Wessel, author of the Nazi anthem, but was considered unworthy and was re-edited to make it a more positive panegyric to National Socialism. Hans

Nikolai Cherkassov as *Alexander Nevsky* (Sergei Eisenstein, 1938).

Nazi Stormtroopers (SA) go to the aid of a Hitler Youth, shot by communists, in *SA-Mann Brandt* (Franz Seitz, 1933).

becomes a martyr to the Nazi cause, gunned down by the communists in the midst of his exertions to rid Germany of Marxist decadence, and earns a lavish funeral, symbolizing the resurrection of the new order out of the ashes of the old. Similar to *Hans Westmar*, but even more overtly 'religious', is Hans Steinhoff's *Hitlerjunge Quex* – 'A film about young people's spirit of sacrifice', explains the subtitle – which also fictionalizes the biography of an actual Nazi martyr (namely Herbert Norkus, murdered by the communists in 1932). The hero is a boy whose misguided father forces him to join in communist youth activities. He finds their behaviour repellent, however, and is attracted to the smart Hitler Youth. After helping the Nazis to overcome a communist plot to blow up a Youth Hostel, he earns his Hitler Youth membership, becomes noted for his courage on hazardous missions, and is eventually murdered by communists while distributing election pamphlets. As he dies, he visualizes the heavens draped with swastikas and his compatriots marching to victory.

Another favourite Nazi theme was established in 1933 with Gustav Ucicky's well-made *Morgenrot* (*Dawn*), a story of heroism, comradeship and self-sacrifice in World War I. After being rammed by a British destroyer, a German U-boat is trapped on the sea-bed. However, there is only sufficient escape equipment for eight out of the ten survivors. The problem is resolved when two of the crew shoot themselves in an act of supreme selflessness ('We Germans may not know much about living,' says the captain, 'but dying . . . we know how to die!'). The film

is notable for its mild pacifist tendencies (not sufficient, though, to invite Party disapproval) and its strong anti-British attitudes.

Ucicky also directed *Flüchtlinge* (*Refugees*) in 1933. A reflection of the idea that, under the Nazis, Germany was once again a land fit for Germans to live in and expatriates could now confidently respond to Rudolf Hess's assertion that 'Germany is home for all Germans from all over the world', this told of a group of Volga Germans who flee from Russian persecution in a stolen train. This theme was reiterated by Paul Wegener in *A Man Must Return to Germany* (1934), about two German engineers who set out on a hazardous journey back to the Fatherland in 1914 in order to join the war, and succeed in spite of relentless attempts by the British to stop them.

These ideas of persecution of *émigrés* and joyful repatriation were taken to extremes in two films made at the beginning of World War II: Viktor Tourjansky's *Feinde* (*Enemies*) and Ucicky's *Heimkehr* (*Homecoming*). In both of these, Germans living in Poland are depicted as a minority being persecuted and terrorized by Poles. In *Feinde*, they return to the Reich; in *Heimkehr*, the Reich goes to the rescue. Both films were designed to justify the Nazi occupation of Poland and gather public support behind this action. Similarly, the plight of the Friesian minority in the border regions of Russia had been depicted in *Friesennot* (1935), though it was subsequently banned during the period of the Russo-German non-aggression pact.

Yet another 1933 prototype was the 'Fridericus' film *The Chorale of Leuthen*, directed

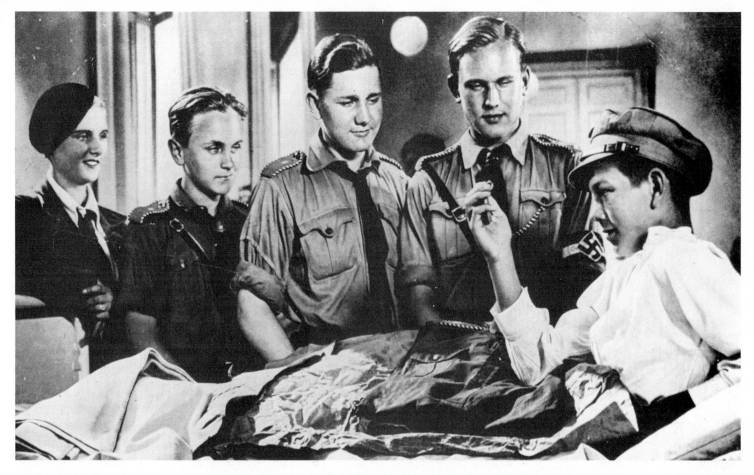

Heini wins his Hitler
Youth uniform in *Hitlerjunge
Quex* (Hans Steinhoff, 1933).

by Carl Froelich, one of a cycle of historical reconstructions glorifying the Fuehrer-like exploits of Frederick the Great (usually played by Otto Gebühr, who had done so in a number of pre-Nazi examples of the genre). From defeating the Austrians at Leuthen, Frederick regresses to his youth, and a lesson in leadership and obedience, in Hans Steinhoff's *The Old King and the Young King* (1935); progresses once again to more military glory by repelling a Franco-Russian invasion in Johannes Meyer's *Fridericus* (1936); and wins the Battle of Leuthen all over again in Veit Harlan's *The Great King* (1942).

The 'leadership principle' was also explored in Wolfgang Liebeneiner's double blockbuster about Bismarck, the Iron Chancellor and architect of Germany unity: *Bismarck* (1940) and *Die Entlassung* (*The Dismissal*, 1942), with Paul Hartmann and Emil Jannings sharing the lead role; and again in (remarkably) Herbert Maisch's *Friedrich Schiller* (1944), about the freedom-loving young poet, and Veit Harlan's *The Ruler* (1927), a fictional study of an industrial chief modelled on Krupp. All of these leadership films were immensely popular with young Germans, a revealing factor when one wonders at Hitler's success in maintaining plausibility and power.

The youth of Germany was, of course, a prime propaganda target. A number of shorts and features were produced with the aim of indoctrinating children, including a homily on labour camps, a special children's newsreel justifying the invasion of Austria and Czechoslovakia, and an alarming animation film,

The Boy Who Wanted to Know What Fear Was (1935), which a UNESCO report of 1946 described as an 'approbation of killing and force coupled with callousness' which 'would either frighten children or encourage sadistic tendencies'. Others glorified the Hitler Youth and the Labour League, such as Froelich's *Me For You – You For Me* (1934); Roger von Norman's *Sky Hounds* (1942) and Alfred Weidenmann's *Young Eagles* (1944), both of which featured the Flying Hitler Youth; and Fritz Peter Buch's *Jakko* (1941), about the Naval Hitler Youth.

Recollections of World War I continued after *Morgenrot*, suitably overlaid with a retrospective Nazi point of view. *Stosstrupp 1917* (*Shocktroop 1917*), directed by Hans Zöberlein in 1934 from his own ultra-chauvinistic book, 'Der Glaube an Deutschland', was the Party's answer to Pabst's *Westfront 1918*, although in the authentic re-creation of barbarous battle scenes it achieved much the same alienating effect as its predecessor. According to one observer of Nazi cinema, Siegfried Kracauer, Zöberlein 'renders the horrors of trench warfare with a realistic objectivity equalling, if not excelling, Pabst's'. He goes on to say, however, that Zöberlein nevertheless 'manages to exclude any pacifist implications by interpreting the last stages of World War I as a struggle for Germany's survival'.

War themes were often aimed at German youth to demonstrate the importance of self-sacrifice, unquestioning obedience, and devotion to the Fatherland. Karl Ritter was the specialist in these. In 1937 he made *Unternehmen Michael* (*Operation Michael*), in which a

German unit fighting in World War I brings about its own destruction along with that of the enemy rather than submit to hopeless odds. Ritter said he made the film to show 'the German youth that senseless sacrificial death has its moral value'! *Leave on Word of Honour* (also 1937) tells a gentler story of soldiers denying themselves the chance of personal happiness to return to the front in 1918. *Pour le Mérite* (1938) sings the praises of those who refused to submit to the Weimar Republic, in this case members of the Richthofen Air Squadron; they maintain a relentless struggle against the democratic government until Hitler comes to power and they are able to re-form their flying unit.

Self-sacrifice and collective responsibility were stressed in three more aviation films, all designed as tributes to the Luftwaffe: Ritter's *Stukas* (1941), in which a pilot regains his will to fight after being shot down; and Herbert Maisch's *D III 88* (1939) and its sequel, *Battle Squadron Lützow* (1941), directed by Hans Bertram.

Ironically, amidst all these expressions of overt militant nationalism, it was an exercise in passive, lyrical veneration which gave the Nazi cinema its one masterpiece: Leni Riefenstahl's dazzling record of the 1934 Party Rally at Nuremberg, *Triumph of the Will*. 'Politics and Film' sums it up neatly: 'One German film demonstrates better than any other artistic work of the period the seductive magic of Nazism. It shows both the upturned faces and the ones looking stiffly ahead, bound by magnetic attraction. The principal character is Adolf Hitler. In a way he is also the originator of the film.' This euphoric deification of the Fuehrer was indeed planned by Hitler himself as much for the camera as for the vast live audience which had come to form part of the hypnotic spectacle. (Leni Riefenstahl wrote later: 'The preparations for the Party Congress were made in concert with the preparations for the camerawork.') The film captured, in unique fashion, the feel of mass emotion being swayed and manipulated by a spellbinding display of pomp and rhetoric. At the same time, it put up an effective smoke-screen against the grotesque realities of Nazism. In short, it remains (in the words of Isaksson and Furhammar) both 'a magnificently controlled work of art' and 'a complex experience'.

Leni Riefenstahl followed this epic piece of propaganda with her equally lyrical two-part record of the Berlin Olympic Games, *Olympiad* (1936) – a paean to athleticism which reflects the Nazi preoccupation with the (Aryan) human body. The cult of sport was also promoted in Alfred Weidenmann's film of the Winter Olympics, *Youth of the World*, while physical purity and the doctrine of 'Blood and Soil' were sentimentally presented in von Pestalozza's' *Der Ewiger Wald* (*The Eternal Forests*, 1936), which symbolized the might of the German people through its indestructible forests.

At the end of the decade, with the outbreak

Heimkehr (Gustav Ucicky, 1933).

of World War II, the darkest aspects of Nazism began to show themselves in propaganda films, most notoriously in a group of despicable exercises in anti-Semitism made in 1940. The most vicious and disturbing of these – the more so because of its technical excellence – was Fritz Hippler's *The Eternal Jew*, a documentary on 'the problems of World Jewry' which set out to 'expose' the alleged decadence of the Jewish people. Shot largely in the poverty-stricken Polish ghettoes, this grotesque indictment compared Jews literally to rats and implied, through horrific scenes photographed in a kosher abattoir, that they were inherently barbaric and unclean. Few would wish to argue with the assessment of 'Politics and Film' that this 'is probably the most evil film ever made'. Veit Harlan's *Jud Süss* (produced by Hippler) ran it a close second, however.

Begun soon after the 'Kristallnacht' (the Nazi swoop on the Jews at the end of 1938), it tells of a Jew, Süss Oppenheimer, who takes evil advantage of his financial hold over the Duke of Württemberg. After a career of criminal debauchery (including the rape of a young girl), he is tolerated no longer by the Duchy, who execute him. The film was 'highly recommended' (by Goebbels) 'for its artistic value and, to serve the politics of the State, recommended for young people'. Teenagers responded obediently by beating up Jews in the street after seeing it.

The third – and mercifully the last – of these gross anti-Jewish fabrications was Erich Waschneck's *Die Rothschilds*, a ponderous attack on the supposedly unscrupulous methods employed by this family of international financiers to build up their fortune. The following year, however, the theme was taken a stage nearer to the 'final solution' with Wolfgang Liebeneiner's *Ich Klage An* (*I Accuse*), a rationalization of the Nazi 'euthanasia' programme subtly

disguised as a tear-jerking drama about a gentle doctor who administers a merciful overdose to his incurably ill wife.

The residue of Nazi hatred was reserved for the British, whose vilification began in the early 'thirties in such features as *Morgenrot* and *A Man Must Return to Germany*. The first blatantly anti-British film, Herbert Selpin's *The Riders of German East Africa* (1934) was actually banned on the grounds that it was pacifist (it tells of two friends, a Briton and a German, at the outbreak of World War I), but Selpin made up for his early mildness with *Carl Peters* (1941), a biography of the German colonialist, whom the British attempt to assassinate in East Africa. The same background serves for *Germanin* (1943), directed by Goebbels's brother-in-law, Max Kimmich, in which a pioneering German doctor's humane medical research is hampered by British oppression. But the scene changes to Ireland for the same director's *The Fox of Glenarvon* (1940) and *My Life for Ireland* (1941), a double exposé of English atrocities in the Emerald Isle; and to

The Fuehrer and his favourite director (Leni Riefenstahl) plan *Triumph of the Will* (1934).

Wunschkonzert (Eduard von Borsody, 1940), a sentimental Nazi propaganda piece about love, sacrifice, and the heroic powers of music.

the mid-Atlantic for *Titanic* (1943), which lays blame for the tragic sinking of the liner on its maiden voyage on the English president of the shipping line, who defies the sensible German first officer and sails the ship at full speed among the icebergs.

The cleverest and most ambitious of the anti-British films, however, is Hans Steinhoff's *Ohm Krüger* (1941) – 'Goebbels's *Battleship Potemkin*', to which the movie-loving Minister of Propaganda seems even to have contributed portions of the script. It re-creates the honourable career of the Transvaal statesman (superbly characterized by Emil Jannings) who led the

Boers in their war against the British at the turn of the century. He is depicted as a simple, authoritative Fuehrer-figure, heroic and determined – in contrast to the British leaders, a set

The Nazi image of Churchill, portrayed by Otto Wernicke as a cruel concentration-camp boss in *Ohm Krüger* (Hans Steinhoff, 1941), with Gisela Uhlen.

of mocking caricatures parodying, with varying degrees of exaggeration and contempt, Cecil Rhodes, Lord Kitchener, Joseph Chamberlain, the Prince of Wales, Queen Victoria (tippling Scotch), and Winston Churchill (as the savage boss of a concentration camp). The corruption, greed, and brutality of these decadent imperialists leads ultimately to the crushing of the dignified Boers, climaxed in a prison-camp massacre of Odessa Steps proportions. Ohm Krüger, in exile and in his dotage, prophesies revenge on the British through the agency of another nation, like the Boers, but stronger.

Smooth, spectacular, humorous and exceptionally well made, *Ohm Krüger* is an expert piece of propaganda, perhaps most mind-boggling in the long run for the utter, shameless cynicism which allows it to accuse the British of inventing concentration camps at a time when its sponsors were perpetrating unspeakable horrors in Auschwitz, Dachau and the like, and to use Nazi slogans to incriminate the enemy ('One must be a dreamer to become a ruler'; 'If a lie is repeated often enough, people will come to believe it in the end').

Goebbels himself stage-managed a fitting finale to the cinema of the Third Reich in 1945 with his personal supervision of Veit Harlan's expensive, dull and monolithic *Kolberg*. This was a massive, manic project designed to prod the German nation into one last do-or-die stand against the imminent Allied invasion by recalling (inaccurately) civilian resistance to Napoleon at Kolberg. All it did, however, was use up vital war resources to no particular purpose, since it was not completed until the final weeks of the war. Virtually its only audience, in fact, was the army besieged at Brest, to whom Goebbels characteristically had a print parachuted in order to bolster the troops' resistance. At the same time, in a speech to his staff, the Fuehrer's faithful sidekick unwittingly drafted the Nazi cinema's ironic epitaph: 'Gentlemen, in a hundred years' time they will be showing another fine colour film describing the terrible days we are living through. Don't you want to play a part in this film, to be brought back to life in a hundred years' time? . . . Hold out now so that a hundred years hence the audience does not hoot and whistle when you appear on the screen.'

Storm Warnings

Paradoxically, it was America, the least threatened or involved of all the future Allies, whose films assumed the strongest jingoistic stance and were the most forthright in taking up the cudgels against Nazism in the late 'thirties. Britain, whose film industry was in a fairly depressed state anyway and resigned to making what it could from exhibiting the Hollywood product it failed so dismally to imitate, contented itself with a few desultory spy movies, while one or two independent film-makers like Paul Rotha continued to turn out brave little documentary tracts urging peace or appeasement. With characteristic English irony, the austerity of war was about to revive the British film, but meanwhile Hollywood continued to rule the free world.

Even America, however, was hesitant about condemning fascism outright before war in Europe had become a certainty, and some ambivalence existed in producers' minds for a while, engendered partly by fear of the other 'ism', communism, partly by the belief that political films spelled death at the box-office. Early pleas for democracy and international peace, such as *Are We Civilized?* (1934), and tentative probings at the nature of Nazism like Frank Borzage's *Little Man, What Now?* (1934, with Douglass Montgomery) were countered by anti-radical, militaristic melodramas with titles like *A Call to Arms* and *Red Salute*. These in turn were slapped down by dramatic exposés of secret Fascist organizations supposedly operating in American cities – for example, *The Legion of Terror* (1936) and *The Black Legion* (1937, with Humphrey Bogart) – and, though producers remained cautious, the common attitude became one of quietly unanimous anti-totalitarianism.

A few independent film-makers chronicled the spread of fascism abroad. Herbert Kline and Alexander Hammid made *Crisis* (1938), about the break-up of Czechoslovakia after the Munich Pact, and *Lights Out in Europe* (1939), a record of the hostilities in Poland, while the conflicts in Spain and China were dealt with in a number of films, both fact and fiction. More accessible was Louis de Rochemont's rather idiosyncratic current-affairs series, *March of Time*, which in 1938 devoted one of its episodes, *Inside Nazi Germany*, to events in the Third Reich. But the main emphasis at home was on militarism and romantic patriotism, expressed through such spectacles as *Annapolis Farewell*, *Flirtation Walk*, *West Point of the Air*, *Navy Blue and Gold* and *Shipmates Forever* (dedicated to the Naval Academy), which, along with rousing forays into the various services like *Here Comes the Navy*, *Tell it to the Marines*, *Follow the Fleet*, *The Singing Marines*, *Wings of the Navy* and *Come On, Marines*, prepared the way for recruitment. Memories of World War I were revived by *Thunder Afloat* (1939), in which Wallace Beery sacrifices himself by tapping on the hull of the German submarine in which he is imprisoned; *The Fighting 69th* (1940), which has James Cagney doing no less by falling on a live grenade; and *H.M. Pulham, Esq.* (1941), with Robert Young reminiscing about the trenches.

It was not until 1939, however, with Roosevelt questioning American neutrality and the pressure of international events bearing down upon it, that Hollywood made its first overt attack on Nazism. This was Anatole Litvak's *Confessions of a Nazi Spy*, which pitted Edward G. Robinson's FBI agent against the fascist villainy of Francis Lederer, George Sanders and Paul Lukas. Based on an actual spy trial, and skilfully blending documentary and fictional techniques, this scathing exposé warned against spies, fifth columnists, German diplomats and any kind of German-American liaison. It was attacked from all sides as being a piece of blatant warmongering, and banned by countries sympathetic to Nazism, but enjoyed considerable success in the United States.

All the same, Hollywood clung uneasily to its official neutrality for another year while the German war machine smashed its way across Europe. The continuing ambiguity was reflected in the fact that war documentaries from both Britain and Germany were imported and received equal screen time – *The Lion Has Wings* thus vied with *Baptism of Fire*, *London Can Take It* with *Victory in the West*. Gradually,

American troops going over the top in *Sergeant York* (Howard Hawks, 1941).

85

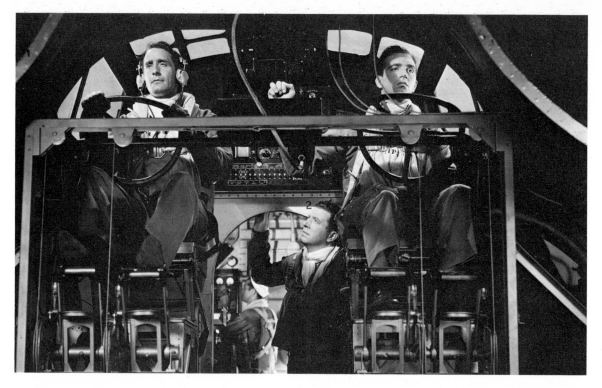

though, the newsreels chipped away at American isolationism by concentrating on the country's defensive preparations on the one hand, and on the plight of England and France on the other; and occasionally the realities and implications of the conflict in Europe were demonstrated by more vivid records of actual events, such as *The Scuttling of the Graf Spee*, *The Siege of Narvik*, and *The Retreat from Dunkirk*.

At last, in 1940, film-makers began to show a real commitment to the Allied cause. Frank Borzage (though Victor Saville has since

claimed ninety per cent of the directing credit) broke new ground with *The Mortal Storm*, setting it inside Nazi Germany, calling Hitler by name, and showing the true nature of Nazism in the first years of its régime. It concerns the persecution of a Jewish university professor (Frank Morgan) who is sent to a concentration camp. His sons (Robert Stack, William T. Orr) become Nazis, and his daughter (Margaret Sullavan), who is attempting to flee Germany with the help of her lover (James Stewart), is shot down at the border. This was too despondent a theme for the box-office, and a number of critics, while praising the film, felt that its message was somewhat belated ('*The Mortal Storm*,' said Bosley Crowther, 'is the sort of picture we should have seen five years ago'). Others could find little evidence for the active pocket of liberal resistance in Germany which the film suggested did exist.

Now that the silence had been broken, the Hollywood conscience more than made up for its tardiness, and there was hardly a single aspect of Nazi frightfulness which went unexposed. Archie Mayo's *Four Sons*, set in Czechoslovakia, continued the theme of family loyalties divided by the swastika, reiterating the anguish and despair of *The Mortal Storm*. Mervyn LeRoy excitingly dramatized the Ethel Vance best-seller, *Escape*, about an American (Robert Taylor) who rescues his German mother (Alla Nazimova, veteran of *War Brides*, in her first talkie) from a concentration camp with the aid of an American-born countess (Norma Shearer). And Irving Pichel's *The Man I Married*, with Joan Bennett and Francis Lederer, contrasted the values of the old Germany with the abuses of the Third Reich.

The most popular of the anti-Nazi films was Alfred Hitchcock's fervent plea on behalf of beleaguered England, *Foreign Correspondent*, a Walter Wanger project which had hiccuped its way to the screen via fourteen scriptwriters and almost as many plot angles, finally settling for a story about an American news-reporter (Joel McCrea) who becomes involved in a web of Nazi intrigue while covering the turbulent political events in Europe. Hitchcock had already squared up to Nazi villainy in one of his last British films, the delightfully clever *The Lady Vanishes* (1938), but the approach had been more sardonic than hateful. *Foreign Correspondent* was much stronger meat, an exciting and timely combination of Hitchcock's special brand of suspense, irony and surprise with the terrifying realities of Gestapo ruthlessness and political assassination. The film ends with newsman McCrea, who has survived several murder attempts and uncovered a Nazi spy-ring, making a radio broadcast to America in the middle of an air raid on London. It is a direct, unfettered appeal to the United States to prepare herself for war. 'The lights are going out in Europe,' he says. 'Ring yourself around with steel, America!' – a well-timed assault on American emotions which undoubtedly helped to sway the nation against neutrality. The film received an unexpected accolade from arch-propagandist Joseph Goebbels, who admired it immensely and allowed that it might 'make a certain impression upon the broad masses of the people in enemy countries'.

Equally impassioned and sincere was Charles Chaplin's ambitious, brave, but rather uneasy satire on Nazi ideologies, *The Great Dictator*. In the case of this film, however, the timing was less than ideal. Conception to completion had taken five years, a period punctuated by protest and attacks from various groups who were unhappy about the production's undenied antifascist theme. By the time it appeared on the

screen, many people felt that the realities of Hitler's régime had become too grim for laughter, and indeed, with contemporary events now clearly visible after thirty years or more, some elements of the film appear distastefully unfunny, notably the whimsical ghetto scenes. Chaplin himself admitted that he might not have gone ahead with the film had he been aware of what was actually happening to the Jews at the time.

It is, nevertheless, a courageous farce, full of effectively barbed ridicule of 'the most dangerous man in the world'. It tells of a mild Jewish

Edmund Gwenn and Joel McCrea in *Foreign Correspondent* (Alfred Hitchcock, 1940).

Charlie Chaplin confronted with an outsize problem in *The Great Dictator* (1940).

barber who, while fleeing from persecution in
the state of Ptomania, is mistaken for the
Dictator, Adenoid Hynkel, conqueror of Auster-
lich. Instead of delivering a victory tirade as
expected, he makes a humanistic speech appealing for international peace and understanding and an end to tyranny. Perhaps the
enormity of Hitler's reign is beyond comic
realization, for as a whole the film now comes
over as blunt, uncomfortable, occasionally
tiresome, and ultimately banal, although
Chaplin strongly, and with fair argument,
defended the serious – and deeply felt – ending
of his film by asserting, 'I had a story to tell
and something I wanted very much to say
. . . the picture is two hours and seven minutes
in length. If two hours and three minutes of it is
comedy, may I not be excused for ending my
comedy on a note that reflects honestly and
realistically the world in which we live, and

I Wanted Wings (Mitchell Leisen, 1941).

may I not be excused in pleading for a better world?'

Anti-Nazi sentiments continued to find expression in American films in the early 'forties, most notably in three 1941 productions, *So Ends Our Night*, *Man Hunt*, and *Meet John Doe*. The first of these, directed with compassion by John Cromwell, is a bitter drama of fugitive workers fleeing from persecution by the Wehrmacht and finding themselves stateless. Fritz Lang's *Man Hunt* is more of a curiosity, an intriguing but rather pointless fantasy (based on Geoffrey Household's compelling story, 'Rogue Male') in which Walter Pidgeon, as a British big-game hunter, sets out, purely for sport, to bag the biggest prize of all – Hitler. Despite getting right into Berchtesgaden and having the Dictator in his sights, he does of course fail, and the main interest of the film lies in his subsequent defiance of the Gestapo (led, as so often, by sinister George Sanders). A novel touch for 1941 was permitting the German characters to talk German to each other, but the film was, on the whole, an unconvincing exercise in wishful thinking. *Meet John Doe* was Frank Capra's *vox pop* contribution to the dossier of warnings against fascism on the home front. Gary Cooper is a down-and-out persuaded by newspaperwoman Barbara Stanwyck to personify 'John Doe', symbol of protest against social injustice, particularly the injustice of financier, oil magnate and fascist, Edward Arnold. In the end he is equated with Christ ('the first John Doe') and America is thus guaranteed God's support in the coming conflict.

With neutrality no longer a viable proposition, American films began to progress away from the rhetoric of anti-Nazism towards the pragmatism of preparedness. *The Ramparts We Watch* (1940), a piece of film journalism from the *March of Time* stables, took the line that an old foe was stirring itself once again and 'the World War we wrapped in old newspapers and laid away for posterity to look back on . . . has suddenly become very much alive'. It urged full rearmament in the belief 'that the war shadow darkens America in 1940 just as ominously as it did in 1914'. Another documentary made in the same year, *The World in Flames*, imparted the same message by highlighting the political and economic events of the decade leading up to the war in Europe and the implicit threat to American democracy.

When compulsory call-up was instituted in the USA, Hollywood responded by filling the cinema screens with military bombast of all kinds. Frank Borzage contributed *Flight Command* (1940, with Robert Taylor, Ruth Hussey and Walter Pidgeon) which was, in effect, a dressed-up training film, describing the activities of a fighter squadron on an aircraft-carrier. Mitchell Leisen's *I Wanted Wings* (1941, with Ray Milland, William Holden, Wayne Morris, Brian Donlevy, Constance Moore, and Veronica Lake) performed the same function for the flying wing of the Army while dramatizing the progress of three unruly young flyers as they strive to become fully fledged pilots. This film was also a display of military strength, putting the new Flying Fortresses on show for the first time. Michael Curtiz directed his favourite actor, Errol Flynn, and Fred MacMurray in *Dive Bomber* (1941), a study of aviation medicine made as a tribute to the Navy Air Corps and its flight

John Loder (*centre*) and Tyrone Power in *A Yank in the RAF* (Henry King, 1941).

surgeons. And Lloyd Bacon put the artillery on parade in his lightweight Jack Oakie vehicle, *Navy Blues* (1941).

All this was made more palatable to potential draftees and their families by a rich leavening of service comedies, which continued as a dominant sub-genre throughout the war. The best of the early ones was David Butler's *Caught in the Draft* (1941), with Bob Hope in excellent

Gary Cooper as *Sergeant York*.

wise-cracking form as a Hollywood star straining, with valet Eddie Bracken's help, to dodge enlistment, but ending up a reluctant hero and romantic catch for Dorothy Lamour. The basic humour of Bud Abbott and Lou Costello found its perfect outlet in military surroundings, as Arthur Lubin's *In the Navy* (1941) demonstrated, and Phil Silvers began his rascally service career in the same year in Lewis Seiler's *You're in the Army Now*.

As the hostilities in Europe spread into Russia and the Atlantic (including the sinking of American ships), so Hollywood's war films took a more aggressive line. The desire to strike back manifested itself in Henry King's pro-British drama, *A Yank in the RAF* (1941), in which Tyrone Power joins the Royal Air Force, partakes in the evacuation of Dunkirk, and wins Betty Grable ('*A Yank in the RAF* may be warmongering,' said critic Howard Barnes. 'That is what makes it a worthwhile screen entertainment'). A similar 'warmongering exercise' was Seiler's *International Squadron* (1941), with Ronald Reagan as an American pilot ferrying bombers to England.

The film which aroused the strongest public emotions prior to the attack on Pearl Harbor was Howard Hawks's *Sergeant York* (1941), which has been described as the 'tragedy of a man rewarded for going against his beliefs'. An unusual film for Hawks, it tells the real-life story of Alvin C. York, a simple Tennessee farmer whose religious convictions caused him to register as a conscientious objector ('War's agin the Book') when he was drafted for war service in 1917. Urged to rethink his attitudes, he was able after meditation to reconcile his duty to his country and to God ('Render unto Caesar . . .'), and while participating in the Battle of the Argonne he became a much-bemedalled hero after single-handedly killing twenty or more Germans and taking 132 prisoners in one vital action.

Although, through the sheer bravado of its story, the film captivated and reassured audiences looking for rationalization of their growing belief that the impending war was necessary and democracy must be defended, Hawks himself was aware of the real underlying theme: 'It was based,' he said, 'on a man who actually was very religious; and so they told him to go out and do everything his religion said not to do, and he became a great hero doing it. So there was bound to be a good deal of confusion in his mind and actually it was a form of tragedy.' The uneasiness of the real York was detectable in his insistence that Gary Cooper play him on the screen, or he would not consent to the film's being made. Cooper responded with a touching, sincere, near-perfect portrayal, which won him a well-deserved Academy Award. So good was his performance, in fact, that it almost hid the film's two crucial weaknesses: the unconvincing glibness of York's conversion to patriotic duty while he communes with nature, and the heroic climax which, though it was excitingly staged and no doubt authentic, verges on the absurd after the

quiet, restrained atmosphere of the domestic scenes.

In 1941, however, *Sergeant York* had an uncomplicated relevance to the contemporary situation and it became a symbolic call to arms. Its effect as such is well summarized by Lewis Jacobs: 'The contemporary impact of the theme, the simplicity of treatment, the fidelity to a real event and a real person gave the picture conviction and made it an eloquent advocate for persuading pacifist-minded men to become war recruits.' As it happened, the idea of non-intervention was in any case finally put to rest at the end of the year by Japan's infamous, unprovoked attack on Pearl Harbor.

Some while before the United States had become engrossed in its moral crisis, before even Britain, France and Germany had become locked in combat, other wars had been fought and resolved: preludes, as it were, to the main event.

In 1935, on some slim, historical pretext, the Italians invaded and subdued Abyssinia, remaining in occupation until the British removed them in the early 'forties. Italy attempted to justify this ignoble deed in a documentary called *Path of the Heroes* (1937), a routine piece of propaganda stressing battle heroics. The Russian-made *Abyssinia* redressed the balance to some extent by concentrating on the arduous social conditions aggravated by Italy's action.

A conflict which achieved much greater emotive impact was the Spanish Civil War. This began in 1936 when reactionary elements, led by General Franco, rebelled against the newly elected left-wing government. The struggle lasted for three years, ending in victory for Franco, by which time over a million people had been killed, half a million dwellings had been destroyed, two million Spaniards were in prison, and half a million had exiled themselves.

Franco's success had been due in no small measure to aid received from Hitler and Mussolini, whereas England and France had committed themselves to non-intervention and the Republicans were given only spasmodic support by Russia.

A number of documentaries were made about the Civil War, chiefly from a Republican point of view. The most moving of these is Joris Ivens's *The Spanish Earth* (1937), which counterpoints the irrigation of newly won land near Madrid with military activity in and around the capital, the one being dependent on the other. The land is worked, recruits are trained, bombs fall, casualties are tended to, a road-bridge is fought over – all to the poignant accompaniment of a folksy, Russian-flavoured choral soundtrack.

Ivens conveyed all this in simple, poetic images which lay bare his sincerity, humanity, and uncomplicated affection for the ordinary people who worked and fought together to preserve their dignity and freedom. His backers were an equally committed group who called themselves Contemporary Historians Inc., one of whom, Ernest Hemingway, wrote and spoke the commentary for Ivens's film.

Other depictions of Loyalist Spain's courageous fight against fascism followed close on Ivens's film. Herbert Kline made *Heart of Spain* for a North American Relief Commission, focusing on the sufferings of people under bombardment and appealing for aid. Luis Buñuel, who had in 1932 exposed the terrible poverty of the Estremadura peasants in *Land Without Bread*, put together *Madrid '36* (subtitled *Loyal Spain Take Arms!*), a dull, scrappy record of events in the first year of the Civil War, rather low on action despite references to the peril the cameramen had put themselves in to achieve some of the shots. The British Progressive Film Unit contributed *Behind the Spanish Lines* and

L'Espoir (André Malraux, 1938).

Anthony Quinn, Dorothy Lamour and Gilbert Roland in *The Last Train from Madrid* (James Hogan, 1937).

Spanish ABC (directed by Thorold Dickinson). Ivor Montagu made *The Defence of Madrid* for showing at pro-Republican rallies in England. And in 1939, the Russian director Esther Shub compiled *Spain*, a brilliantly edited account of the war based on a series of newsreels shot and sent home by Roman Karmen and Boris Makaseyev.

Dramatization of the struggle in Spain took various forms, the most powerful being novelist André Malraux's *L'Espoir* (1938). This re-creation of incidents in the Civil War, made in mid-battle, as it were, achieved a raw authenticity by employing a cast of actual combatants and shooting many of its exteriors in a Barcelona airfield in between bombardments. The arrival in Barcelona of Franco's army disrupted work on the film, which was eventually completed in France.

Although carrying a veneer of careful reconstruction, *L'Espoir* contains some remarkable scenes: realistic street fighting, including a kami-kaze car drive in which a young Republican destroys both himself and a strategically placed gun by crashing into a fascist artillery post at great speed; a hazardous, heroic bombing raid on an enemy airfield, the pilot relying on navigational guidance from local peasants who fail to recognize their own countryside from the air; and a climactic descent by Republicans, carrying dead and wounded airmen, from a mountainside on which one of their bombers has crashed. It is, above all, a film with considerable emotional pull, courageous and dignified.

British and American treatments of the Civil War were not as impressive. Alex Bryce's *The*

Last Barricade (1938), a trite adventure story about a reporter who saves a spy's daughter from prison, typified the English contribution. American film-makers came on a little stronger, using a topical Spanish background for the first time in *The Last Train from Madrid* (1937). This, however, was no more than a romantic melodrama, uncommitted, uncontroversial, non-political ('Its sympathies,' said the 'New York Times', '. . . are clearly on the side of the Ruritanians').

Of greater significance was William Dieterle's *Blockade* (1938), a more positive statement about the Civil War (although it cautiously declined to differentiate between Rebel and Republican), used by producer Walter Wanger partly to preach preparedness, partly to arouse American feelings against the fascist threat, partly to test the box-office reception to politically controversial films. A shrewd publicity rumour that Franco had banned the film (which he then obligingly did) ensured it a measure of success, helped further by the casting of Henry Fonda and Madeleine Carroll. Although a simple-minded, inadequate piece of propaganda, Dieterle's film was, for Hollywood, strong politics. It clearly sided with the radical cause, and Fonda's impassioned appeal into the camera at the end ('This is not war but murder. Where is the conscience of the world?') was considered remarkably bold. By focusing on and deploring war's effects on civilians, *Blockade* was also, in its naïve way, a genuinely humane film.

Hollywood hid its commitment in similar fashion when it returned to Spain in 1943 with Sam Wood's adaptation of Hemingway's *For Whom the Bell Tolls*, with Gary Cooper, Ingrid Bergman and Akim Tamiroff. Producer Adolph Zukor called it a film 'without any political connotation – we are neither for nor against anyone', but it was still banned in Spain.

A third source of pre-World War strife was Japan's undeclared war against China, begun as early as 1931 with the attack on Manchuria and intensified in 1936 when Japanese troops invaded China itself.

Predictably, Western film-makers failed on the whole to treat this act of blatant aggression with more than remote interest or indignation. Britain and Hollywood, in fact, used it simply as an excuse to set their screen melodramas against a freshly topical setting. *Incident in Shanghai* (1938), directed by John Paddy Carstairs, showed a British pilot flying for the Chinese; *Too Hot to Handle* (1938), with Clark Gable and Myrna Loy, and *Exiled to Shanghai* (1937) were both stories of newsreel men in China; *Daughter of Shanghai* (1938) was principally about smuggling; and two more 1938 productions, *International Settlement* and *West of Shanghai*, focused on the bombing of Shanghai. Even as late as 1943, fantasy was still proving stronger than reality as Alan Ladd exterminated large portions of the Japanese Army while lending Chinese guerrillas a helping hand in *China*. A film with a little more substance to it was Lewis Milestone's *The General Died at Dawn* (1936), a spy story set in Manchuria which worked in a message or two about feudal oppression.

One exception to the blandness was Joris Ivens's *The 400 Million* (1938–39), another project set up by Contemporary Historians,

The 400 Million (Joris Ivens, 1938–39).

whose company by now included stars like Fredric March, Franchot Tone and Luise Rainer. Ivens's film is about the efforts of the people of China to repel the Japanese invasion, centring on a battle in which the former were indeed victorious, although this was not to be their common experience. Georges Sadoul called it (in 1939) 'one of the most striking documents ever produced on any war'.

Japanese film-makers themselves betrayed a remarkable ambiguity towards the policy of military aggression, at least for a year or two until the government clamped down on unaligned thinking. During the brief period of grace, two directors, Tomotaka Tasaka and Kimisaburo Yoshimura, were able to turn out three exceptional war films based on the Sino-Japanese conflict (single surviving prints of which have only recently been unearthed).

The finest of these was Tasaka's *Five Scouts*

adventures. What they do experience is the full horror of war, presented by Tasaka in a terrifying, abstract way, making effective use of the soundtrack.

This unusual film, shot with a surprising technical virtuosity, set the pattern for a number of subsequent Japanese movies, not all of which, however, managed with such skill to question the validity of war while prudently paying lip-service to patriotism, duty and self-sacrifice.

One which did was Tasaka's next odyssey of war, *Mud and Soldiers* (1939), a virtually plotless affair designed officially to encourage public support for the Chinese adventure but containing very little propaganda. Tasaka manages to convey such a realistic feeling of battle, in fact, that it is difficult not to interpret his attitude as one of rejection of war.

The third of this intriguing trio of films was Yoshimura's *The Story of Tank Commander Nishizumi* (1940), in which the humanistic values are probably the strongest of all. In contrast to the traditional occidental image of Japanese savagery during war, Yoshimura's hero is outwardly friendly towards enemy civilians, and gives aid to a Chinese woman and her child.

Alas, by this time the Japanese government was already enforcing a code of film-making to take account of war preparation and to encourage 'the national Japanese philosophy . . . and the spirit of complete sacrifice for the nation', and it became impossible for Tasaka and Yoshimura to mine fully the rich vein of their promise. Japan's thinking was now approximately in line with that of Goebbels and global warfare was just one bomb attack away.

(1938), Japan's first major war film – this genre never having had cause to develop in Japan's film history, and the classic pacifist movies such as *All Quiet . . .* and *Westfront 1918* having been banned from Nippon screens. A story of five ordinary soldiers out on patrol, *Five Scouts* is really about survival: the soldiers are not heroic, they have a sense of duty but not of divine mission, they are not particularly nationalistic, and they experience no great

The Necessary War

The Fight for Democracy

It is a little disquieting to observe that it took a world war to revive Britain's sagging cinema. The 'thirties had not been short of talent – Korda, Hitchcock, Saville, Reed were all active – and some good films had been produced, but in terms of quality the overall record was a dismal one: British films tended, with few exceptions, to be dull, insipid, unimaginative, studio-bound, technically hidebound, and pathetically derivative. There was no reason to suppose that this decline would be halted by the outbreak of war in September 1939, but (in the words of Dr Roger Manvell, writing in the near-Biblical 'International Encyclopedia of Film') 'the miracle happened. British feature film-making was born of an entirely new spirit of austerity and strenuous work. The stupidities, extravagances and dishonesties of the passing decade were all but eliminated as if at a single stroke. . . . Quality

began to emerge as if the industry had received shock therapy.' In short, World War II proved to be, from a film-making point of view, Britain's finest hour.

The key to this renaissance lay in the character and style of the one branch of British cinema which had built up a decent reputation: the documentary movement led and inspired by John Grierson. The distinctive, highly original factual films turned out by Grierson's team of talents were regarded by the industry as a clever, but marginal and uncommercial by-product. Suddenly, however, their realism, dry pragmatism and concern with the life and problems of the ordinary British citizen seemed perfectly suited to the social atmosphere of the times. They were, moreover, already geared to the kind of practical, flexible, fast, low-budget film-making dictated by wartime conditions, and were at once promoted to the forefront

Model aircraft fly across a cardboard island in *Ships with Wings* (Sergei Nolbandov, 1941).

Sally Gray and Anton Walbrook in *Dangerous Moonlight* (Brian Desmond Hurst, 1941).

Tommy Trinder, Michael Wilding and Claude Hulbert in *Sailors Three* (Walter Forde, 1940).

Ralph Richardson and Merle Oberon in *The Lion Has Wings* (Michael Powell, Brian Desmond Hurst and Adrian Brunel, 1939).

Michael Wilding (*left*), John Clements and David Hutcheson (*all standing*) in *Convoy* (Pen Tennyson, 1940).

of production; meanwhile while the feature side paused for readjustment. When feature films started to re-emerge in quantity (a relative term since output of features during the war was restricted to between fifty and sixty a year, compared with 225 in 1937), they reflected the sober realism of the documentaries and succeeded in projecting the peculiar nature of the war and the character, personality and attitudes of the people who were fighting in it. They still retained a few bad habits from the past, but at their worst they were the product of a recognizable, indigenous culture. At their best they formed a perceptive and convincingly human portrait of a nation at arms.

The war unified the British in an unusual way, lowering class barriers, providing both a common cause and a sense of national identity, and engendering in the people as a whole a modest self-respect and quiet determination to safeguard the white cliffs of democracy. Confronted with German notions of 'superiority', the British took a collective pride in being 'ordinary', and the phenomenon of an entire populace mentally rolling up its sleeves is remarkably well conveyed in the war features of the period. These films also share, in varying degrees, a number of other characteristics. They are gritty, serious (though never without a sense of humour), realistic, informative, emotionally restrained, not given to expressions of overt nationalism, and relatively tolerant towards the enemy. War is still a game, but one in which it is more important to win than to take part.

These qualities and traits, which gave the best wartime films an intrinsic value as propaganda and entertainment, did not, of course, appear the moment war was declared. On the contrary – *The Lion Has Wings*, the first feature backed by the Ministry of Information, rushed out for release in November 1939, was considered (at least by the cognoscenti) a fairly disastrous miscalculation of mood. Produced by Alexander Korda (who, according to the film's story-writer, Ian Dalrymple, cashed in his life insurance to pay for it) and directed by Michael Powell, Brian Desmond Hurst and Adrian Brunel, it is a scrappy, sentimental, jingoistic account, semi-dramatized (Ralph Richardson as a wing commander, Merle Oberon as a fervently patriotic nurse), of the events leading to the outbreak of war and the RAF raid on the Kiel Canal. The Establishment and the Press, preconditioned, liked the film, but the MOI realized it was a mistake, and the documentary-makers were quick to counter with their unique brand of unpretentious realism. Fiction features were rarely guilty thereafter of carrying such hollow propaganda.

The next two years saw audiences, seeking escape, companionship, and moral comfort, swell to an unprecedented level, while film-makers tried out a variety of themes and formulas, the documentarists leading them progressively nearer to the new realism. Routine heroics were supplied by Michael Powell in his espionage thriller, *Contraband* (1940), with Conrad Veidt, as a Danish merchant captain, helping girl agent Valerie Hobson to outwit German spies. Marcel Varnel's *Neutral Port* (1940) has another merchant skipper (Will Fyffe) avenging the loss of his ship by stealing a German supply vessel and ramming a U-boat. Maurice Elvey attempted to dramatize Britain's first naval triumph of the war, the sinking of the German pocket-battleship the Graf Spee, in *For Freedom* (1940), throwing in for good measure an early impersonation of Hitler by Billy Russell. Brian Desmond Hurst tackled the problem of traumatic amnesia (albeit in rather moody, romantic fashion) in *Dangerous Moonlight* (1941) –

Eric Portman in *49th Parallel* (Michael Powell, 1941).

famous for its popular theme music, 'The Warsaw Concerto' – about a Polish pianist (played by the excellent *émigré* actor Anton Walbrook) who escapes to the West, marries a rich reporter (Sally Gray) and loses his memory after taking part in the Battle of Britain. And Jiri Weiss contributed a slight, rather banal fantasy called *John Smith Wakes Up* (1940), in which a man (Eliot Makeham) is encouraged to join the fight for freedom by a dream in which he sees Britain conquered by the Nazis. Meanwhile, escapism and war linked arms in such thoroughly pleasant entertainments as Varnel's *Let George Do It* (1940), which had George Formby, ukelele in hand, unmasking spies in

Robert Beatty (*left*), Emrys Jones (*third from left*) and Bernard Miles in *One of Our Aircraft is Missing* (Michael Powell and Emeric Pressburger, 1942).

Noël Coward in *In Which We Serve* (Coward and David Lean, 1942).

Norway, and Walter Forde's charming, lively *Sailors Three* (1940), a 'breezy nautical comedy' with songs, in which Able-Seamen Tommy Trinder, Claude Hulbert and Michael Wilding capture an enemy battleship.

The most popular film of 1940 was the Ealing production, *Convoy*, directed by Pen Tennyson, a prestige production which offered an effective reply to Nazi propaganda films with its story of a British cruiser, outgunned and under heavy fire, engaging a German battleship long enough to save a convoy of merchant vessels. The 'Monthly Film Bulletin' hailed it as 'the most exciting, lifelike and restrained account of the Navy's work in wartime yet seen on the screen'. The officer class was represented by Clive Brook and John Clements, Albert Lieven appeared in one of his countless German roles, and a long cast included many stalwarts of the

period, with a newcomer, Stewart Granger, bringing up the rear.

The heroics in another Ealing tribute (this time to the Fleet Air Arm), Sergei Nolbandov's *Ships with Wings* (1941), are much more of an old-fashioned, romanticized, phlegmatically English kind, with the hero (John Clements) redeeming himself after a blemished career by flying his aeroplane self-sacrificially into a vitally important, Axis-held dam (cleverly taking with him his arch-enemy, a German pilot). Effective scenes shot on board the aircraft-carrier Ark Royal give the film a modicum of interest, but mostly it is imperialistic melodrama, marred by some disastrously obvious model-work. Everything, in fact, from the dam to the planes to a whole Greek island, is so clearly made of ticky-tacky that Noël Coward was moved to describe it as 'Gamages, dear boy, pure Gamages'. In their shame, Ealing began after this to strive for greater realism, and eventually even gained a reputation for doing so.

The theme of resistance by Germans to their own régime – part fact, part wishful thinking – was tackled in two features at this time. John and Roy Boulting's *Pastor Hall* (1940) cast Wilfrid Lawson in a role freely based on religious resistance hero Martin Niemöller. A moving, dignified film, it recounts the tragedy of a village pastor who, in 1934, denounces the Nazis, is arrested and tortured, escapes, refuses to flee the country, speaks his mind once again, and is shot by stormtroopers as he leaves his church. Anthony Asquith's *Freedom Radio* (1941), a skilful, if unremarkable film, tells of an anti-Nazi Viennese throat specialist (Clive Brook) who establishes a secret radio link with like-minded Germans in order to broadcast the truth about Hitler's régime. Contemporary

Refugees take cover from strafing aircraft in *The Foreman Went to France* (Charles Frend, 1942).

100

Ad hoc surgery for the Chief Engineer . . . Barry Letts, Ralph Michael, Walter Fitzgerald and Robert Beatty in *San Demetrio – London* (Charles Frend, 1943).

critics liked the story's 'unstressed heroism' and the proficiency of Brook, but found the plot generally unconvincing.

Asquith made two further competent but conventional war features before rediscovering his old touch. *Cottage to Let* (1941) is a spy story set in Scotland, in which John Mills (disguised as an RAF pilot) turns out, rather improbably, to be a Nazi agent seeking the plans of a new bombsight. *Uncensored* (1942) is similar to *Freedom Radio*, except that the setting is Belgium and instead of radio the medium of resistance is a newspaper, 'La Libre Belgique', run by a popular cabaret entertainer (Eric Portman).

One of the subtler and more beguiling pieces of propaganda from this formative period was Leslie Howard's gentle, entertaining *Pimpernel Smith* (1941) which, with humour and hints of self-mockery, contrasts the traditional, historical 'goodness' of the British (the upper classes, at least) with the vulgarity, smugness and stupidity of the new breed of upstart Germans. It makes the (dangerous) assumption, one made frequently in British films in the early war years, that the innate corruptness of the

Nazi régime will cause Germany to collapse quickly from within, and the forces of democracy will achieve a swift and inevitable victory. Howard himself took the part of Professor Horatio Smith, a refined, aristocratic, whimsical university don – in German eyes, the archetypal joke Englishman – behind whose elegant, silly-ass façade there is the cold-tempered steel of a fearless British agent. He is, of course, a reincarnation of The Scarlet Pimpernel (played also by Leslie Howard in the 1935 film version), infinitely superior to his adversaries and able to outwit them with effortless ease at every turn. The Nazis, as deliciously embodied in a grotesque Himmler-Goering imitation by the inimitable Francis L. Sullivan, are, to a man, dim, brutal and humourless. The film ends with Smith, having delayed the invasion of Poland and eluded his enemies yet again, delivering a homily to the audience on the meaning of the war and the ultimate victory of the weak (but morally strong) over the strong (but morally weak). For the times, it was a stirring, seductive, finely calculated blend of message and massage.

The basic plot of *Pimpernel Smith* concerns

British Tommies come to the aid of a Nazi-held English village in *Went the Day Well?* (Alberto Cavalcanti, 1942).

the rescue of political prisoners from Nazi Germany, in particular the escape of a Polish journalist, Ludmilla Koslowski (Mary Morris). Carol Reed used a similar theme, though more conventionally, in his excellent early film *Night Train to Munich* (1940), in which Intelligence man Rex Harrison poses as a Nazi in order to effect the rescue of a Czech inventor (James Harcourt) and his daughter (Margaret Lockwood). Paul Henreid (then known as Paul von Hernried) played a Gestapo agent, and Basil Radford and Naunton Wayne gave a repeat of their performances in *The Lady Vanishes* as English commuters a long way from home.

The most prominent – and profitable – film of 1941 was Michael Powell's *49th Parallel*, an ambitious, two-hour variation on one of Powell's favourite themes, respect for the enemy. It had a high-calibre cast (Laurence Olivier, Leslie Howard, Raymond Massey, Anton Walbrook, Eric Portman, Glynis Johns, plus strong support from the likes of Finlay Currie and Niall MacGinnis), was scripted by Powell's imminent partner, Emeric Pressburger, and edited by David Lean, and was one of the first war features to show tangible signs of the documentary influence. It is an episodic account of the efforts of a group of survivors from a U-boat sunk in the Gulf of St Lawrence to escape to the neutral USA via Canada. They are all committed Nazis, a fact demonstrated by their ruthlessness and brutality; their leader (Portman, in a performance which made his reputation) is especially intransigent. On their wanderings the group come across a settlement of Herrnhuters (fugitives from Nazi Germany) and make an unsuccessful attempt to infiltrate them. One of the party is struck by the sincerity of his ex-countrymen, but is shot for his pains when he tries to speak up on their behalf. The message is that while the free world might be fighting a Germany which had become rotten, there were still good Germans to be found. Partly financed by the British government, *49th Parallel* was both effective propaganda and a thoroughly well-made film, full of authentic touches such as showing the Germans photographing the death-throes of a ship they have just sunk.

Michael Powell, rapidly laying the foundations for an arguable claim to being the finest British director of this period, if not of all time, was less subtle, less generous towards the enemy in his next film, *One of Our Aircraft is Missing* (1942) – possibly because it was dedicated to Holland, whose people had suffered intensely at Nazi hands. All the same, Powell used ridicule against the Germans rather than malice. The first Powell-Pressburger joint production (they also co-directed and co-scripted the film), this was, in effect, a dramatized, bigger-budgeted version of Harry Watt's 1941 documentary, *Target for Tonight*, in that it dealt with bomber crews and showed Britain as the aggressor. The film is an uneasy mixture of documentary and fictional techniques, beginning with a tense, realistic bombing raid over Stuttgart, and developing, when the bomber crashes, into a rather improbable escape odyssey as the crew repatriate themselves with the help of the Dutch underground. Notable features of the film include the spectacle of the bombing raid, overlaid with a fantastic fire and studded with parachutes and flak; the use of natural sound only; the aura of confidence and sangfroid which surrounds the airmen and is clearly meant to be conveyed to the audience ('With such confidence one could take careful aim' – Isaksson and Furhammar); the lack of love-interest, a novelty in 1942; Pamela Browne's upstaging performance as a no-nonsense Dutch schoolmistress; and an astonishing cast list, headed by Godfrey Tearle, Eric Portman and Hugh Williams, and on which the *last* five names are Robert Helpmann, Peter Ustinov, Alec Clunes, Roland Culver and Stewart Rome.

In 1942 and 1943, the British war feature reached maturity and a steady flow of good-quality films helped to keep the cinemas full. Perhaps the most significant production to appear at this time was Thorold Dickinson's *The Next of Kin* (1942), a military training film on the dangers of careless talk which mixed documentary and fiction so successfully that it was released in the commercial cinemas and continued to draw audiences long after the war.

This new technique launched by Dickinson was used to good effect in several subsequent productions. The biggest and best received of these was Noël Coward's ineffably class-conscious naval drama, *In Which We Serve* (1942), the most popular film of the period and a rare success for English film-making in America, where it was voted most outstanding film of the year by both the National Board of Review of Motion Pictures and the New York Critics. For Coward, who produced, co-directed (with David Lean, whose directorial début this was), scripted, composed the music, and starred in the film, it was virtually a one-man venture, and it bears his unique stamp in its restraint, poignancy and defence of English values. It is the unheroic story of an English destroyer, HMS Torrin, and the men who serve in her, told in flashback from the time of her sinking in the Battle of Crete. The film concentrates on the musings of three survivors – the Captain (Coward), the Chief Petty Officer (Bernard Miles), and an Able Seaman (John Mills) – who recall their lives both on board the Torrin and ashore with their wives and families.

Although Coward's film has become something of a museum-piece, with time devaluing its propaganda effect and blunting its credibility, it can still be admired for its integrity, its empathy with the servicemen it is portraying, and above all for the acting of its fine cast, among whom is a teenaged Richard Attenborough in his movie début, commencing his typecast career below decks as a cowardly stoker.

A leading exponent of the new realism in fiction films was Charles Frend, who directed three notable features during the middle-war period. The first of them, *The Big Blockade* (1942), was a straightforward piece of propaganda dramatizing the blockade of Germany by the Ministry of Economic Warfare, the Navy and the RAF ('Fighting is one side of war. There is another side – that is, stopping the enemy from fighting').

Frend followed this with *The Foreman Went to France* (1942), the intriguing story (based on an actual incident involving one Melbourne Johns) of a factory foreman (Clifford Evans) who goes to France in 1940 to retrieve some special-purpose machines in order to prevent them getting into German hands. With the help of two soldiers (Tommy Trinder and Gordon Jackson, the latter making his screen début) he survives fifth-columnists, strafing, lack of food, fire and other dangers and completes his mission.

More downbeat is *San Demetrio – London* (1943), another incredible fact-based story, directed by Frend in a self-effacing, almost matter-of-fact style which makes it seem all the more truthful and dramatic – 'a film narrative,' said the 'New Statesman', 'that really comes out of the national temperament'. It is about a group of seamen who abandon ship during an attack on their convoy, drift for days in an open boat, miraculously rediscover their original vessel, the San Demetrio, burning but still afloat, reclaim her and set her limping home to England with only a school atlas to give navigational guidance. With the cast under-acting almost to the point of anonymity, this is one of the most restrained and (in terms of both image and mood) accurate of the Ealing war features.

Two leading members of the documentary movement, Harry Watt and Alberto Cavalcanti, turned to feature film-making for Ealing, thus

Rosamund John, David Niven and Leslie Howard in *The First of the Few* (Howard, 1942), the story of Spitfire-designer R.J. Mitchell.

resists menial war work at first, but eventually knuckles down and falls in love with the factory foreman (Eric Portman). It is unsensational stuff, but handled with conviction, humour and humanity.

Women, and their contribution to the war effort, are paid an even stronger tribute by Leslie Howard (co-directing with Maurice Elvey) in *The Gentle Sex* (1943), which recounts the experiences of seven diverse girls who join the Auxiliary Territorial Service and do their bit at an anti-aircraft station.

Leslie Howard directed himself once again in *The First of the Few* (1942), a romantic film biography of R. J. Mitchell, the designer of the Spitfire prototype, which co-starred David Niven as test-pilot Geoffrey Crisp. But this dealt mainly with the inter-war years, and a good account of the Battle of Britain had yet to be made.

Not all the leading talents were entirely sold on the documentary style. Asquith, for example, resisted being depersonalized by the demands of the new realism and happily did not forsake his natural lyricism and wit to accommodate it. He did, though, find a satisfactory compromise with *We Dive at Dawn* (1943), a tribute to the submarine service which also marked a solid return to form. This quietly absorbing film tells of a voyage into the Baltic by the submarine Sea Tiger in pursuit of the German battleship Brandenburg. The submarine hunts down the battleship and attacks it with torpedoes, but is immediately beset by destroyers and forced to lie low. Out of fuel, it puts into an occupied Danish port and, with the help of local patriots, manages to refuel and escape back to England.

Leaving aside some rather stagey and inadequate onshore scenes designed to shed light on the character and home life of the ordinary seaman ('the trouble may be that very few English actors have the vaguest idea of how anyone below a duchess behaves in normal circumstances,' remarked the 'Documentary News Letter'), Asquith's film is a first-rate action drama, tense, low-keyed and nearly always believable. The torpedo attack on the Brandenburg is particularly well handled, with the periscope going up and down like a yo-yo and an authentically irritable atmosphere prevailing. And the acting throughout, especially from John Mills and Eric Portman, is admirably plain and self-effacing. On the debit side, a false note is struck by portraying the Germans simply as archetypes (they are all either arrogant or cowardly); the script at times takes British understatement close to parody ('One comes in, another goes out,' muses a member of the top brass poetically, watching two subs pass each other at the harbour entrance. 'Just like running a ruddy bus service!'); and the much-copied routine of firing chattels and dead bodies through a torpedo-tube to simulate being sunk, though undoubtedly novel at the time, has the air now of a well-worn cliché. But the film was, in its best moments, a welcome confirmation of Asquith's real ability.

setting the seal on the new form. Cavalcanti made *Went the Day Well?* (1942), a Graham Greene story, about a quiet English village whose occupants offer stiff resistance to invading German paratroops – a rather surprising blend of fantasy and feasibility, but handled with immaculate control by its director. Watt contributed *Nine Men* (1943), the story of a rearguard action against the Italians by a handful of soldiers holed up in a derelict Libyan tomb. On this the documentary influence was emphatically apparent, and 'the result,' said the 'Monthly Film Bulletin', 'comes as near to a native style of British film-making as anything which has yet been seen. . . . One feels that justice has been done in a film to all these qualities in the British character in wartime of which we are proud.'

Frank Launder and Sidney Gilliat adapted the new realism to the home front in their modest but much admired *Millions Like Us* (1943) which, set in an aircraft factory, concentrates on the lives and courage of ordinary people, mostly women. One young girl (Patricia Roc) marries a pilot (Gordon Jackson) who is reported missing shortly afterwards; another (Anne Crawford), from a middle-class family,

The vein of irony and self-mockery which was always present as an undertone in Asquith's films came to the surface in his next venture, *The Demi-Paradise* (1943), a comedy about Anglo-Russian relations (the first friendly gesture towards the Soviet Union in British films) which held an amiable mirror up to English foibles. The plot concerns a young Soviet marine engineer (brilliantly played by Laurence Olivier) who has invented a new type of propeller and makes two trips to England to supervise its manufacture there. On the first, made early in 1939, he is disconcerted to find the English smug, obsessed with tradition, and possessed of a most peculiar sense of humour, along with other idiosyncrasies. On the second, made in 1941, he sees the country at war and recognizes the latent qualities of friendliness and warmth in the British character. He has, meanwhile, fallen in love with the grand-daughter (Penelope Dudley Ward) of an eccentric shipowner (Felix Aylmer) and promises to return to her when the war is over.

This gentle satire, tending at times to exaggeration and caricature (a result, possibly, of the script having been written by an expatriate Russian, Anatole de Grunwald) has retained its charm and still merits the praise it drew from contemporary critics. The 'New Statesman' called it 'the nearest thing yet to English René Clair'; Dilys Powell observed, with reference to Asquith, 'that a natural talent is at its best when working in its own manner'; and the 'News Chronicle' decided that 'a certain glossy charm carried it along, and the misty sentimentality of Anthony Asquith's direction is consistent'. For all that, though, America found the film alienating, Bosley Crowther of the 'New York Times'

deciding 'the prospect is not very rosy that this picture will generate many Anglophiles. For not only is it rather stuffy in its regard for British temperament, but it lacks the intended quality of popular comedy-romance. And also, to be more explicit, it has an oddly patronising air towards the gentleman visitor from Russia, whom it presumes to educate to British ways . . . this is a limp and dampish hand across the sea.'

Other home-front films which put the English character on display included Maurice Elvey's saga of the (lower middle-class) Bunting family, *Salute John Citizen* (1942), with Edward Rigby and Stanley Holloway, and *The Bells Go Down* (1943), a semi-documentary comedy drama (no mean feat in itself) about the Auxiliary Fire Service, directed by Basil Dearden and starring Tommy Trinder and James Mason. Dearden had previously directed (with comedian Will Hay) a more conventional war comedy, *The Goose Steps Out* (1942), a fairly unsubtle send-up of the Nazis mostly remembered now for a minor piece of scene-stealing by a young, bespectacled Peter Ustinov as a repulsive German schoolboy.

Among the more routine features made during this prolific period, espionage and resistance continued to be popular topics. Harold French almost made a career out of them, directing in quick succession in 1942 *Unpublished Story*, an uninspired drama about a war correspondent (Richard Greene) who exposes a peace organization as a Nazi sabotage agency; *The Day Will Dawn*, a strongly cast (Ralph Richardson, Deborah Kerr, Hugh Williams, Griffith Jones, Francis L. Sullivan . . .), decently scripted (Terence Rattigan, de Grunwald) action picture, set in

Eric Portman and John Mills in *We Dive at Dawn* (Anthony Asquith, 1943).

105

Laurence Olivier as a Soviet marine engineer in *The Demi-Paradise* (Anthony Asquith, 1943).

Norway in which a reporter and a seaman's daughter are rescued by commandos after destroying a U-boat base; and *Secret Mission*, a story about agents in France, with Hugh Williams, James Mason and Michael Wilding. Other films in this category were John Harlow's *This Was Paris* (1942), with Ben Lyon, in which an American fashion-designer is suspected of being a spy; Lance Comfort's *Squadron Leader X* (1942), which has a Nazi war hero (Eric Portman) posing as a British pilot in his efforts to return to Germany; Harold Bucquet's *Adventures of Tartu* (1943), a rather fanciful affair, set in Czechoslovakia, in which a British officer (Robert Donat) poses as a Rumanian ex-diplomat in order to blow up a poison-gas plant; and George King's *Candlelight in Algeria* (1943), which tells how a British agent and an American girl (James Mason, Carla Lehmann) co-operate to save a photograph of an Allied rendezvous from spies.

There was also a brief but curious vogue for films depicting resistance fighters posing as collaborators to achieve their ends. George King set this particular ball rolling with

Tomorrow We Live (1942), with John Clements and Greta Gynt, and the theme was quickly adopted by Vernon Sewell and Gordon Wellesley in *The Silver Fleet* (1943), with Ralph Richardson and Googie Withers; by Sergei Nolbandov in *Undercover* (1943) – John Clements again; by Lance Comfort and Mutz Greenbaum in *Escape to Danger* (1943), Eric Portman starring; and by Herbert Wilcox in *Yellow Canary* (1943), with Anna Neagle and Richard Greene.

The theme of Americans crossing the Atlantic to support the European war effort was revived temporarily by Walter Forde in *Flying Fortress* (1942), about an American pilot who joins the RAF and takes part in a raid on Berlin. Of greater interest, however, were those war films which attempted to get out of the rut and express themselves in new ways. The most intriguing of these was *Thunder Rock* (1942), directed by Roy Boulting and produced by his brother John. In this, a journalist in Canada in the late 'thirties (Michael Redgrave) retires in disgust to a lighthouse when his campaign against fascism fails to arouse support. During

his sojourn, he conjures up incarnations of European immigrants who drowned in a storm ninety years earlier. They recount their life histories and the journalist realizes that their tribulations were greater than his own frustration. Also unusual, in concept if not in execution, was Jeffrey Dell's *The Flemish Farm* (1943), with Clive Brook and Clifford Evans, in which a Belgian airman returns to his occupied homeland to retrieve the squadron's flag, buried on a dead friend's farm.

Powell and Pressburger stole everybody's thunder in 1943 with the release of their two-and-threequarter-hour blockbuster, *The Life and Death of Colonel Blimp*, at £1,000,000 the most expensive film made in Britain up to that time, and considered by many to be one of the greatest of any period. Felicitously described (by Leslie Halliwell) as 'a mischievous account of the British military character', the film is a daringly timed satire on red-necked, dyed-in-the-wool, professional English soldiery, a breed whose built-in obsolescence is more than outweighed by its durability and instinct for survival. Woven into this theme is the parallel,

contrasting one of how other nations (particularly the Germans) conduct their martial affairs – usually, in Blimp's eyes, in a far more pragmatic and ruthless but largely inefficient and unsporting way.

Blimp's real name is Clive Wynne-Candy (beautifully played by Roger Livesey as a well-intentioned, good-hearted, bumbling, blink-ered, big-game-hunting jingoist), whose life is traced from his days as a VC-winning hero of the Boer War to his dotage in World War II. On the way, he befriends a sensitive, intelligent German officer (Anton Walbrook), a liberal realist who eventually flees to Britain on the eve of war and teaches Blimp the true nature of the struggle: 'This is not a gentleman's war. . . . If you lose, there will be no return match next year.' Blimp remains uncomprehending, and in a Home Guard exercise he is humiliated by a younger officer who breaks 'the rules' by making his move before the appointed time. The message, for a country engaged in a war against incorrigible evil, is clear: if Britain is to win she must play the Nazis at their own game, without compromise or chivalry, using the enemy's own distasteful methods.

The ambiguity of Michael Powell's achievement is in making Blimp such a sympathetic figure, a symbol of nostalgia and sportsmanship (not necessarily abhorrent things, though they may be irrelevant and dangerous in 1943) – a kind of English Everyman. It is this element, together with its marvellous evocation of England itself, which makes the film, like Blimp and his kind, such an enduring creation.

Curiously, Powell and Pressburger followed *Colonel Blimp* with a brief (forty-six-minute), anti-climactic exercise in down-the-line propaganda called *The Volunteer*, in which Ralph Richardson played himself and Pat McGrath played his dresser, who goes off to join the Fleet Air Arm and wins the DSM. During which time, presumably, the future Sir Ralph has to dress himself.

After 1943, there was a pronounced decline in the number of war films put before the British public, barely a dozen being produced in the eighteen months leading up to the end of the war. One of them, *For Those in Peril* (1944), a shortish tribute to Air/Sea Rescue with David Farrar, marked the modest directing début of Charles Crichton, who was to make some of the best Ealing comedies, such as *The Lavender Hill Mob*. Others tackled an assortment of themes with varying success. Maurice Elvey's *A Medal for the General* (1944), with Godfrey Tearle and Jeanne de Casalis, dramatized one of the more curious home-front phenomena, evacuation, which abruptly threw together people of different classes (in Elvey's film, cockney evacuees are billeted on an old general, with happy results) and caused more social ripples than is commonly supposed. Frank Launder directed an oddity called *2,000 Women* (1944), about two British pilots who parachute into a women's internment camp in France, of interest mainly for its line-up of Rank actresses, including Phyllis Calvert, Patricia Roc, Anne Crawford and Jean Kent. Vernon Sewell's *The World Owes Me a Living* (1945) starred David Farrar once again, this time as an amnesiac who gradually recalls how, as a pilot in a flying circus, he once helped

Anton Walbrook, Deborah Kerr and Roger Livesey in *The Life and Death of Colonel Blimp* (Powell and Pressburger, 1943).

to devise a troop-carrying glider. Max Greene's overlong *The Man from Morocco* (1945) had Anton Walbrook as a Czech who escapes to London with important secret information. And John Boulting made *Journey Together* (1945), from a Terence Rattigan story, about an RAF trainee (Richard Attenborough) who fails to make the grade as a pilot but succeeds in becoming a navigator; Edward G. Robinson and Bessie Love gave the film a touch of class.

Patriotism, meanwhile, received one last big boost in Laurence Olivier's wholly delightful adaptation of Shakespeare's *Henry V* (1945) – made with victory in mind – with its splendidly rousing speeches, its emotional appeals to national sentiment, its spectacular battle scenes, and its pervasive generous air of firm reconciliation.

The best of the films brought out as the conflict neared its close were those which probed the background and psychology of those at war. Sidney Gilliat's *Waterloo Road* (1945), for example, an atmospheric melodrama about a cockney soldier (John Mills) who goes absent without leave to set about the man who has seduced his wife, uses an authentic South London background. Although dated now, this was a novel touch at the time and Leslie Halliwell sees the film as the beginning of the British realist movement which eventually led to *Saturday Night and Sunday Morning*.

The Way Ahead (1944) studied the reactions of civilians called up into the Army after Dunkirk. Directed by Carol Reed from a script by Eric Ambler and Peter Ustinov, and photographed by Guy Green, it began as a military propaganda short and grew into a prestige tribute to the British Army, with a long cast of stalwart English actors led by David Niven, Raymond Huntley, William Hartnell and Stanley Holloway. The film follows the lives and fortunes of seven reluctant conscripts as they progress from training to active service in North Africa, blending comedy and action and ending on a note which anticipates final victory.

One of the best and most satisfying films of the war came right at the end – Asquith's memorable and convincing portrait of RAF and USAF pilots, *The Way to the Stars* (1945), a triumphant peak in the collaboration between Asquith, de Grunwald (producer) and Rattigan (story and scriptwriter). Eschewing, to remarkable effect, scenes of actual combat, it describes the lives, loves and deaths of British and American bomber pilots on an English airfield in 1940. Opening with a camera tour of the deserted, desolate airfield, with its nostalgic reminders of more active times (an idea flatteringly used by Henry King in *Twelve O'Clock High* a few years later), the film flashes back to the early war years. Two pilots, Peter and David (John Mills and Michael Redgrave), become friends. Peter falls in love with Iris (Renée Asherson) but refuses to marry her when David is killed, leaving behind a wife (Rosamund John) and son. A contingent of American pilots, among them Johnny and Joe (Douglass Montgomery and Bonar Colleano), joins the base. Mutual distrust springs up, soon to change into friendship and understanding. Johnny dies, Peter and Iris are reunited – and all the while, the whole business of flying and organizing operations is carried through in counterpoint.

The film contains many fine touches, in addition to the overall quality of the acting which lends depth and subtlety to some familiar character types. There is effective and disturbing reference to the poem 'Johnny Head-in-Air'; a marvellously moving rendering of 'Let Him Go, Let Him Tarry' by the sixteen-year-old Jean Simmons; an embryonic cameo

from another newcomer, Trevor Howard; and a magnificent score by Nicholas Brodsky, subsequently one of the most familiar and popular of any British film bar *Genevieve*.

As with many of the major films of the war (*In Which We Serve*, *The Way Ahead*, etc.), some of the values and sentiments of *The Way to the Stars* seem dated and inappropriate now, but much of the contemporary opinion holds good. The late Ernest Lindgren, writing in the 'Monthly Film Bulletin', rightly regarded it 'as a film of atmosphere . . . so successful and so entertaining that it must rank as one of the outstanding British films of the war years. No other film has so subtly and so truthfully portrayed the life of the airman in war, its problems, its hazards, its exaggerated casualness towards death, its courage, its humour, its comradeship.' Richard Winnington described it as 'a moving film . . . which somehow catches the rhythm of war and the baffled courage of men and women who cannot sort out the vast thing that grips them, a war film without slogans and brilliant heroics'; an assessment echoed by Dilys Powell, who wrote that the film 'flawlessly revives the mood of the war'. More important, perhaps, was Asquith and Rattigan's treatment of Anglo-American relations, analysed best by Pat Jackson in 'Our Time': 'The film accepts that we are two very different peoples, with very clear-cut misconceptions, prejudices, and a good deal of jealousy about each other. . . . In facing up to this indisputable fact and bringing the conflicting issues of it out into the open, the air is cleared, and many prejudices thrown into the ash-can, so that the instinctive desire of friendliness amongst most human beings gets a real chance of establishing itself.'

However it is judged in retrospect, *The Way to the Stars* made a fine finale to one of the healthiest periods of British film-making.

David Tomlinson and Trevor Howard in *The Way to the Stars* (Anthony Asquith, 1945).

David Niven, William Hartnell, Stanley Holloway, John Laurie and (*in front*) Jimmy Hanley in *The Way Ahead* (Carol Reed, 1944).

111

Hollywood Joins Up

To an America entering the war late, its mind finally and abruptly made up after months of hesitation by Japan's surprise attack on Pearl Harbor on 7 December 1941, the issues were gratifyingly clear-cut: the United States and the Allies were the goodies, the Japs, the Germans and the Italians were the baddies. The one side was fighting for something called 'freedom', which the other side was striving to suppress. There was rarely any attempt in war films to delve deeper than this, to explain the underlying issues or to probe the enemy's philosophy or motivations. The war was a straightforward melodrama made up of heroes and villains: America was the cavalry come to relieve the beleaguered fort of Europe, to keep the Pacific prairie safe from the marauding Nippon savages; Uncle Sam was the knight in shining armour riding to rescue the fair damsel of democracy from the Axis dragon.

The apparent simplicity of the situation was, from Hollywood's point of view, decidedly convenient. 'The movie city,' wrote Parker Tyler, 'was, like one of the many factories made over to manufacture guns and planes and other *matériel*, ready with very little reconversion to start on war production.' Unlike the British industry, for which the war spelt a new lease of life, and whose wartime films took on a subtlety, a humanity, a self-awareness and an identity previously unknown, Hollywood merely carried on as before, using the same codes and formulas for the new genre as it had been doing for Westerns, gangster films and, latterly, political spy dramas. The conflict simply gave the movie industry new sensations to explore: sensations which could be indulged with a clear conscience, on the grounds that this was a just and necessary war.

'The American war movie,' says Arthur F. McClure in his essay, 'Hollywood at War', 'was probably more important as an historical phenomenon than as an artistic achievement.' Its purpose was to stimulate rather than inform, to wrap the war up in attractive packaging and sell it to the people. Thus, for much of the duration, the bulk of the war films which came out of Hollywood 'sprang (as Isaksson and Furhammar explain it) less from reality than from currently popular preconceptions which, in turn, they served to reinforce. War was an exciting adventure; politics a superior form of romance; morality a matter of morale. In this treatment, death was painless, decorative and even, ultimately, a blessing.' The average American war film was smooth, lively, efficiently made, naïvely heroic, unashamedly patriotic, far removed from reality, predictable, unforgiving, indistinguishable from a dozen others of the same type, and, at its middle-brow level, undeniably entertaining. The various themes of war could, moreover, be made to fit almost any genre – musical, crime thriller, cartoon – with only minor adjustments to style and content.

As the war progressed, it is true that the glamour and escapism began to be replaced by greater honesty and realism, and a few brilliant films were made – accurate studies of men at war, perceptive, moving and humane. But generally speaking, it is difficult to argue with the opinion of historian Charles Alexander that American war films 'absorbed and diffused the experience of war, but received little inspiration from it. Just as Hollywood had eluded most of the realities of Depression America, so it refused to deal honestly with the realities of America at war.'

What the American war movie lacked in quality and truth, however, it certainly made up for in quantity. Hollywood virtually mobilized along with the armed forces, and of 1700 features produced between 1942 and 1945, over 500 were war films of one kind or another. Producer Walter Wanger was moved to predict: 'When future historians write the story of World War II a bright chapter will be assigned to the contributions of America's motion picture industry in winning the war' – an over-optimistic assertion, perhaps, yet it is a fact that films were considered officially in the light of how they could 'usefully serve the National Defense effort'. Film became 'a potent instrument of national policy . . . promoting the aims and goals of the war effort' (Lewis Jacobs), and from the start the government offered resources and advice and drew up guidelines as to how the motion-picture industry might best present that war effort on the screen. Hollywood responded happily – at least in the early stages – by glorifying the waging of the war in the same way that it might exalt the busting of a crime syndicate or celebrate the winning of the West.

Few of the films made during the first year of America's involvement in the conflict attempted to treat the themes of war in an original or thoughtful way. Most of them simply, and simplistically, adjusted the familiar entertainment formulas to a wartime setting or combined them with more or less relevant propaganda. George B. Seitz's *A Yank on the Burma Road*, for example, was a quick, cheap, action-and-romance B-feature rushed out after Pearl Harbor, the archetype for dozens of puerile adventure stories with a war framework.

Also plentiful, though scarcely more profound, were the films designed to stimulate recruitment by detailing and dramatizing the training methods of various branches of the armed forces. Two of the earliest, both released in the first months of 1942, were Michael Curtiz's *Captains of the Clouds*, a Technicolor tribute to the Royal Canadian Air Force with James Cagney and Dennis Morgan, and Bruce Humberstone's *To the Shores of Tripoli* (with John Payne, Maureen O'Hara and Randolph Scott), which highlighted the United States Marines. This kind of film continued to be made throughout the war, a later, trumpet-blowing,

and very popular example being Darryl F. Zanuck's eulogy on the Army Air Corps, *Winged Victory* (1944), adapted from a play by Moss Hart and directed by George Cukor. Half-documentary, half-jamboree, this glorification of air combat blended excellently handled training scenes with the standard emotionalism of young guys going off to war, the whole being sentimentalized by some corny love-interest and regular bouts of marching and singing.

The reluctance of Hollywood to relinquish its favourite themes, even in the extraordinary circumstances brought about by a world war, meant that a large, ceaseless sub-genre of spy films grew up, some of them contriving cleverly to involve gangster-figures converted to the common cause for the duration.

Humphrey Bogart and Alan Ladd led the field in this respect, Bogart starting the ball rolling in Vincent Sherman's *All Through the Night* (1942). This fast-paced thriller pits a whole gang of hoods (led by Bogart as 'Gloves' Donahue) against a Nazi spy-ring headed by Conrad Veidt and Peter Lorre, who intend to blow up a battleship in New York Harbor. Bogart played a more conventional secret agent in John Huston's spy story, *Across the Pacific* (1942), a reunion of Bogart, Sidney Greenstreet and Mary Astor from Huston's classic private-eye thriller, *The Maltese Falcon*. Set in the period just prior to Pearl Harbor, this lively melodrama cast Bogart as an army officer posing as a traitor in order to save the Panama Canal from Japanese intrigue.

The same year, Bogart created his most characteristic and best-loved role as the cynical, politically ambivalent nightclub-owner Rick

Blaine, in one of the most popular and magical entertainment films ever made, Michael Curtiz's *Casablanca* (1942). Fortuitously well timed – its release coincided with the Casablanca Conference and the Allied invasion of North Africa – *Casablanca* captivated audiences with its perfect blend of patriotism, liberal idealism, heroism and heady, unashamed romanticism. Expertly constructed (in spite of having been scripted and filmed in chaotic, piecemeal fashion) and engagingly acted by an inspired cast (Ingrid Bergman as lost lover, Sidney Greenstreet as disarmingly corrupt black-

Kevin McCarthy entertains fellow airmen (among them Don Taylor, Edmond O'Brien and Ronald Reagan) in *Winged Victory* (George Cukor, 1944).

Ingrid Bergman and Humphrey Bogart in *Casablanca* (Michael Curtiz, 1942).

113

Nazi interrogation in
Berlin Correspondent
(Eugene Ford, 1942).

Greer Garson protects her
family (Claire Sanders and
Christopher Severn) and her
maid (Brenda Forbes) from
the bombs in *Mrs Miniver*
(William Wyler, 1942).

marketeer, Peter Lorre as doomed double-dealer, Claude Rains as charming, amoral police official, Conrad Veidt as ice-cold Nazi officer, plus a host of harmonized supporting players), Curtiz's 'lesson in film contrivance' tells how Blaine's indestructible love for Ilsa (Bergman) changes him from an embittered introvert into a champion of democracy. The trenchant dialogue crackles with hard-bitten wit ('What's your nationality?' 'I'm a drunkard'); the atmosphere – authentic or not – is enchanting; Bogart's brand of self-sacrificial heroism is irresistibly inspiring; the propaganda set-pieces (such as the war exiles' rendering of the 'Marseillaise' drowning the German officers' stentorian patriotic song) push all the correct emotional buttons; and the music – dominated by the strains of 'As Time Goes By' – is calculated to break down any remaining vestiges of resistance to the film's other hypnotic qualities. An enduring favourite among Hollywood movies, and undeniably a masterpiece of escapist cinema, *Casablanca* epitomizes more than any other film the dreams, ideals and style of wartime America.

The same combination of sex, politics and cynical hero cropped up again two years later in Howard Hawks's enjoyable version of Ernest

Youthful defiance in *The Pied Piper* (Irving Pichel, 1942).

Robert Preston (firing gun) and William Bendix (*right*) in *Wake Island* (John Farrow, 1942).

115

Jack Benny and Sig Rumann in *To Be Or Not To Be* (Ernst Lubitsch, 1942).

Nazis Otto Kruger and Tim Holt watch a sterilization operation in *Hitler's Children* (Edward Dmytryk, 1943).

Hemingway's *To Have and Have Not*, revamped as a resistance melodrama set on the French Caribbean island of Martinique, with Bogart as an uncommitted boat captain closely related to the Rick of *Casablanca*. The film is best remembered for introducing the feline charms of Lauren Bacall, whose 'husky, underslung voice' could turn the most innocent line of dialogue ('Anybody got a match?') into a *double entendre*.

Another star to make a sensational début in the early 'forties was Alan Ladd, whose portrayal of the professional killer harnessed to the war effort in Frank Tuttle's *This Gun for Hire* (1942) made him an instant box-office

draw. This was another reshaping of a famous novel for topical reasons – Graham Greene's 'A Gun for Sale'. Ladd and Tuttle were asked to reiterate the thesis that American gangsters are nicer than Nazis in the ludicrous *Lucky Jordan* (1943), in which Ladd is a racketeer who resists the draft but ends up a patriotic hero. 'It's still cops and robbers, no matter how you slice it,' said the 'New York Herald Tribune'.

Most of the post-Pearl Harbor melodramas touched upon the war in trivial terms, but a few attempted to make a serious, if not particularly profound, comment on the war situation as it affected the United States. Richard Thorpe's *Joe Smith, American* (1942), for instance, an informative piece of propaganda highlighting the production-front workers, offered some credible reasons for the war. It tells of a skilled aircraft mechanic (Robert Young) whose knowledge of a new bombsight causes him to be kidnapped by Nazi agents. He is tortured and beaten, but refuses to reveal his secrets. Finally he escapes, and helps the FBI to round up his captors. It is an honest tribute to the ordinary American, his values, his courage, and his indomitable spirit.

The same theme was handled in inimitable and far more sensational fashion by Alfred Hitchcock in *Saboteur* (1942), a contrived but exciting chase melodrama in which Robert Cummings, as an aircraft-factory worker, takes on a gang of shop-floor fifth-columnists who have framed him for murder. Clever touches include investing the villainous saboteurs with

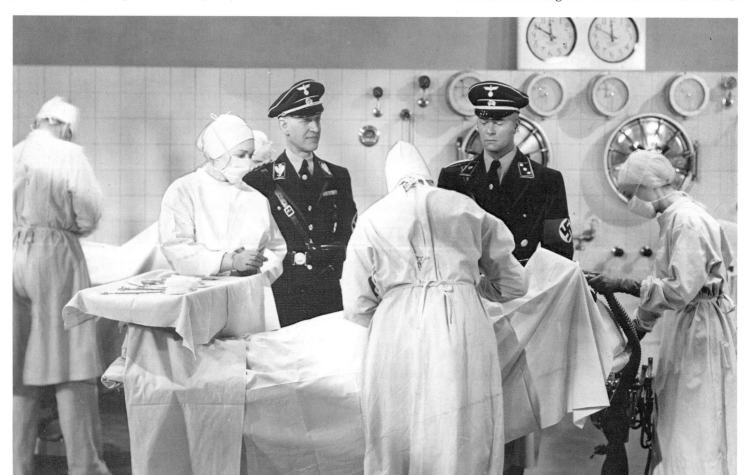

a sober anonymity which makes them indistinguishable from ordinary, law-abiding citizens, and there is a classic Hitchcock climax in which hero Cummings and traitor Norman Lloyd fight symbolically to the death in the torch of the Statue of Liberty. Unfortunately, the official law-enforcement agencies emerged in a rather dim light, making it appear, as Bosley Crowther pointed out, 'that the nation's safety depends entirely on civilian amateurs'.

Three of the most interesting of the home-front espionage films were made towards the end of the war, beginning with Fritz Lang's strongly anti-Nazi adaptation of another Graham Greene novel, *Ministry of Fear* (1944), with Ray Milland and Marjorie Reynolds. This was followed in 1945 by the semi-documentary, *The House on 92nd Street* (1945), a quasi-realistic re-creation of authentic FBI counter-espionage activities, cleverly directed by Henry Hathaway and produced by newsreel expert Louis de Rochemont. This film's fast-paced, journalistic technique, reminiscent of de Rochemont's current-affairs series, *March of Time*, proved highly influential. The cast (Lloyd Nolan, William Eythe, Signe Hasso, Leo G. Carroll) was supplemented by actual G-men and authentic FBI footage was plumbed into the film, with the result that the finished product was both convincing and entertaining. The third film of this trio kept the anti-Nazi theme going long after the armistice. This was *The Stranger* (1946), in which Orson Welles directed himself as a particularly evil ex-Nazi hiding from retribution by posing as a mild New England professor. The

intention was to proffer a chilling reminder that the spirit of Nazism had not necessarily died with Hitler, but in spite of Welles's flair and the presence of attractive co-stars (Edward G. Robinson and Loretta Young) the exercise was less than convincing.

The contrast of free and fascist ideologies was effectively dramatized in the Herman Shumlin/Dashiell Hammett adaptation of Lillian Hellman's emotional play *Watch On the Rhine*, originally set in 1941 when many Americans still chose to ignore the barbarism which was shaking Europe. A German refugee resistance leader (Paul Lukas, earning himself an Oscar) and his wife (Bette Davis) return to the latter's home in Washington, where the imminent global struggle between liberty and fascist oppression is rehearsed in embryo in a dignified American household.

Similar in intent was Leslie Fenton's *Tomorrow the World* (1944), in which an average small-town American family has its liberal principles tested by the arrival of an orphaned, but still intractable Hitler youth (Skippy Homeier, later to shoot Gregory Peck in *The Gunfighter*). In time, of course, the boy is converted to the democratic ideals which America is fighting for.

A few films shifted the intrigue to Germany itself. Jules Dassin's first feature, *Nazi Agent* (1942), offered two Conrad Veidts for the price of one in a tense, intriguing story about German-born twin brothers, one a Nazi, the other an American agent who impersonates him. And in *Berlin Correspondent* (1942), an

Secret German agent George Coulouris (*centre*) attempts to win the confidence of concentration-camp prisoners Paul Guilfoyle (*left*) and Carl Esmond in *The Master Race* (Herbert J. Biberman, 1944).

117

Hans V. Twardowski (*right*) as Reinhard Heydrich in *Hangmen Also Die* (Fritz Lang, 1943).

the national pastime ('358 for 3. England seems to be doing pretty well.' 'Well, we can still play cricket'). Then the Nazi onslaught begins to impinge upon and disrupt their way of life. Their older son joins the RAF; bombs fall, and they read 'Alice in Wonderland' to their younger children in the air-raid shelter; Mr Miniver goes to Dunkirk to rescue British soldiers; Mrs Miniver captures a crashed German pilot; they mourn the death of their son's bride. Finally, they assert their faith in the bombed village church as RAF aeroplanes

unlikely melodrama directed by Eugene Forde, war correspondent Dana Andrews borrows the same device of posing as a Nazi officer in a bid to escape from Berlin with important Axis military secrets. That he succeeds is a tribute more to luck and the Germans' stupidity (Sig Rumann, a frequent player of Nazi buffoons, is one of his dupes) than to the quality of his impersonation. This is one of many spy films which attempted to ridicule Nazism.

The American attitude to Britain, of course, continued to be one of total admiration. One of the cleverest and most popular Hollywood films of the early war years was a glowing tribute to the fine, enduring traditions of middle-class England and the calm, solitary courage of the British in the Blitz: William Wyler's *Mrs Miniver* (1942), winner of six Academy Awards. This remarkable dramatization of the Anglo-Saxon character through the war experiences of an 'average' English family came to symbolize what the Allies were fighting for: the right to lead a free and civilized life within a tolerant and well-ordered society.

Shot entirely, with great virtuosity, in the MGM studios with emigrant English actors, the film is, from the point of view of setting, pure pastiche. Against this mythical backdrop, a patriotic fable unfolds. The Minivers (Walter Pidgeon and Greer Garson), in spite of the growing threat of war, go blithely about their village idyll, growing roses, patronizing the flower show (and their servants), discussing fly overhead, and the soundtrack's triumphant rendering of 'Land of Hope and Glory' confirms the film's central message, expressed by one character in appropriately horticultural terms: 'There will always be roses and there will always be an England.'

This emotional portrayal of English middle-class mores looks, in retrospect, laughably quaint, artificial and over-idealized, but contemporary audiences were enraptured by its skilfully seductive propaganda: they were able to identify with the Minivers and to recognize

and take comfort from their inherent qualities of fortitude, solidarity and self-confidence. (A 1950 sequel, *The Miniver Story*, which had the good lady dying of cancer, itself died at the box-office.)

Another emotive vehicle for Hollywood-based British actors was the all-star production, *Forever and a Day* (1942), which consisted of episodes in the life of an English family from 1804 to 1942. Several directors had a hand in the film, including René Clair, Cedric Hardwicke, Victor Saville and Herbert Wilcox, and

Cedric Hardwicke (*second from right*) in *The Moon is Down* (Irving Pichel, 1943).

119

profits went to the British Red Cross. The subject of British class differences was dealt with more directly in Anatole Litvak's *This Above All* (1942), in which Tyrone Power played a disillusioned, lower-middle-class hero of Dunkirk who deserts as a protest against risking his life for the upper classes. He is finally persuaded that England's cause is a just one and that social reform, however desirable, can only be tackled once England has been saved.

MGM continued to pay periodic tribute to the British character in its wartime productions. Greer Garson starred again in Mervyn LeRoy's *Random Harvest* (1942), about an amnesiac (Ronald Colman), shell-shocked in World War I, who marries a dancer. Miss Garson caused a minor sensation by revealing her legs. Two years later, Metro tried to repeat the success of *Mrs Miniver* with *The White Cliffs of Dover*, about a courageous American girl (Irene Dunne) who loses her English husband in the first World War and her son in the second. A well-acted but excessively sentimental film, 'Newsweek' described it as 'Anglophile . . . with knobs on'. More perceptive was W.S. Van Dyke's *Journey for Margaret* (1942), a moving, fact-based film about the plight of Britain's war orphans, with Robert Young playing an American correspondent who adopts two bombed-out children (Margaret O'Brien, making a stunning appearance at the age of five, and William Severn). The film observed with compassion and restraint the effect of war on its most innocent victims. Children were

also the subject of Irving Pichel's *The Pied Piper* (1942), the story of an ageing Englishman (Monty Woolley) who finds himself playing courier to a growing band of refugee children as he attempts to escape from France in 1940.

The first combat movies, although occasionally quite harsh in treatment, stuck to basic heroics and made little attempt to be realistic. Arthur Lubin's *Eagle Squadron*, with its British setting and sizeable cast headed by Robert Stack, Diana Barrymore and John Loder, was one of the more ambitious examples. So was David Miller's *Flying Tigers*, a tribute to the volunteer American airmen who fought against the Japanese on behalf of China before Pearl Harbor.

The first significant departure from the romantic, recruiting-poster approach to the fighting was John Farrow's *Wake Island*, a semi-fictional account of a courageous but doomed defensive action in the Pacific by a handful of under-equipped marines, which inspired a small but welcome cycle of more realistic battle movies. 'Although the United States has been at war for nine months,' said 'Newsweek', '*Wake Island* is Hollywood's first intelligent, honest, and completely successful attempt to dramatize the deeds of an American force on a fighting front.'

The heroics in this stirring, immensely popular re-enactment of a gallant defeat were still Hollywoodian, but of a sterner kind than hitherto ('Tell them,' says Brian Donlevy to his radio operator, who has received an invitation

Walter Huston, Ann Sheridan and Errol Flynn in *The Edge of Darkness* (Lewis Milestone, 1943).

from the Japs to surrender, 'to come and get us!') and the action scenes rang truer. The acting, too, from an impeccable tough-guy cast led by Donlevy, Robert Preston, Macdonald Carey, William Bendix and Albert Dekker, was of the best bantering, self-effacing, ensemble kind, at pains to show that this was the ordinary guy at war.

In subsequent front-line films, this motif of the classless-group, studded with occupational types (apple-grower, salesman, butcher, garage mechanic, etc.) but acting as a harmonious unit to preserve a fondly remembered way of life, became more formalized. Often the group would have an international, immigrational flavour, answering to a string of easily recognizable ethnic names like Murphy, Larsen, Schwartz, Kowalski, Salvatore, Schmitt, and Jackson who might occasionally be black, to stress their adopted country's democratic ideals. Officers, moreover – unlike their British counterparts – were depicted as being much closer to the men they commanded in both class and conversation, the main difference being that they had either been to West Point (in which case they were usually stuffy martinets) or came from a professional background (medicine, the law), making them paternal, philosophical and highly intelligent. It all added up to one thing – this was 'the people's war'.

Perhaps the most outstanding war film of 1942 was *émigré* Ernst Lubitsch's bitter, bizarre,

controversial send-up of the Nazi myth, *To Be Or Not To Be*, a kind of *Great Dictator* without the Chaplin soft centre. Set in Warsaw at the time of Hitler's invasion of Poland, the plot concerns the efforts of a theatrical troupe, led by Carole Lombard and Jack Benny, to undermine the Germans and escape the Nazi occupation, which they eventually do by means of a hilarious accumulation of impersonations, including one of the Fuehrer himself by a terrified bit-player. Like Chaplin's film, only more so, Lubitsch's flippant farce was attacked for being callous, tasteless and irreverent about a

Spencer Tracy (*centre*) in
The Seventh Cross (Fred Zinnemann, 1944).

Stalwart Nazis Alan Hale and George Coulouris in *Hotel Berlin* (Peter Godfrey, 1945).

121

Mission to Moscow
(Michael Curtiz, 1943).

subject of deadly seriousness, whereas the intention, brilliantly achieved, was to reduce to ridicule the ogres of Nazism. Lubitsch's trick was to combine real tragedy with running gags, authentic suspense with merciless satire. Against the clown figures, like Benny's conceited ham actor and Sig Rumann's joke German, were set perfectly straight characters such as an Allied agent (Robert Stack) and a Polish traitor (Stanley Ridges). The film can best be described as a grim burlesque, a justifiable portrayal of the idiocy of war and warmakers. How much of the criticism levelled against it was an emotional reaction, caused by the tragic death of Carole Lombard in a plane crash soon after it was completed, cannot, of course, be assessed.

To Be Or Not To Be gave rise to a whole clutch of frivolous, slapstick farces ridiculing the Nazi hierarchy, usually with Bobby Watson and Joe Devlin doing their respective impersonations of Hitler and Mussolini. *The Devil with Hitler* (1942) and *That Nazty Nuisance* (1943) were two popular examples.

As Hollywood became bolder and more experienced, however, so its portrayals of the enemy became more serious and more concerned with Nazism's underlying psychology. An effort was made to expose and analyse the enemy's amorality, brutality and lack of ethics. Occasionally this was done in sensational, B-feature fashion, as in Steve Sekely's *Women in Bondage* (1943), but other attempts were more thoughtful. One of the first was

Edward Dmytryk's low-budget but immensely successful film ('One of the great sleepers of movie history' according to Griffith and Mayer), *Hitler's Children* (1943). This also indulged in profitable sensationalism, exposing such atrocities as the flogging of sexually uncooperative women and compulsory sterilization, and ultimately it got bogged down in an intrusive love-plot involving its two leads, Tim Holt and Bonita Granville. It tried hard, however, to give a serious, if not sober, account of the indoctrination of young Germans with 'Mein Kampf' ideology, and to describe the savagely oppressive nature of the Nazi régime.

The Hitler Gang (1944), directed in quasi-documentary fashion by John Farrow, is a braver and far more intriguing study of the Nazi character – or at least, Hollywood's view of it; Parker Tyler described it as 'a sort of glorified *March of Time* into the private life of the Fuehrer'. Using mostly relatively unknown expatriate German actors (although Bobby Watson – now called Robert – was back in his Hitler role) to impersonate as realistically as possible the Nazi leaders, Farrow's film attempted to chronicle the rise of the Third Reich and the ruthlessness and degeneracy of its architects. The script, according to producer B.G. DeSylva, had been 'authenticated from every available source . . . (and) is true insofar as decency will permit'. The background and detail are certainly convincing. The film's main flaw is in its depiction of Hitler as an insane clown and his henchmen as petty gangsters; they

122

were gangsters all right, but something more than petty.

A more subtle approach to the insidious influence of Nazism was provided by Herbert J. Biberman's *The Master Race* (1944), in which George Coulouris played a German colonel posing as a Belgian patriot who incites a community of freshly liberated Belgians to rebel against their new occupiers, the Americans.

Far *less* subtle was Douglas Sirk's excessively horrific account of the life, crimes and assassination of Reinhard Heydrich, Nazi overlord of Czechoslovakia, in *Hitler's Madman* (1943), with John Carradine as Heydrich. 'Here in one lurid diatribe,' said the 'New York Times', 'MGM's assortment of authors have summed up practically every indictment against the Nazis that they could crowd into one film.'

The Heydrich killing was handled with much greater sobriety and realism in Fritz Lang's *Hangmen Also Die* (script by Bertolt Brecht), which concentrated on the heroic resistance of the Czechs against their Nazi persecutors. This was, in fact, one of several notable films of 1943 which dramatized the fight-back against a supposedly invincible enemy and helped to stimulate the idea of nations linking arms to combat fascism, both from without and from within.

Resistance under the Nazi yoke was a theme which, as the war progressed, Hollywood occasionally came to handle well. The simple melodramas of espionage, sabotage and escape produced during the uncommitted years began to give way to stories which portrayed with care and feeling the plight of the ordinary citizen under occupation, and which were prepared to analyse the nature of fascism and to debate the morality of resistance (or non-resistance) rather than merely show its mechanics.

Among the best of these was *This Land is Mine* (1943), the second Hollywood project of refugee French director Jean Renoir. Written by Dudley Nichols, this contemplative film examined in a sane, sensitive way the inner conflict between submission and protest experienced by ordinary people in a state of tyranny. The main character is a mild schoolmaster (played by Charles Laughton) who chooses to oppose his oppressors and makes a climactic (and rather improbable) court-room speech about freedom. The film was variously described as 'one of the most eloquent statements of the basic issues of the war' (Writers' War Board), 'the first United Nations anti-fascist film' (John McManus) and as revealing 'the ultimate verities behind the present struggle' (Howard Barnes). According to the script, it was meant to be 'symbolic of all occupied countries', but its resemblance to France at a time when the Gallic worm was beginning to turn was not purely accidental.

Intrinsic qualities aside, Renoir's film also did much to dispel the fatuous impression of resistance heroism given by such potboilers as Jules Dassin's *Reunion in France* (1943) – contemptuously dismissed by 'Time' as 'a Joan

Crawford version of the fall of France' – which suggested that the French social élite was leading the internal struggle against Nazism.

Another theatre of resistance – Norway – was the setting for two more 1943 films, released almost simultaneously: Irving Pichel's *The Moon is Down*, and *Edge of Darkness*, directed by Lewis Milestone. The first of these was a skilful, well-meaning, dispassionate and downbeat adaptation of the John Steinbeck novel about the enslavement and martyrdom of a Norwegian mining village, which resists the

Erich von Stroheim and Martin Koslick (*right*) in *The North Star* (Lewis Milestone, 1943).

Gregory Peck and Tamara Toumanova in *Days of Glory* (Jacques Tourneur, 1944).

Robert Walker in
See Here, Private Hargrove
(Wesley Ruggles, 1944),
with Keenan Wynn, George
Offerman Jr and Bill Phillips.

Eddie Bracken
(*centre*) and William
Demarest (with ribbons) in
Hail the Conquering Hero
(Preston Sturges, 1944).

German invaders with tragic consequences. It was too cool for contemporary audiences, who were put off by its detachment and lack of romanticism. The plainer heroics and simple, direct story-line of Milestone's dashing film, in which a similar community, armed with British guns and led by Errol Flynn, rises up and destroys the overbearing enemy, was much more acceptable.

The German war scene was tackled seriously in some later films. Fred Zinnemann's *The Seventh Cross* (1944) echoed *The Mortal Storm* in attempting to show that not all Germans were bad, that there was another Germany ready to emerge once the Nazis had been crushed (Zinnemann, of course, being another director of German origin). Spencer Tracy played, with great conviction and restraint, an escaped prisoner from a concentration camp who flees across Germany with the help of a few decent, sympathetic countrymen. It was a convincing re-creation of the social atmosphere of a fascist state, though criticized on its release for being less than vituperative towards the German people.

Another film which questioned whether all Germans were bad was Peter Godfrey's *Hotel Berlin* (1945), a kind of *Grand Hotel* in a Nazi setting, written by Alvah Bessie (one of the Hollywood Ten who were jailed and blacklisted after the war for defying McCarthyism), and outstandingly acted by a cast which included Helmut Dantine, Raymond Massey, Faye Emerson and Peter Lorre.

One of the last films about the resistance movement was Gregory Ratoff's *Paris Underground* (1945), the story of two women (Constance Bennett and Gracie Fields) who smuggled Allied fliers out of occupied France. One of the oddest was *Dragon Seed* (1944), directed by Jack Conway and Harold S. Bucquet, and based on a Pearl Buck novel – a rather obvious attempt to cash in on the earlier success of *The Good Earth*. Excellent players like

Katharine Hepburn, Walter Huston, Aline MacMahon, Akim Tamiroff and Hurd Hatfield were suitably orientalized to portray Chinese farmers, which they did well enough to make a few telling points about the nature of the war.

The bravery of the Russians in their stand against Hitler, and the need to cement the alliance with the USSR and sell it to a suspicious America, led to a minor sub-genre of pro-Soviet films, the most memorable and controversial of which was Michael Curtiz's *Mission to Moscow* (1943). This was a grand-scale, highly expert piece of semi-documentary screen propaganda, based on a book by US Ambassador Joseph E. Davies (portrayed in the film by Walter Huston), whose experiences in pre-war Russia the film recounts. Davies himself introduced the movie ('There was so much prejudice and misunderstanding of the Soviet Union, in which I partly shared, that I felt it was my duty to tell the truth . . . as I saw it, for such value as it might have') which then goes on to re-create the highlights of his sojourn in the USSR, all designed to show the sincere desire of Stalin and his people for peace, democracy and truth. Among the film's more remarkable sequences is one which contrives to white-wash the purge trials of 1937, and episodes such as this provoked bitter debate. John Dewey called the film 'anti-British, anti-Congress, anti-Democratic and anti-truth'; others condemned it as a scandal and a lie. An equal number praised its intentions and hailed it as 'an epoch-making film for America'. It remains a fascinating picture, both for its technical brilliance and boldness (exemplified by strikingly accurate impersonations of Stalin, Roosevelt, Churchill, Trotsky and other historical notables) and for its social interest (i.e. as a manipulator of contemporary American attitudes towards Russia).

Mission to Moscow was followed by other tributes to the heroic Russian people, equally well intentioned and naïve. Lewis Milestone's *The North Star* (1943), a $3,000,000 Sam Goldwyn epic, extolled the hard-pressed Russian peasants (Anne Baxter, Walter Huston, Walter Brennan and Farley Granger among them) and their guerrilla activities, but mixed realism and romantic fancy rather jarringly. Gregory Ratoff's *Song of Russia* (1944), with Robert Taylor as an American orchestra conductor caught up in Russia's early mobilization against the Nazis, was pure romanticism and audiences practically laughed it off the screen. Jacques Tourneur's *Days of Glory* (1944) was mainly notable as the charismatic début of the young, devastatingly handsome Gregory Peck, playing a guerrilla leader in love with a ballerina (Tamara Toumanova). And Zoltan Korda's *Counter-Attack* (1945), with Paul Muni as a Soviet paratrooper keeping eight Nazi prisoners at bay in a bomb-blasted cellar, paid tribute to the simple heroism of the Russian soldier.

All of these harmless eulogies became an acute embarrassment to Hollywood in the murky period after the war when the House

Committee on Un-American Activities began to investigate communism in the movie industry. Their creators were cross-examined ('Just crazy,' said Dore Schary, '. . . like saying *Mrs Miniver* was a plot to get us to become a monarchy') and at least one witness, Robert Taylor, turned 'friendly' and was moved to regret his involvement in the ludicrous *Song of Russia*.

Back on the home front, civilian morale was

Robert Walker, Jennifer Jones and Guy Madison in *Since You Went Away* (John Cromwell, 1944).

John Hodiak and Lana Turner in *Marriage is a Private Affair* (Robert Z. Leonard, 1944).

Robert Walker and Judy Garland in *The Clock* (Vincente Minnelli, 1945).

The 'Head in the Clouds' number from Irving Berlin's lavish patriotic musical, *This is the Army* (Michael Curtiz, 1943).

kept buoyed up by a heady mixture of comedies, romances, musicals, dramas, or any combination of all four, adapted to war themes. Humour, in particular, was employed to mock and alleviate the inconveniences and frustrations brought about by the war.

One small group of comedies made light of the incredible overcrowding problem in wartime Washington, caused by an escalation 'of the innumerable government agencies, civil service employees, and priority-bent visiting businessmen whose conglomerate efforts, despite avalanches of complaint, somehow launched the most stupendous war effort in history' (John Gassner and Dudley Nichols). The best of these was George Stevens's *The More the Merrier* (1943), with Jean Arthur, Joel McCrea and Charles Coburn vying for

bed-space in the house-scarce capital. Later came James V. Kern's adaptation of a hit Broadway play, *The Doughgirls* (1944), with Ann Sheridan, Alexis Smith, Jack Carson and Jane Wyman; and Joe May's *Johnny Doesn't Live Here Any More* (1944), with Simone Simon and James Ellison.

Service comedies, especially those depicting camp life, were numerous and rarely rose above the rudimentary antics of Abbott and Costello's *Buck Privates* or the mercifully brief farces featuring William Tracy and the eternal sergeant of American movies, Joe Sawyer. One which did was Wesley Ruggles's *See Here, Private Hargrove* (1944), a satirical demonstration that the Army could turn the wildest misfits into first-rate fighting men. This was a genuinely funny adaptation of a book about army training by an actual GI, Marion Hargrove, made the more effective by a sympathetic performance from the then relatively inexperienced Robert Walker in the lead part. Elliot Nugent's lively and amusing *Up in Arms* (1944) brought stardom to another newcomer, Danny Kaye, who played a reluctant, hypochondriacal draftee who captures thirty Japanese soldiers single-handed.

Two war comedies which were sharper and wiser than most came from one director, Preston Sturges. *The Miracle of Morgan's Creek* (1943) is an outrageous satire on wartime morals, in which a small-town girl (Betty Hutton) gets drunk at a party and marries a soldier whose name she subsequently can't remember. Pregnant, she is ostracized by society, but eventually becomes a national heroine by producing sextuplets. Betty Hutton's co-star, Eddie Bracken, was also the 'hero' of Sturges's *Hail the Conquering Hero* (1944), an acid, sometimes serious satire on hero-worship in which a soldier discharged

from the Marines because of chronic hay fever is put up for mayor of his home town on the strength of a non-existent war record.

A more serious and realistic evocation of the home front and the tribulations and frustrations of a 'typical' family in 'that fortress, the American Home' was provided by the blockbusting David O. Selznick production, *Since You Went Away* (1944), directed by John Cromwell. This sentimental epic paid tribute to the stoicism of American women whose menfolk had gone to war in the same way that *Mrs Miniver* had praised the British. It chronicled the nation's triumphs and tragedies and dramatized its hopes and fears through the experiences of Mrs Average American (Hollywood version, in the shape of Claudette Colbert), and like *Mrs Miniver* it was very popular.

The sadness of families disrupted by the departure of fathers, husbands and boy-friends for the war was depicted in several home-front movies, more notably Irving Cummings's *The Impatient Years* (1944), with Ginger Rogers and Joseph Cotten. The problems of wartime attachments were the subject of Robert Z. Leonard's *Marriage is a Private Affair* (1944), which starred Lana Turner as a young woman uncertain about her love for the soldier she has married. One of her co-stars was John Hodiak, who appeared again soon afterwards in Lloyd Bacon's quiet, pleasantly modest *Sunday Dinner for a Soldier*, about a lonely GI who falls in love with the oldest member (Anne Baxter) of a poor, orphaned Florida family who have invited him home for a Sunday meal. A minor variation of the enlistment theme was provided by Alfred E. Green's *Mr Winkle Goes to War* (1944), which cast Edward G. Robinson, somewhat improbably, as an ageing but adventurous bank clerk who opts for combat duty, in spite of his wife's objections, and becomes a war hero.

Perhaps the most charming of all the war romances was Vincente Minnelli's *The Clock* (1945), which gave Judy Garland her first straight role as a young New Yorker swept into love and marriage by a shy soldier (Robert Walker) on a forty-eight-hour leave. It is a film made timeless by her melting performance, and by Minnelli's fresh handling of cliché situations (like the bureaucratic difficulty of getting married in haste).

Musicals achieved their greatest popularity during the war, accounting for 40 per cent of all production from 1943, and many of them managed to find a link, no matter how tenuous, with the war itself. A typical programmer, for example, was *Private Buckaroo* (1942), directed by Edward F. Cline, which wove a banal call-up story round some excellent music by Harry James and the Andrews Sisters.

A number of memorable spectaculars were produced, however, one of the most entertaining being Michael Curtiz's massive biography of showman George M. Cohan, *Yankee Doodle Dandy* (1942). James Cagney played the irrepressible, ultra-patriotic song-and-dance man (winning an Oscar for his trouble) with rousing, nationalistic fervour, giving prominence to

The American forces' favourite pin-up, Betty Grable, in the pose that made her famous.

such stirring numbers as 'Over There', 'You're a Grand Old Flag' and the title-song. In the same year, Busby Berkeley directed Judy Garland in the energetic *For Me and My Gal*, which used a First World War setting to make a patriotic gesture towards the Second. Gene Kelly made his début as an entertainer who maims himself to avoid the draft, only to find redemption in an act of heroism while on duty as a non-combatant. Judy Garland, meanwhile, patriotically entertained the troops – and audiences ever after – with 'After You're Gone', 'When You Wore a Tulip' and 'For Me and My Gal'.

Michael Curtiz made another blockbuster to follow *Yankee Doodle Dandy* – *This Is the Army*, the big hit of 1943. Based on Irving Berlin's stage show and containing no less than seventeen of his songs, this was an unashamed piece of flag-waving, for which many of the stars (who included George Murphy, Joan Leslie and Ronald Reagan) donated their services free, all profits from the film going to Army Emergency Relief.

Berkeley replied again with his first colour film, *The Gang's All Here* (1943), a loosely plotted Alice Faye musical built round a war

Hollywood Pets at War I:
Lassie becomes a war hero
in *Courage of Lassie* (Fred
Wilcox, 1945), with Bill
Wallace and Tom Drake.

bond fund-raising show. The production numbers, culminating in 'The Lady in the Tutti-Frutti Hat' in which giant bananas pay homage to Carmen Miranda, all but parodied the ingenuous eroticism of Berkeley's choreographic fantasies of the 'thirties.

Peculiar to wartime, but oddly reminiscent of the very early musicals like *Hollywood Revue* and *Show of Shows*, were the multi-star, let-your-hair-down demonstrations of how much Hollywood was doing for the boys in uniform. Almost the entire complement of a studio's movie stars and support players would take part in these omnibus entertainments, revered gods and goddesses such as Bogart, Flynn and Bette Davis frequently finding themselves doing bizarre, unexpected party-pieces in endless revues. Warners contributed *Thank Your Lucky Stars* (1943), directed by David Butler, and Delmer Daves's *Hollywood Canteen* (1944); United Artists came up with Frank Borzage's *Stage Door Canteen* (1943), a tribute to the services' entertainment centre in New York; and Universal produced Eddie Sutherland's *Follow the Boys* (1944). No star, it could be said, was left unturned.

The most glamorous and consistently popular musical star of the war period was Betty Grable, whose trivial, nonsensical films, like *Pin Up Girl*, *Coney Island* and *Sweet Rosie O'Grady*, became less of a legend than her legs.

Hollywood made the occasional intriguing war film which it is impossible to categorize. *A Guy Named Joe* (1943), for example, a romantic melodrama directed by Victor Fleming and scripted by Dalton Trumbo, starred Spencer Tracy as the ghost of a dead airman who guides young pilots and his earthly girl-friend (Irene Dunne) through the pitfalls of the war. Contemporary audiences ignored the film's inconsistencies and its trivialization of immortality, and flocked to see it.

Alfred Hitchcock made, in 1943, what many acclaim as the profoundest and most objective contemporary fictional statement on the war – the closely confined, semi-allegorical *Lifeboat*. This was an ambitious attempt to depict the thoughts and reactions of a handful of survivors from a U-boat attack on a freighter, including the U-boat commander himself. As they drift in an open boat, the individuals in this microcosmic group reveal themselves as character types (cynic, humanitarian, liberal, tyrant, etc.) and ethnic representatives (Negro, Nazi, immigrant, and so forth), and their plight comes to symbolize the war situation itself as the German at first proves himself to be the only dominant, decisive person among them. Eventually the 'Allied' group overcomes the devious Nazi, by which time Hitchcock has rammed home his message that the enemy should not be underestimated and that the Allies must act in harmony to protect their traditional freedom. Hitchcock was well served by his actors in this grim, unheroic drama, particularly Tallulah Bankhead as a caustic journalist, and Walter Slezak as the Nazi, treacherous, ruthless, but commanding one's admiration and respect.

It was not until the war was well advanced that the atrocities of the enemy began to be exposed. One film which tackled this theme in a powerfully emotive way was Lewis Milestone's

The Purple Heart (1944), an imagined reconstruction by Darryl Zanuck of the fate at Japanese hands of some of the first American pilots to bomb Tokyo. Known to have been tried and executed, they were assumed to have also been tortured in an attempt to extract strategic information, and this film was a tribute to their courage. Once again, stress was laid on the moral strength to be gained from inter-racial comradeship, helped by restrained performances from such solid actors as Dana Andrews, Richard Conte and Sam Levene. Milestone's direction was, despite the hate-stirring subject of the film, equally sober, adult and unsensational, even eschewing direct representation of the Japanese abuses, preferring to imply them by the physical results.

One of the bravest and (at over $5,000,000) costliest films of the war was Darryl Zanuck's tradition-breaking production, *Wilson* (1944), directed (in Technicolor) by Henry King, about the tragic political career of the World War I President who devoted his life to peace and whose failure (in the words of Gassner and Nichols) 'had momentous consequences to be told only in terms of the blood, sweat and tears of a world in travail'. Zanuck explained his motives for undertaking the project: 'The war and my own experiences on the fighting fronts played their full part in fashioning this film. . . . I saw how destructive of humanity war was, and how innocent of its causes were those who had to do the fighting. Again and again as I saw our boys dying and suffering the thought occurred: why had not something been done to prevent this futile sacrifice?'

Wilson, he felt, had shared this sentiment and envisaged prevention of future wars by leading America into the League of Nations. But the isolationists had had their way. Zanuck warned against a repetition of this mistake.

Zanuck had offered his film to the government as a documentary but had, not surprisingly, been turned down. The result was, in his hands, a big, controversial, idealistic piece of hagiography, well intentioned but rather too broad and over-simplified in treatment, with a deliberate underscoring of its dramatic and entertainment values for the sake of the popular market. Zanuck did,

Charles Russell, Dana Andrews, Farley Granger, Sam Levene, John Craven and Richard Loo in *The Purple Heart* (Lewis Milestone, 1944).

however, have the sense to use an appropriate-looking actor (Alexander Knox), not a big star, to play the part of President Wilson.

The bulk of Hollywood's war films were, of course, the combat movies, which proliferated after *Wake Island* and began to develop away from simple flag-waving and to attempt, on occasion, a serious re-enactment of fighting conditions. This trend towards greater toughness and realism was influenced by two factors: the necessity to shoot on location following a War Production Board decree that no more than $5,000 could be spent on set-building for any one film, and the inescapably authentic picture of the war which emerged in documentaries and newsreels. Romanticization of the war and glamorous notions about death and the enemy gave way to stern truth and defiant violence, and the best combat films began, in the words of Lewis Jacobs, 'to socialize the butchery and profanity of war, its soberness and attrition, the fighting man's dignity, his acts of conscience and personal decision, his fulfillment in group responsibility. . . . On all battlefronts . . . the camera became an articulate and penetrating witness to the pain, bitterness and horror of war.'

The theatre of operations which occupied

Richard Jaeckel, Preston Foster and Lloyd Nolan in *Guadalcanal Diary* (Lewis Seiler, 1943).

Hollywood most in 1943 was the Pacific, evoked with particular effectiveness in Lewis Seiler's *Guadalcanal Diary*, a film close in atmosphere and technique to *Wake Island*. This was a dramatization of the best-selling book by war correspondent Richard Tregaskis, although considerably more restrained than the original, which had spared no detail in its description of the horrors of combat: 'Everywhere one looked there were piles of bodies; here one with a back-bone visible from the front, and the rest of the flesh peeled up over the man's head like the leaf of an artichoke; there a charred head, hairless but still equipped with blackened eye-balls; pink, blue, yellow entrails drooping; a man with a red bullethole through his eye; a dead enemy private, wearing dark, tortoise-shell glasses, lying on his back with his chest a mass of ground meat.'

Naturally, little of this found its way into Seiler's film, but on its own conventional terms it gave a convincing, if inaccurate, account of the Guadalcanal offensive, restrained, un-romantic and aware of the exigencies of jungle warfare. Once again, stress was laid on the group motif, the cross-section of American social types acting in harness without losing their individuality: Lloyd Nolan as the tough sergeant, William Bendix as a Brooklyn taxi-driver, Anthony Quinn as the courageous Indian, Richard Jaeckel (in his début) as the excited, raw recruit, and Preston Foster as the saintly chaplain ('Father, you'd better not go in with the first wave.' 'Why not? That's when I'll be needed most'). There was the continual suggestion also that the Japs fought unfairly but were too stupid to capitalize on the fact.

Ethnic stereotypes with whom filmgoers could easily identify played an even more prominent part in Tay Garnett's *Bataan*, a tense, emotional piece of fiction about a sacrificial rearguard action by thirteen Ameri-can fighting men to aid the withdrawal from the Philippines. It was less subtle and more melodramatic than *Wake Island*, but it con-veyed the full tragedy of the Bataan retreat in a strong, personal way which deeply affected contemporary audiences.

The forging of men into soldiers was the primary theme of two other Pacific-oriented films, *Gung Ho!* and *Salute to the Marines*. The latter, directed by Sylvan Simon, and featuring Wallace Beery, Fay Bainter, Reginald Owen, Ray Collins and Marilyn Maxwell, is mainly remarkable for its unusually mature cast. The livelier *Gung Ho!*, directed by Ray Enright and starring Randolph Scott, re-created a real-life mission by six hundred marines who were packed off in two submarines to take the Japanese-held Makin Island. The best scenes are the early ones, which show in convincing detail the special training given to this fighting force.

William Nigh's *Corregidor* recalled the battle of that name and managed some realistic war effects, but allowed an irritating and unlikely love triangle between Otto Kruger, Elissa Landi and Donald Woods to intrude.

The Pacific war film also took to the air, and never more excitingly than in Howard Hawks's spectacular *Air Force*, described variously as 'an absolute masterpiece' and 'a permanent classic of the American Cinema'. The story concerns the fortunes of a Flying Fortress and its crew as they battle their way across the Pacific from San Francisco to an Australian beach. The group (under Hawks's direction a credible and highly professional one) is again of importance, intended as representative of many crews whose experiences writer Dudley Nichols culled from Army Air Corps files.

Forming an irresistible sub-genre were the films which paid tribute to women in the front line, though the credibility of even the best of them was undermined by what Bosley Crowther described as 'the studiously dishevelled glamour' of their leading ladies – an ambi-valence mildly satirized later on in Edward Buzzell's *Keep Your Powder Dry* (1945), with Lana Turner, Laraine Day and Susan Peters. The two which tried hardest were Mark Sandrich's *So Proudly We Hail* and Richard Thorpe's *Cry Havoc*, both of which saluted the courage of the combat nurses at Bataan during

Emotive symbol of the heroic resistance at *Bataan* (Tay Garnett, 1943), which starred Robert Taylor, George Murphy, Thomas Mitchell, Lloyd Nolan, Robert Walker and Desi Arnaz.

the desperate withdrawal from the island.

When the United States took the war into the Far East with the Doolittle raid over Japan, Hollywood dutifully followed. Edward Dmytryk used the raid in *Behind the Rising Sun* (1943) as an excuse to catalogue Japanese atrocities against the Chinese, including rape and infanticide. Robert Florey made it the climax to his pious biography of Colonel Robert Lee Scott, *God is My Co-Pilot* (1945), the true story of a thirty-four-year-old airman (played by Dennis Morgan) who defied efforts to ground him because of his age and became a hero with the Flying Tigers.

Destination Tokyo (1943), Delmer Daves's feature début as a director, dealt with the war adventures of a submarine, the USS Copperfin, and in particular its daring mission to get right into Tokyo Bay to help set up the Doolittle raid. Under the smooth captaincy of Cary Grant, the sub. does this and more, finally torpedoing a Japanese aircraft-carrier, surviving a depth-charge attack, and limping into San Francisco Bay. An exciting, efficient, effectively photographed film, it was also convincing enough to be used as an instructional film in the US Navy.

Thirty Seconds Over Tokyo (1944), directed by Mervyn LeRoy, dealt with the Doolittle raid itself. Spencer Tracy portrayed the lieutenant-colonel who planned and gave his name to the first American bombing attack on Japan in April 1942, and Van Johnson played the pilot, Captain Ted Lawson, who chronicled the dramatic events. Long, heroic, realistic and technically very proficient, the film was warmly

Randolph Scott in *Gung Ho!* (Ray Enright, 1944).

Gig Young, Arthur Kennedy and James Brown in *Air Force* (Howard Hawks, 1943).

132

praised, being described as a story 'told with magnificent integrity and dramatic eloquence' and 'one of Hollywood's finest war films to date'.

By contrast, opinions of Cecil B. DeMille's hammy, cliché-ridden epic of simple heroism, *The Story of Dr Wassell* (1944), were somewhat less than ecstatic. Wassell (played by Gary Cooper) was an actual Navy doctor who evacuated a number of seriously wounded men to Australia when the Japanese invaded Java. Said Howard Barnes: 'The director has taken a true story of heroism . . . and jangled it into a cacophony of dancing girls, phoney self-sacrifice and melodramatic romance.'

The war at sea also received variable treatment. Tyrone Power's last film before he donned a uniform in real life, *Crash Dive* (1943), was really just one of his swashbuckling, Technicolor adventures updated to a submarine setting – causing Bosley Crowther to wonder 'blankly whether Hollywood knows that we're at war'. Anne Baxter and Dana Andrews made up the other two sides of a triangular sub-plot, and Archie Mayo directed. Robert Z. Leonard's *Cargo of Innocents* (1943), a patriotic drama about the exploits of a veteran destroyer, also failed to take off, despite a cast led by Robert Taylor, Charles Laughton, Brian Donlevy and Walter Brennan.

Altogether more successful was Lloyd Bacon's *Action in the North Atlantic* (1943), an exciting, much-merited tribute to the merchant seamen who heroically maintained the Atlantic supply-lines to the Allies. Humphrey Bogart and Raymond Massey were a captain and mate who set out to lure and destroy a bothersome U-boat. This was another movie considered a sufficiently faithful re-creation of real events to be used as a training film (this time by the Merchant Marine) – a considerable compliment to the ten-thousand-ton Liberty ship which Warner Bros had specially constructed in the studio. Another branch of the Navy, its construction engineers, was given its due in Edward Ludwig's *The Fighting Seabees* (1944), with John Wayne, Susan Hayward, and Dennis O'Keefe.

Lloyd Bacon stayed with the Navy for the time being, recounting a factual story of five brothers who lived and died together as sailors in *The Fighting Sullivans* (1944). This modest family saga concerned itself more with the home front than with actual combat, emphasizing America's more parochial values and her pride in parenthood as well as the nature and necessity of extreme sacrifice. Anne Baxter and Thomas Mitchell headed the otherwise unknown cast.

The ubiquitous Humphrey Bogart added another campaign medal to his collection in *Sahara*, one of a handful of Hollywood excursions into the North African desert filmed in 1943. Skilfully directed by Zoltan Korda, this was 'the first film to popularize the spirit of the United Nations' – not that that made its story any less preposterous. It tells of a tiny and ever-diminishing group of Allied soldiers, British, American, French and Sudanese wandering in the Libyan desert in a tank during the retreat

Veronica Lake and Claudette Colbert in *So Proudly We Hail* (Mark Sandrich, 1943).

Japanese rearguard action in
Behind the Rising Sun
(Edward Dmytryk, 1943).

from Tobruk; and of how Bogart, virtually single-handed, contrives to defeat a whole German battalion in a way that makes Sergeant York look like a fumbling Boy Scout. Front-line troops, when they saw it, resented the film ('That kind of crap gives the folks at home the wrong idea about what we are up against', said one GI colourfully), but the unlikely heroics apart, it was well made, exciting, and un-ashamedly entertaining.

Henry Fonda's desert bravery in John Stahl's *Immortal Sergeant* was of a more modest kind, intended to demonstrate how the mildest man in the ranks can be spurred on by his sense of duty to become a courageous leader of men. Again, the plot revolves round a small group of men (all allegedly British this time, though none too convincing, some of them) up against great odds in hostile terrain; and again, the well-staged battle scenes are the film's best feature.

Billy Wilder's *Five Graves to Cairo*, also set in the North African desert, was more con-cerned with intrigue than action, offering the not-too-serious conjecture that a British agent (Franchot Tone) outwitted Field-Marshal Rommel (an enjoyably inaccurate impersona-tion by Erich von Stroheim) and thus secured secret information vital to a British victory at the Battle of El Alamein. This was simple,

unpretentious, entertaining, free of excessive ideological debate, and lifted by Wilder's witty direction and the excellent playing of Tone, von Stroheim, Akim Tamiroff and Peter van Eyck (a blond German actor setting out on a thirty-year career of inevitable typecasting).

From 1944, there was a marked decline in the number of war films produced in Hollywood. There were several reasons for this: the pro-duction process had become much more compli-cated and expensive, particularly where loca-tion work was involved, and studios preferred to lavish their bigger budgets on more popular genres, such as musicals; there was less un-certainty about the outcome of the war and thus a less urgent need for widespread patriotic propaganda; a growing awareness of the mounting carnage and destruction was causing a general distaste for war films; and, finally, the public had, quite simply, had enough of this type of movie.

On the other hand, the few films which were being made in 1945 carried larger proportions of realism, honesty, objectivity and human kind-ness than hitherto. In the best of them, said Lewis Jacobs, 'there was implicit a rationale that attempted to define the moral consequences of fighting and dying'. One or two films, like *Objective, Burma!* and *Back to Bataan*, still mindlessly depicted the enemy as sadistic

134

automatons, but war movies were mostly concerned now with the preoccupations and anxieties of the average American soldier.

America's developing conscience was put tentatively on show in Henry King's unsung *A Bell for Adano*, in which war-movie veterans John Hodiak and William Bendix, as military administrators of a Sicilian town newly liberated from the fascists, gradually win over a suspicious populace and revive their community spirit. Symbolically they also replace Adano's revered town bell, and witness the return of its prisoners of war in one of the film's most effective moments.

Back to Bataan, with Edward Dmytryk directing John Wayne as a guerrilla leader in the Philippines, is more conventional, and not quite as good as its reputation suggests. Nevertheless, it is an honest tribute to Filipino resistance (embodied most colourfully in Anthony Quinn) with sober, near-documentary qualities, and a vivid re-enactment of the Corregidor victory.

Raoul Walsh's *Objective, Burma!*, by contrast, has an unjustifiably adverse reputation clouded by hysterical British claims that it gave a risibly biased account of American deeds in Burma. There is, it is true, more than a suggestion at the end that the Allied invasion of Burma has been made entirely possible by Errol Flynn's successful mission to knock out a Japanese radar station, but at the same time an introduction has already stated that 'this production covers a single, typical [!] operation. The actors are American. But they enact experiences common to British, Indian and Chinese forces who victoriously fought the grim jungle war.' Perhaps this was added

Destination Tokyo (Delmer Daves, 1943).

Van Johnson, Robert Walker, Tim Murdock, Gordon McDonald and Don Defore in *Thirty Seconds Over Tokyo* (Mervyn LeRoy, 1944).

Gary Cooper and Laraine Day in *The Story of Dr Wassell* (Cecil B. DeMille, 1944), with Paul Kelly (*below right*).

retrospectively, but in any event it hardly matters: Walsh's film remains one of the fastest-paced, most exciting combat movies of the war, and one in which not even Errol Flynn is gilded with false romanticism.

There are, of course, a number of the fictional elements common to the more fanciful films, British and American: after the paratroopers' mission has been achieved with miraculous

Humphrey Bogart and Pat O'Moore in *Sahara* (Zoltan Korda, 1943).

efficiency, Flynn asks, 'Any of our boys dead?' and one of them replies, 'No sir, but we sure were lucky!' (It is, in fact, reel ten before a GI is actually *seen* being shot.) There is also a certain amount of ambivalence, particularly in a scene where the Americans, having smilingly massacred a whole encampment of Japs without a murmur, proceed to show excessive indignation when the enemy hits back. And it is hard to suppress a giggle when one of the paratroopers, having come upon a colleague butchered by the Japs, says falteringly: 'That's Harris . . . isn't it?'

These clichéd moments, however, detract little from an efficient, entertaining film in which James Wong Howe's photography (particularly in the parachute-jumping scene and a night-attack sequence) and the ensemble playing of a convincing cast (including old hands Henry Hull and George Tobias) are especially noteworthy.

John Ford, although not a director noted for his commitment to the conventional type of war film (though he made some notable documentaries), nevertheless came up with one of the most admired in *They Were Expendable*. This was a solemn and somewhat overdue tribute to the small band of men who pioneered and operated the motor torpedo boats which played a crucial forestalling role during America's defeat and withdrawal from the Philippines. Robert Montgomery and John Wayne, acting with almost melancholic restraint, pointed up the gallantry and devotion to duty of the men chosen to effect the historic evacuation of General MacArthur at the end of the campaign. The film wavers rather oddly between sentimental melodrama (with a highly patriotic soundtrack) and straight reporting, but, with the help of Joseph August's superlative camerawork (this was his last of fourteen films with Ford), it achieved some fine moments, especially in the scenes showing the torpedo boats in action.

The two finest films depicting the ordinary front-line American soldier came right at the end of the war – William Wellman's *The Story of GI Joe* and Lewis Milestone's *A Walk in the Sun*. Wellman's film, based on the writings of popular war correspondent Ernie Pyle (portrayed in the film by Burgess Meredith), was a humane hymn of praise to the infantryman, a 'sultry poem' focusing on a small group of soldiers who battle their way from North Africa to Rome via Sicily, Southern Italy and Cassino. Even though Robert Mitchum has a prominent role, there are no mock heroics – one sees only the hunger, misery, fear, boredom and weariness of the foot-soldiers amidst a confusing nightmare in which 'different campaigns became one interminable campaign; romance wore a death-mask' (Gassner and Nichols). To American eyes, turned roseate by Hollywood's incessant glorification of the war, *GI Joe* was intensely realistic, a 'distillation of the war documentaries' and 'far and away the least glamorous war picture ever made'. Ernest Lindgren, however, in the British 'Monthly Film Bulletin', found its style 'in considerable contrast to the British blend of documentary and fiction techniques. Its realistic scenes are more impressionist and hazy, and in its dramatized scenes one is more conscious of the actor'. Either way, it was universally praised – James Agee called it 'a tragic and eternal work of art', Sam Fuller reckoned that, 'with its feeling of death and mass murder', it was the only war

film he'd seen which wasn't 'adolescent, completely insincere', and the Fifth Army (many of whom had participated in the film) said, 'This is it!' In cinematic terms, it stripped the myth from the war movie.

A Walk in the Sun is even more microcosmic in its concentration on a single platoon spending a single morning progressing from a beach landing at Salerno to the capture of a German-

Raymond Massey and Humphrey Bogart in *Action in the North Atlantic* (Lloyd Bacon, 1943).

Henry Fonda as *The Immortal Sergeant* (John Stahl, 1942), with Thomas Mitchell (*left*) and Allyn Joslyn.

Franchot Tone, Peter van Eyck and Erich von Stroheim (as Rommel) in *Five Graves to Cairo* (Billy Wilder, 1943).

held farmhouse six miles away. It is a rhythmic, folkloric parable of combat, punctuated by pleasantly incongruous ballads (one of which tells of some men who 'came across the sea to sunny Italy, and took a little walk in the sun') and concerned exclusively with the characters, foibles, actions and reactions of soldiers suddenly confronted with decision-making and

death. Robert Rossen's brilliant script is full of cadences, effective repetitions ('Give me a butt!' says Richard Conte's cynical machine-gunner every few minutes) and strikingly original touches, such as the habit of one soldier (John Ireland) of commentating on the action by composing letters in his head (sometimes with bitter irony, as in his last missive,

John Hodiak, Henry Morgan, John Russell and William Bendix in *A Bell for Adano* (Henry King, 1945).

138

Paul Fix, John Wayne and J. Alex Havier in *Back to Bataan* (Edward Dmytryk, 1945).

Errol Flynn in *Objective, Burma!* (Raoul Walsh, 1945), with (*at rear*) Henry Hull as a war correspondent.

Burgess Meredith
as war correspondent Ernie
Pyle in *The Story of GI Joe*
(William Wellman, 1945).

Right: George Tyne and
Richard Conte in *A Walk in
the Sun* (Lewis Milestone,
1945).

John Wayne, Robert
Montgomery and Jack Holt
in *They Were Expendable*
(John Ford, 1945).

muttered matter-of-factly after the final costly attack: 'This morning we captured a farmhouse. It was easy . . .'). The acting throughout is harmonious and uniformly inspired, with Dana Andrews (subjugating his star status), as a sensitive but competent sergeant, and Herbert Rudley, as a shell-shocked platoon leader, outstanding.

A Walk in the Sun is not pacifist in the sense that Milestone's *All Quiet on the Western Front* is pacifist, but it is distinguished by an intense compassion and humanity which, in the context of a war which had to be fought, comprise an equally strong statement about the futility and tragedy of war. 'It is,' said Penelope Houston, 'concerned with the immediate realities of a situation rather than its deeper implications and the mood is, therefore, one of acceptance of the fact of war rather than rebellion against it.' It was a high note of quality and maturity on which to conclude Hollywood's contribution to the war effort.

During the war years, attendance at cinemas in America grew to an unprecedented level, and film-makers bore the greatest responsibility for keeping the public informed about the war and maintaining its morale. This they did with a remarkable output of entertainment and propaganda, much of which was naïve and superficial but which had an over-all effect of keeping the issues clear while engendering in the public a powerful emotional involvement. The American people knew what the war was about – that good was being assailed by evil – and they cared.

A majority of the five hundred or more war-oriented films produced in this period were shallow, trite, bloodthirsty, mindlessly jingoistic and far removed from reality – shoddy items which served a contemporary purpose but are now best forgotten. A few, however, survive as works of cinematic art or as monuments to one of mankind's grosser demonstrations of its inability to live at peace with itself.

140

The War: Official

The best and most enduring films to emerge from World War II, on either side of the Atlantic, were those which set out not to entertain (though many of them did), but to record the war and to inform, persuade, stimulate and reassure the citizenry on whose behalf it was being fought. By the end of the war, the British, Americans, Russians and Germans had between them accumulated a superb, in-depth record of the conflict in all its aspects – a mass of unique, historical film which has still to be fully tapped and utilized.

In Britain, the war documentary has come to be recognized as the zenith of the country's cinema, and its principal contribution to the art of the film. A maturing of the erratic but inspired documentary movement of the 'thirties, it appeared to thrive on austerity as well as on the brilliance of its exponents, and its exposition of the war was inimitably lucid, factual and beguiling, sometimes lyrical and always distinctively British. The potential of film as propaganda was not underrated, and the war began with a shot-gun wedding of the Government and Service film units and the best of the independent documentary companies. Numerous films of an instructional nature were eventually turned out, the propaganda purpose behind them ranging from the practical (how to cope with food, health, weapons, machinery, etc.) to the political (war information, ridicule of the enemy, moral preparedness, and so on). Mobile film units set up by the Ministry of Information supplemented the cinemas by disseminating these wares to the towns and villages of Britain for showing in factories and public halls. Latterly, certain sections of the home front even received their own tailor-made magazine films, like *Worker and War-Front*.

Initially, there was a lack of co-ordination among the documentary film-makers placed under the bureaucratic control of the Ministry of Information, which was not at first much interested in documentaries. Few projects were started, and the only films of note during the first year of the war were those made on the independent initiative of the talented members of the GPO Unit. One of these was *The First Days*, a mood-piece depicting London's reaction to the declaration of war ('people joked, but in their hearts was devastation'), made as a private collaborative effort by Humphrey Jennings, Harry Watt, Pat Jackson and Alberto Cavalcanti. Watt followed this with *Squadron 992*, the first General Post Office film to be officially commissioned by the MOI. It was a simple, strikingly photographed study of an anti-aircraft balloon unit in training and protecting the Forth Bridge. Neither of these films was liked, and they became dated before they could be properly distributed.

The situation improved rapidly after the summer of 1940, when the MOI's Films Division was reorganized, the Crown Film Unit set up (absorbing the GPO Unit), and a definite production programme and policy laid down. Thereafter, Crown and many other sponsored units, such as Shell and Paul Rotha, got down to the task of pumping out propaganda in films ranging from two-minute flashes to feature-length documentaries. Many of the film-makers involved, now working for the Establishment, had been known in the 'thirties for their radical political views, and Harry Watt has since pointed out the irony of these 'armchair left-wingers . . . making films to win the war'.

Unlike the Americans, British audiences took readily to documentaries, possibly because – in contrast to feature films, which concentrated on the officer class – they gave an honest portrayal of the country's class structure and respected the viewer's intelligence and opinions. One of the most popular of the early documentaries was *London Can Take It* (1940), directed for Crown by Humphrey Jennings and Harry Watt, which told the story of the first big bombing raid on London at the beginning of the blitz in the form of a news bulletin delivered by the American correspondent Quentin Reynolds. It showed, with sympathy and feeling, the stoicism of the British learning to live with war, and it had the double purpose of inspiring confidence at home and dramatizing to those abroad how their own democracy might be threatened.

Jennings was the poet – perhaps the genius – of the documentary movement. The bulk of his films belong to the general propaganda war effort, yet they also transcend it. They are, with their warmth and spontaneity of feeling, brilliant evocations of the atmosphere of Britain and the mood of its people in wartime. 'No one else,' according to Lindsay Anderson, 'has put British people so truthfully and so worthily on the screen', and his achievement is all the more remarkable in that he went against the dominant trend of the documentary film by trading in emotion rather than pragmatism.

Alan Lovell and Jim Hillier, in their book 'Studies in Documentary', have described how 'Jennings responded very quickly, artistically and personally, to the war and his response seems to have been analogous to that of the new generation who went into uniform, finding . . . "that they lived in a world without peace"'. His early films as a director were straightforward contributions to the propaganda drive to involve people in the war effort. *Speaking from America* (1939) described the transatlantic telephone link and contained an oblique appeal to the United States to ally itself with Britain; *SS Ionian* (1939) was about merchant ships in the Mediterranean and the role played by the Royal Navy in protecting them; *Welfare of the Workers* (1940), made with Pat Jackson, was a perceptive study of working conditions in wartime; and *Spring Offensive* (1939) described, with lyrical force, the reclamation and care of farmland in East Anglia for the war effort.

Jennings's technique of divining the character, culture and traditions of Britain by weaving a film poem out of evocative images and sounds, reached its culmination in his three 1941 documentaries, *Heart of Britain*, *Words for Battle*, and *Listen to Britain*. The first of these contrasts city and country scenes with shots of bomb damage and war activity, against a soundtrack which alternates between lyrical commentary and classical music. The message is simple: 'No one with impunity troubles the heart of Britain.' *Words for Battle* is a call to arms in which poetic quotations (spoken by Laurence Olivier) are applied to contemporary events. *Listen to Britain*, made in collaboration with Stewart McAllister, again strings together impressionistic images of a country at war, but this time eschews commentary altogether, relying entirely on natural sounds and music. The effect is splendidly moving as the noise of factories and dance-halls, tanks and canteens, gives way to the characteristic music-making of Flanagan and Allen and Dame Myra Hess.

Jennings's next film, generally acknowledged to be his masterpiece, was *Fires Were Started* (1943), an 'unpretentious memorial' to the firemen of London which painted 'an astonishingly intimate portrait of an isolated and besieged Britain' (Peter Morris). More narrative in style than Jennings's previous films, this dramatization (using real firemen) of a day and a night in the life of one unit of the Auxiliary Fire Service in the middle of the blitz, captured with unerring truthfulness all

the tragedy and the heroism of civilians at war. Most memorable, in an unforgettable human document, are the fire-fighting scenes and their aftermath, and the fireman's rendering of 'One Man Went to Mow' as they await the call to action.

The blending of documentary and fictional techniques was continued by Jennings in his next two films, *The Silent Village* (1943) and *The True Story of Lilli Marlene* (1944). The first of these transposed the story of Lidice, the Czechoslovak mining village liquidated by the Germans after the assassination of Heydrich, to a similar Welsh village. It was an appealing idea, but Jennings's lyricism was ill-suited to such a dramatic subject. *Lilli Marlene*

Listen to Britain (Humphrey Jennings and Stewart McAllister, 1941).

Fires Were Started (Humphrey Jennings, 1943).

attempted to re-create the story of the song which had caught the imagination of both the British and German armies, but again the symbolism proved elusive.

Jennings returned successfully to his old style in *The 80 Days* (1944), about the V1 attacks on southern England, although the mood was more sombre than before. A measure of gloom as well as hope also pervades *A Diary for Timothy* (1945), a picture of Britain in the last months of the war, with various characters (including a baby) looking to the uncertain future. Using characteristic, often familiar images, and enriched with an E.M. Forster commentary spoken by Michael Redgrave, this stands as one of Jennings's justly more famous documentaries.

Jennings signed off his own unique commentary on the war with *A Defeated People* (1945), which dealt with the German experience after the armistice. It showed sympathy and understanding but could not compare with the earlier, British-oriented films.

Jennings's best work makes the rest of Britain's war documentaries look largely unsubtle and mundane. Many of them, however, were extremely well made and effective in their

144

avowed intent. Morale was boosted in various ways: conventionally, as in *Britain at Bay* (1940), with J.B. Priestley contributing; pragmatically, as in Geoffrey Bell's Shell film, *Control Room* (1941), a reassuring description of the organization of Air Raid Precautions in a big city during an attack; or with satire, as in *Lambeth Walk, Germany Calling* (1941), and Cavalcanti's caricature of the pompous Italian dictator Benito Mussolini, *Yellow Caesar* (1940).

Various aspects of war service were depicted in *Mastery of the Sea, They Also Serve, Men of the Lightship* (all 1940), J.B. Holmes's *Merchant Seamen* (1941), the full-length *Coastal Command* (1942), and many similar tributes to the defenders of Britain. The food situation was described fancifully, as in Len Lye's *When the Pie Was Opened* (1941), an imaginative presentation of a wartime recipe for vegetable pie; or seriously, as in Paul Rotha's feature-length documentary, *World of Plenty* (1943), the first to get a full-circuit release in Britain. Rotha's film surveyed the global food problem with clever, journalistic techniques derived from *The March of Time* and which he developed further in *The Land of Promise* (1945).

Anthony Asquith contributed three short films in association with the Ministry of Information: *Channel Incident* (1940), an unconvincing dramatization (with Peggy Ashcroft, Gordon Harker, Robert Newton and Kenneth Griffith) of the Dunkirk 'armada'; *Two Fathers* (1944), in which an Englishman and a Frenchman pay tribute to the Maquis in France; and *Welcome to Britain* (1943), a shrewd, penetrating, humorous guide to the British for the benefit of American servicemen, with Burgess Meredith, Bob Hope and Beatrice Lillie.

Among the best documentaries of the war were those depicting actual operations and combat, especially welcomed at a time when newsreels were being trivialized by censorship. The most imaginative of these was Harry Watt's *Target for Tonight* (1941), a feature-length film about an RAF bombing raid, filmed at a time when Britain was beginning to go on to the offensive. An actual bomber crew played themselves in this sober reconstruction of a routine mission, notable for its attention to detail and its sympathetic portrait of men facing extreme danger with quiet courage and practised calm.

Similar homage was paid to the merchant seamen in *Western Approaches* (1944), made in

Marjorie Rhodes in *World of Plenty* (Paul Rotha, 1943).

Opposite above: The inhabitants of Cwmgiedd, in South Wales, re-enacting the tragedy of Lidice in *The Silent Village* (Humphrey Jennings, 1943).

Opposite below: Yellow Caesar (1940), Cavalcanti's satirical portrait of Mussolini.

145

colour by Pat Jackson, which reconstructed the sinking of a U-boat by a merchantman in the Atlantic. Again, the sailors were all played by serving officers and men, and the film achieved a remarkable degree of authenticity and realism.

Most of the major campaigns of the war were recorded on film and edited into documentaries. *Lofoten* (1941) was a brief newsreel account of the Anglo-Norwegian raid on the Lofoten Islands near Narvik. More ambitious were the series of 'Victory' films photographed by the Services Film Units: *Tunisian Victory* (1944), Roy Boulting's *Burma Victory* (1945), and *Desert Victory* (1943), the same director's efficient account of the defeat of Rommel in North Africa. Best of all, however, was the prestige Anglo-American compilation recounting the defeat of the Germans on the Western Front – *The True Glory* (1945) – put together from an alleged six million feet of news film by two of the brightest directors of the time, Carol Reed and Garson Kanin. Cleverly edited to emphasize the part played in the final offensive by the ordinary fighting men of all the Allied nations – Britain, America, Canada, France – *The True Glory* still retains a strong emotional impact and remains one of the finest of all the World War II documentaries.

Starved of encouragement and support, the British documentary film went into a rapid decline after 1945, achieving since only spasmodic reminders of the halcyon days of Jennings, Watt, Cavalcanti, Jackson, and the many other talented film-makers of the war years.

The American contribution to the documentary in wartime was an outstanding one, particularly in its staggering reportage of front-line combat. Hollywood, as part of its general mobilization for the war effort, contributed a large number of personnel to the services film units (including directors of the calibre of William Wyler, Frank Capra, Anatole Litvak, John Huston and John Ford) and, after a spasmodic start, coverage of the conflict became vivid, thorough and uncompromisingly detailed. American war cameramen, even by the standards one applies to such men, were incredibly brave, and many were killed.

A German general said early in the war that the opponent with the best cameras would be the victor, and the US War Department responded by spending an annual sum of $50,000,000 on factual film-making in order to swing the odds America's way. Massive amounts of combat footage were used for military study, to show to the troops, and to make into newsreels for public consumption. And while the main emphasis throughout was on factual reporting and technical instruction, leading to a scarcity of documentaries which put forward ideas, shaped opinion, or provoked thought, in the end an incomparably comprehensive chronology of the war had been compiled.

America's first war documentaries were made as a reaction to the 'woefully cheap make-believe' then being churned out by the movie city. Said Bosley Crowther: 'What we want in our war films is honest expression of national resolve and a clear indication of realities unadorned with Hollywood hoop-la.' The Office of War Information deplored the lack of reality and truth about the war in motion pictures, and took the initiative by showing to film-makers a series of clear, concise, military-made documentaries as a demonstration of what could be achieved within a propaganda framework.

Among these films was most of Frank Capra's significant and highly influential series *Why We Fight* (1942–45), made to persuade the public to relinquish isolationism, and to promote knowledge of the enemy and the reasons for the war. Made by Capra in conjunction with Litvak and Anthony Veiller, with Walter Huston doing the commentary, *Why We Fight* was an expert and sustained piece of propaganda 'turning unpleasant facts into breathtaking entertainment' (Leslie Halliwell). The series consisted of seven features – *Prelude to War*, *The Nazis Strike*, and *Divide and Conquer* (depicting the rise of fascism and the German attacks on European countries), *The Battle of Britain*, *The Battle of Russia*, and *The Battle of China* (highlighting the courage and resistance of the Allies – marred in *China* by the omission of tricky political elements such as reference to the communist armies) and *War Comes to America* (examining the impact on American opinions of the war's events) – each compiled from film from a variety of sources, including the enemy, enlivened by diagrams, optical effects and Dimitri Tiomkin's music. Their tone is stridently persuasive, partisan and (in the tributes to the Allies) unstintingly effusive, and the achievement of the series is that it works both as entertainment and as didacticism.

Why We Fight and other, less ambitious documentary projects inspired film-makers thereafter to produce far more meaningful and authentic war pictures, which in turn influenced the tone of fiction films about the war.

Capra himself was involved in a number of subsequent films either as producer or director, including *Two Down, One to Go* (1945) and Roy Boulting's *Tunisian Victory*. He also inspired a bi-weekly, twenty-minute newsreel specifically designed for the armed forces, called *The Army-Navy Screen Magazine*.

As in Britain, all aspects of the war were dealt with in factual films. Civilian morale was kept up with home-front documentaries like Irving Lerner's *A Place to Live* (1941) and Willard van Dyke's *War Town* (1943). Munitions workers were given added incentive by being shown such emotive scenes as (in *The Enemy Strikes*) German soldiers smoking cigarettes taken from dead American troops. And the soldiers themselves were manipulated in various ways by

Merchant seamen re-staging the Battle of the Atlantic for Pat Jackson's dramatized documentary, *Western Approaches* (1944).

Desert Victory (Roy Boulting, 1943).

official films: *Baptism of Fire* (1943) and *Resisting Enemy Interrogation* were simple, dramatic, effective devices to prepare soldiers for the experience of combat (and inevitable fear) and its possible consequence. *The Negro Soldier* (1944) was a miscalculated attempt to allay prejudice against coloured soldiers. *Twenty-Seven Soldiers* (1944) showed Allied soldiers of twenty-seven nationalities fighting together in perfect harmony on the Italian front. *Your Job in Germany*, made just before the Normandy invasion, stressed non-fraternization with the enemy (and included footage of the concentration camps which was later withdrawn). Veiller's *Know Your Ally, Britain* (1944) prepared American troops quartered in the British Isles and was fairly sensible, though inadequate as a guide to the British. And *These are the Philippines* performed a similar function in a different part of the world, just prior to the islands'

148

British troops entering Brussels during the relief of Belgium – a scene from *The True Glory* (Carol Reed and Garson Kanin, 1945).

recapture by General Douglas MacArthur.

The best of America's war documentaries, however, were those from the front line. As Lewis Jacobs described it, films like *The Battle of the Beaches* (1943), *With the Marines at Tarawa* (1944), *The Battle for the Marianas* (1944), *Attack: Invasion of New Britain* (1944), *To the Shores of Iwo Jima* (1945), and *Fury in the Pacific* (1945) 'truthfully projected the dirty business of fighting. These pictures were imbued with conviction and unavoidable horror. They documented unflinchingly the desperate involvement of men in close quarters with each other, the shattering muteness of men before the anonymity of death, and the bewildering sense of war's toll and waste.' Parker Tyler added: 'We know . . . that . . . to make us, war-conscious, propaganda documentaries unaffectedly set out to shock our sensibilities and abash our inadequate awareness of soldier suffering.'

Some of these combat films used the *Target for Tonight* technique of concentrating on one fighting unit. Wyler's *The Memphis Belle* (1944), following the fortunes of a Flying Fortress, conveyed eloquently the realities of aerial combat, while both *The Life and Death of the USS Hornet* (1944) and *The Fighting Lady* (1944, beautifully photographed in colour by Edward Steichen) combined the flying theme with a naval one in their studies of aircraft-carriers in action.

In curious contrast to *The Memphis Belle* was Walt Disney's feature-length cartoon, *Victory Through Air Power* (1943), aimed at persuading the public that air domination was the only way to win the war. This was an extraordinary use of such an entertainment medium for propaganda purposes. Skilfully animated, and a powerful plea on behalf of the air force, it was nevertheless simplistic and naïve. It envisaged the war carrying on well past 1945, and bombers being developed as invulnerable super-weapons bristling with guns and capable of bringing down fighters in droves.

Perhaps the finest front-line films came from the cameras of Ford and Huston. *The Battle of Midway* (1942), with some of Ford's favourite actors (Henry Fonda, Jane Darwell, Donald Crisp) contributing a commentary, left its director wounded but clutching an Oscar. His next documentary, *December 7th* (1943), about

Victory Through Air Power (Walt Disney, 1943).

149

Above: The enemy identified in *Prelude to War* (1942), the first part of Frank Capra's influential propaganda series, *Why We Fight*.

Below: The heroine of William Wyler's *The Memphis Belle* (1944), in which Wyler and cameraman William Clothier flew actual combat missions armed with a hand-held camera.

the attack on Pearl Harbor and its aftermath, also won an Academy Award.

John Huston began his war career with the pleasant, non-sensational colour documentary, *Report from the Aleutians* (1943), a study of ordinary soldiers on a little-known posting in the North Pacific, notable for its airstrip sequences showing bombers preparing for take-off.

Huston went on to make two of the finest films of the war, *The Battle of San Pietro* (1944) and *Let There Be Light* (1945). The first of these, a poignant on-the-spot account of Allied attempts to capture a German-held Italian village, contrasted military objectives with human courage and carnage and pulled no punches. Death in action is plainly seen and there are some telling sequences showing bodies being wrapped in white 'shrouds' and heaved around like sacks of flour. 'These lives were valuable,' says Huston himself on the soundtrack. 'Valuable to their loved ones, to their country, and to the men themselves.' Finally, the objective is taken and the villagers, starved and oppressed, stagger out of the ruins (to the accompaniment, unfortunately, of a slushy heavenly choir – a rare lapse). The film's deep-seated humanity and scenes of slaughter (of American troops significantly, not the enemy) caused the War Department to condemn it as pacifist and demoralizing ('It's against war,' a general is supposed to have complained to Huston, who replied: 'Well, sir, whenever I make a picture that's for war – why, I hope you take me out and shoot me') and it was hacked down in length from fifty minutes to thirty. As it stands, however, it is still a powerfully compassionate statement on the waste and futility of war.

Let There Be Light also met with official opposition. Asked to make a film about the treatment of soldiers suffering from war-

150

The Battle of San Pietro
(John Huston, 1944).

The Fighting Lady (1944),
a study of a United States
Navy aircraft-carrier,
photographed by Edward J.
Steichen and narrated by
Robert Taylor.

induced neuroses which would show industry that these men (who had faced 'death and the fear of death') were not permanently insane, Huston came up with an intensely human document with wide general implications about mental disorder and the terrible effects of war. The War Department banned it, and despite changing attitudes over the years, its exhibition is still restricted. Humane, unpatronizing, unsensational and full of hope, this remains a relevant and revealing film even today, so cleverly and honourably did Huston transcend his terms of reference. 'It was the most hopeful and optimistic and even joyous thing I had a hand in,' said Huston. 'I felt as though I were going to church every day out in that hospital.'

The American documentary movement, if it can be called that, fizzled out at the end of the war almost as abruptly as it had begun. A number of intriguing films, like *Thunderbolt* (a 'terrifying account of aerial warfare in Italy'), completed as the conflict came to a close, were never even distributed. In spite of their consistent high quality and the admiration shown for them, documentaries had never cut much ice with the American box-office, and now audiences turned their backs on them completely and demanded a diet of total escapism once again.

151

Friend and Foe

While film-making in Britain and America thrived during the war, and even retained a measure of artistic freedom together with some liberality of expression, production in many other countries either diminished, or was disrupted, or came under the strict ideological control of whatever régime was in power. Nazi-occupied Czechoslovakia was reduced to turning out a trickle of escapism; in Poland, also occupied, film-making virtually ceased until the commencement of liberation. Denmark managed to maintain a spark of life by producing subtly disguised anti-Nazi documentaries; and France did the same with a handful of beguiling features. Germany, Japan, and (despite formative rumblings from Visconti, De Sica, and Rossellini) Italy simply poured out a familiar stream of fiercely militaristic, patriotic propaganda. Neutral Sweden, by contrast, enjoyed a creative period free of political pressure, though she overtly sympathized with her oppressed neighbours in such films as Gustaf Molander's celebrated resistance drama *Det Brinner en Eld* (*A Fire is Burning*, 1943).

Russian cinema, like that of its two principal allies, was stimulated by the war, especially in the areas of newsreel and documentary. The aim of Soviet film-making at this time was, according to the Russian All-Union Cinema Committee, 'to depict the greatness of the period and help in the moral, political and military defeat of Fascism', and the documentary-makers – never previously a prominent breed – pursued this end with skill and enthusiasm after Germany's violation of the non-aggression pact (in honour of which Dovzhenko had, in 1940, made the pro-German *Liberation*).

Once Russia was committed to war, the film industry set to work producing numerous propaganda shorts and newsreels, which were expanded into a remarkable cycle of documentaries by such talents as Dovzhenko, Leonid Valamov, Roman Karmen and Yuli Raizman, and others who were, like Raizman, essentially feature directors. Unlike the feature films being made at the time, however, these war records were surprisingly restrained, as factual and unemotional as their titles indicate: *In the Line of Fire* (1941), Dovzhenko's *Defeat of the Germans Near Moscow* (1942) and *Victory in the Ukraine* (1945), *Leningrad Fights* (1942 – Karmen), *Liberation France* (1945 – Yutkevitch), *Defeat of Japan* (1945 – Zarkhi and Heifitz), and so forth. Among the more ambitious newsreel compilations were Valamov's *Stalingrad* (1943); Solntseva's *Battle for the Ukraine* (1943), supervised by her husband, Dovzhenko, who allegedly gave the twenty-four front-line cameramen involved detailed briefings as to the kind of pictures he wanted; *A Day of War* (1942), a huge co-operative effort compiled from the contributions of a hundred cameramen covering the entire battlefront; and Raizman's *Berlin* (1945), photographed by Karmen and forty other cameramen, and famous for its shots of the Red Flag going up on the Reichstag, the summary cremation of Goebbels and his family after their suicide, and the bemused people of Berlin wandering among the ruins.

Russian feature films of this period were mainly escapist and inspirational, ranging from musicals to historical tributes to Tsarist heroes such as Pudovkin's *Suvorov* (1940) and Petrov's *Kutuzov* (1944). A number of war-oriented dramas were made, however, taking in the Finnish War (Eisimont's *The Girl from Leningrad*, 1941), resistance (Pudovkin and Vasiliev's *In the Name of the Fatherland*, 1943, and Pyryev's *We Will Come Back*, 1942), and the home front (Kozintsev and Trauberg's *Plain People*, 1945, and Gerassimov's *Mainland*, 1944).

A favourite theme was the indestructible spirit of the Russian people, however fierce the onslaught, portrayed usually through the stoicism and bravery of partisan heroines. Friedrich Ermler's *She Defends Her Country* (1943) was about a peasant woman (brilliantly played by Vera Maretskaya) who hit back at the Nazis after the murder of her husband and child by fighting with the partisans. Leo Arnstam's *Zoya* (1944), an 'optimistic tragedy' made in semi-documentary style, told of a sixteen-year-old girl partisan hanged by the Germans.

German atrocities were the theme of several films, including Mark Donskoy's *How the Steel Was Tempered* (1942), which recalled Ukrainian resistance to the German invaders in 1918; the same director's contemporary sequel, *The Rainbow* (1944), a grim, dramatized catalogue of reprisals taken against the women and children of a partisan village; and Mikhail Romm's *Girl No. 217* (1944), which dealt with the deportation and treatment of Russian women as slaves – all the more effectively for not exaggerating or caricaturing the German characters.

One of the most highly regarded of the Russian war features was Ermler's *The Great Turning-Point* (1945), an account of the Battle of Stalingrad seen from the point of view of the generals who had to bear the strain of military command and strategic decision-making. Although static and wordy, with few scenes of action, it was a successful and popular study of the psychology of warfare.

Sadly, the vein of originality and creative elbow-room which pertained in Soviet film-making during the war years was severely suppressed in the cause of socialist realism after 1945. Any signs of 'formalism' – even a peak of artistic achievement like the second part of Eisenstein's *Ivan the Terrible* – were condemned, and the Russian cinema moved into one of the dullest and most uninspiring periods of its development.

French film-making, with the country under the control of the collaborationist Vichy government, was totally disrupted by the war. Most of the principal directors (Orphüls, Clair,

Renoir) fled, and the period was notable mainly for the emergence of talented new directors like Bresson, Becker and Clouzot. Occasionally, however, film-makers managed to instil apparently innocuous features with hidden meanings accessible to anyone receptive enough to detect them. Carné's *Les Visiteurs du Soir* (1942), for example, though set in medieval times, contrived to be an allegory of the resistance, if somewhat obscure (the Devil persecutes a young couple and turns them to stone – but their hearts go on beating). Similarly, Grémillon's *Lumière d'Eté* (1943) contained an allusive attack on the ruling classes strong enough to get it banned by the Vichy censors. There was, though, a reverse side to this coin. Jean Delannoy's handsome, stylish film, *L'Eternel Retour* (1943), an updating by Jean Cocteau of

the Tristan and Isolde legend, was criticized for being defeatist and for favouring its blonde, Aryan hero and heroine; and Jacques Feyder's delightful *La Kermesse Héroique*, although made in 1935 and describing the Spanish occupation of a Flemish town, was allegedly redistributed by the Nazis on the grounds that it argued in favour of collaboration.

After liberation, there was an abrupt change of attitude, best exemplified by the resistance films which suddenly emerged. These ranged from raw actuality (for example, the *Journal de la Résistance*, made by the resistance workers themselves) to stereotyped fiction (e.g. *Behind These Walls*, in which fifty French civilians are condemned to death for the sabotage of a German supply train, but escape when the RAF bombs the walls of the chapel where they are

Nikolai Cherkassov as the heroic Tsarist General, *Suvorov* (Vsevolod Pudovkin and Mikhail Doller, 1940).

A moment's respite for two Russian generals at the Battle of Stalingrad . . . Andrei Abrikosov and Mikhail Derzhavin in *The Great Turning-Point* (Friedrich Ermler, 1945).

As a reprisal for acts of sabotage carried out by the French Resistance, railway workers are picked out at random to be shot in *La Bataille du Rail* (René Clément, 1945).

imprisoned). The best and most moving tribute to the resistance was René Clément's *La Bataille du Rail* (1945), which singled out the part played by the railwaymen. Exciting, atmospheric, authentic, this semi-documentary reconstruction of sabotage acts and reprisals launched a new 'realism' in French cinema, comparable with that in contemporary Italy.

Two fine documentaries were also produced in France at the war's end: *Le Retour*, a moving record of the liberation of inmates of German prisoner-of-war camps and their journeys

of repatriation to their homelands; and *Le Six Juin à l'Aube*, an austerely impressionistic account by Grémillon of the Normandy landings and the tragic consequences of war.

Other countries made noteworthy statements about resistance and survival as the war lumbered to a close. From Denmark came *Your Freedom is at Stake*, and from Norway, Olav Dalgard's *Vi Vil Leve* (*We Want to Live*), followed in 1947 by an ambitious Franco-Norwegian co-production directed by Titus Wibe Müller, *The Battle for Heavy Water*, an account of the sabotaging of Germany's heavy water plant (vital for atomic research) in Telemark. Switzerland made a rare contribution – Leopold Lindtberg's *The Last Chance*, a sincere, realistic, deeply felt allegorical drama about two Allied soldiers, an Englishman and an American, escaping from fascist-held Northern Italy in 1943. They join a group of civilian refugees of mixed nationalities and make an arduous journey into Switzerland, proving symbolically that alien peoples can live in peace together.

The Axis nations, meanwhile, continued purposefully to pump out their single-minded propaganda with acknowledged skill and efficiency. Germany maintained an unflagging newsreel, *Die Deutsche Wochenschau*, up to the end of the war, as well as producing numerous short record films describing aspects of the war effort, such as the work of the Nazi Army Hospital Service or the activities of U-boats. Added to this regular diet were the occasional prestige documentaries, like H. Bertram's *Baptism of Fire* (1940), which praised the part played by the Luftwaffe in the invasion of Poland, and the two by Dr Fritz Hippler, *Campaign in Poland* (1940) and *Victory in the West* (1940). However obnoxious their intentions, these many and varied actuality films did represent the work of cameramen as courageous as those of any other country, and they form a major contribution to the over-all film record of World War II.

German feature films carried on in the same vein as before the war, merely adjusting their themes to take account of the conflict. *Submarines Head West* (1941), for example, glamorized the U-boat service, showed the Germans to be decent, chivalrous men and portrayed the English as cowards.

Japan's output of militaristic war films was prodigious and, once the early humanistic 'aberrations' like *The Five Scouts* had been put aside, as proficient and mindless as that of any of the other combatant nations. At their best they were simple appeals to duty with little stress on the issues at stake or the rightness of the Nippon cause. Themes were strong and straightforward; characters were typical and ordinary rather than super-heroic or larger than life; and death and horror were shown to be a part of the war scene. They evidently impressed Frank Capra more than somewhat ('We can't beat this kind of thing. We can make

films like these maybe once in a decade'), but by and large they differed little from Western war films.

The leading exponents of the mainstream nationalistic battle movie were Yutaka Abe and Kajiro Yamamoto. Abe favoured flying subjects, using extensive, authentic aerial footage for the first time in Japanese films in *The Burning Sky* (1940), *Nippon's Young Eagles* (1941), and *South Seas Bouquet* (1942). A print of *Nippon's Young Eagles*, about the training and heroism of young Japanese pilots, was presented to Hitler to commemorate the German-Japanese alliance. Yamamoto went in for epic dramatizations, such as *The War at Sea from Hawaii to Malaya* (1942), judged the top film of its year, which extolled 'the Navy spirit as culminated at Pearl Harbor'. It was acclaimed for its very effective realistic special effects and model shots. The same grandiose treatment was used for *General Kato's Falcon Fighters* (1944), except that the action was transferred to the air, while *Torpedo Squadrons Move Out* (1944) tackled yet another topic, human torpedo work.

The war in the air was a favourite theme, occurring again in Eiichi Koishi's semi-documentary *Soaring Passion* (1941); Kunio Watanabe's popular air-cadet story, *Towards*

Jules Berry as the Devil in *Les Visiteurs du Soir* (1942), Marcel Carné's medieval allegory of the Resistance.

155

The aftermath of the Normandy landings in *Le Six Juin à l'Aube* (Jean Grémillon, 1945).

Refugees struggling to reach the Swiss border in *The Last Chance* (Leopold Lindtberg, 1945).

the *Decisive Battle in the Sky* (1943); and *Navy* (1943), Tasaka's film about the airmen who took part in the attack on Pearl Harbor.

Front-line conflict was depicted in Tetson Taguchi's *Generals, Staff and Soldiers* (1942) and Tadashi Imai's *The Suicide Troops of the Watchtower* (1942), set in North China and Korea respectively. The home front, meanwhile, was taken care of by Shiro Toyoda's *A Record of My Love* (1941), in which a nurse marries a disabled soldier; Také Sado's interesting *Chocolate and Soldiers* (1941), the story of a village clerk who is drafted into the army, experiences the horrors of war, and sends chocolate wrappers home to his son, who wins a competition with them and, after the clerk's death in a suicide attack, has his education sponsored by the chocolate company; and Toyoda's *The Daily Battle* (1944), a compassionate look at the life of lower-middle-class people in wartime.

A large number of films were devoted to attacking Britain and the United States, often in a historical context. These included Daisuke Ito's *International Smuggling Gang* (1944); Masahiro Makino's *The Opium War* (1943), which claimed that it had once been a British tactic to stupefy the Chinese with opium;

Masanori Igayama's *If We Go to Sea* (1943), which dramatized Japan's opposition to the international naval disarmament conference in the 'twenties; Shigeo Tanaka's *The Day England Fell*, which recounted the occupation of Hong Kong; and, the most virulent of them all, Daiei's *You're Being Aimed At* (1942), one of the first films about bacteriological warfare, which imagined American agents plotting to spread a deadly disease throughout Japan.

Japan's documentaries were in the German style, glorifying Nippon exploits and the superiority of the conqueror over the conquered. Typical were *The Capture of Burma, Occupation Sumatra* (both 1941), *Divine Soldiers of the Sky* (1942), a salute to Nippon parachute troops, and *Malayan War Record* (1942), which inspired Koji Shima's dramatized version of this theatre of the war, shot on location, *All-Out Attack on Singapore* (1943).

Japan's war – and with it everyone else's – came to an abrupt end with the dropping of the atomic bombs on Hiroshima and Nagasaki. The combatant nations of World War II, bludgeoned and exhausted, paused to take stock, lick their wounds, and bury their dead before dreaming up new causes for armed conflict and new ways of going about it.

Aftermath

In 1945, Allied victories and anticipation of a swift end to the war had led American film producers to start abandoning war pictures even before an armistice was in sight. In the general air of relief and subdued optimism, the public demanded, and got, escapist entertainment, leavened by only the gentlest reappraisal of the immediate past. Battle movies, for the time being at least, were dead.

Hollywood had, nevertheless, been exposed to strong doses of realism and social awareness, the effects of which could not readily be shaken off. Everyone's troubles did not automatically evaporate with the Japanese surrender in September 1945, and a trickle of serious, probing films acknowledged the fact.

John Huston's courageous, controversial documentary, *Let There Be Light* (as already described) dealt vividly and compassionately with one set of human problems engendered by the war: battle neurosis in front-line troops. There were others, mental, physical and social, which became the subject of a handful of feature films.

The first serious study of the rehabilitation of disabled soldiers was Delmer Daves's *Pride of the Marines* (1945), based on the true story of Al Schmid, a young marine blinded at Guadalcanal. John Garfield played the war hero who had trouble adjusting both to his affliction and to post-war social conditions, but who finally pulled through with the devoted help of his forbearing girl-friend (Eleanor Parker). The film was sincere and realistic (notably in its handling of combat scenes) and spoke with a liberal voice on a number of knotty issues, including racialism and class.

Physical disablement also formed part of the theme of William Wyler's justly acclaimed, three-hour 'tribute to the lost innocence of American society', *The Best Years of Our Lives* (1946), in which three veterans of the war return to face the problems of readjustment. One is an air force officer (Dana Andrews) who can come to terms with neither his old job (serving in a drugstore) nor his unsuitable war-bride (Virginia Mayo); another (Fredric March) is a middle-aged ex-banker faced with having to get to know his wife (Myrna Loy) and daughter (Teresa Wright) all over again; the third is a sailor (Harold Russell) who has lost both hands and fears the pity of his fiancée (Cathy O'Donnell), family and friends. Their predicaments were representative of the sufferings of many in real life (Russell, a non-professional, played himself in all but name), and were accurately, sincerely and touchingly portrayed thanks to the excellence of both the writing (screenplay by Robert Sherwood) and the acting. 'This American masterpiece,' wrote Griffith and Mayer, '. . . came as near perfection as popular art contrives to be. . . . It showed Americans as they are, presented their problems as they themselves see them, and provided only such solutions – partial, temporary, personal – as they themselves would accept. The picture's values are the values of the people in it.' The film's immense popularity and unanimous acclaim were reflected in its seven Academy Awards, recipients of which included March, Russell, Wyler and Sherwood.

Four years later Fred Zinnemann dealt more specifically with the problems of paraplegic war veterans in *The Men*, in which Marlon Brando made his striking screen début as a cripple embittered by his condition. This was an early and effective piece of social campaigning by producer Stanley Kramer, notable for its honesty, restraint and compassion. Brando prepared for his role with characteristic thoroughness by living for a while with actual paraplegics.

Zinnemann made two other substantial contributions to the cinema's study of post-war problems. In *The Search* (1947), a part-Swiss production shot on authentic location, he focused on the plight of refugee children through the story of one small boy, shocked into speechlessness, who is cared for by an American soldier (Montgomery Clift) and a nurse (Aline MacMahon) until found again by his mother. One unforgettable scene shows a group of children panicking in an ambulance which they are convinced is a gas chamber. In *Teresa* (1951), Zinnemann probed the weaknesses and uncertainties of a young man (John

Ericson) unable to reconcile his wartime marriage to an Italian girl (Pier Angeli) with the domination of him by his mother (Patricia Collinge). With the help of psychiatric treatment he is eventually able to face up to his situation and his responsibilities.

Other aspects of post-war domestic disruption were explored in William Dieterle's *The Searching Wind* (1946) and Mervyn LeRoy's *Homecoming* (1947). Dieterle's film, which starred Robert Young and Sylvia Sidney, was a dull, inconclusive piece about internecine strife in a solid American family, but it made a few rare and bold attempts to question the worthiness of the cause which had just been fought for. *Homecoming* was a smooth, starry attempt to deal with the sensitive subject of infidelity during wartime. Clark Gable played an army surgeon who falls in love with his nurse (Lana Turner) although he has a wife (Anne Baxter) back home. With the nurse dead and the war over, the surgeon confesses to his wife in a dramatic climax and asks for her patience and understanding.

One taboo significantly weakened by the war was that against open discussion of racial prejudice. The first film to test the climate was Edward Dmytryk's thriller, *Crossfire* (1947), a disturbing, violent portrayal of anti-Semitism, adapted from a novel which was originally about homosexuality (a subject which *was* too strong for Hollywood at this time). Robert Ryan played (superbly) a brutal, bigoted GI, who, during the demobilization period, murders a Jew with the connivance of a group of fellow veterans and is slowly ensnared by a patient policeman (Robert Young). This was one of the best of the American 'conscience' movies, a gripping study in fear and intolerance which both allegorized the war situation and spoke volumes about the casting out of motes and beams.

Crossfire launched a brief but energetic cycle of films arguing for racial justice, among them the double Oscar winner *Gentleman's Agreement* (1947), a study of anti-Semitism in high society directed with admirable cool by Elia Kazan. Gregory Peck played a journalist who masquerades as a Jew in order to investigate prejudice at first hand; John Garfield was the Jewish serviceman who acts as his catalyst.

Two years later, Stanley Kramer established his long-standing reputation as a liberal producer (with the help of director Mark Robson and writer Carl Foreman) with *Home of the Brave* – adapted from a play about anti-Semitism but substituting a Negro for the Jewish hero. The Negro (played with dignity and power by James Edwards) is one of a fractious group of volunteers who undertake a dangerous wartime mission in the Pacific. Beset by bigotry, his own hypersensitivity, and the death of his best friend, he breaks down and loses the use of his legs. Happily, an Army psychiatrist (Jeff Corey) unravels his hang-ups (shades of *Let There Be Light*), and when he understands his inhibitions he is able to walk again. Despite its glib conception and facile happy ending (Kramer characteristics which have not altered in twenty-five years) this was a timely, courageous film which spoke plainly about America's second-class citizens.

Sadly, Hollywood failed to sustain its blitz on the conscience of the United States and quickly returned to safer, less uncomfortable themes. The subject of war psychiatry has been revived from time to time, as in the David Miller film *Captain Newman MD* (1963 – with Gregory Peck, Tony Curtis and Angie Dickinson), but rarely in a more than conventional, superficial, Kildare-ish manner.

Apart from rehabilitation and social conscience sub-genres, Hollywood made few war-

oriented films in the five years between World War II and Korea. Fritz Lang came up with a solitary spy-thriller, *Cloak and Dagger* (1946), with an up-to-date plot about a nuclear physicist-turned-agent (Gary Cooper) who rescues an Italian atomic scientist from the Nazis. It was slick and exciting, but unexceptional – noteworthy only for an eye-catching Hollywood début by Lilli Palmer, and for the way in which Warner Bros, by lopping off Lang's original ending, turned the film from an implicit condemnation of the atomic age into a cosy, uncontroversial melodrama.

The Marx Brothers, meanwhile, were gleefully sending up the whole war-espionage genre, with the help of director Archie Mayo, in *A Night in Casablanca* (1946), which had the mad trio hindering Nazi efforts to get at a fabulous treasure hidden in a Casablanca hotel. Groucho, in fez and greasepaint moustache, was the hotel manager; Chico ran the Yellow Camel Company; and Harpo was a crazy bell-hop. Warner Bros filed a feeble complaint that the word 'Casablanca' could cause confusion with their own box-office hit, but without satisfaction.

Chaplin also satirized war in the most

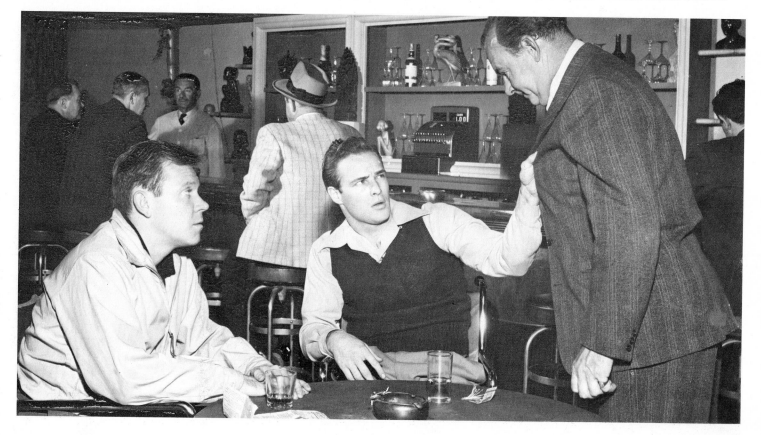

161

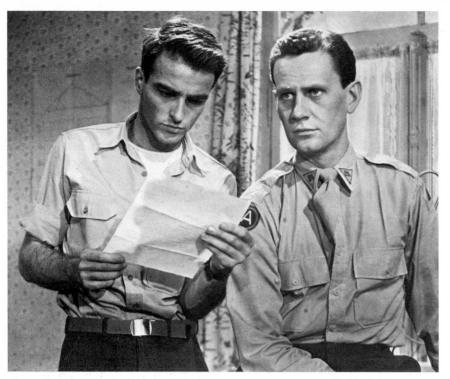

Montgomery Clift and
Wendell Corey in *The
Search* (Fred
Zinnemann, 1947).

unusual of his comedies, *Monsieur Verdoux*
(1947). Suggested by the crimes of Landru and
based on an idea by Orson Welles, this tells of
a bank clerk who becomes a seducer and murderer of rich women during the Depression.
'Von Clausewitz said that war is a logical extension of diplomacy,' explained Chaplin. 'Verdoux feels that murder is a logical extension of
business.' Verdoux himself says, after he has
been imprisoned: 'Wars, conflict, it's all business. One murder makes a villain; millions a
hero. Numbers sanctify.' For once, the Chaplin
screen character was elegant, intelligent and
anti-heroic. The film's cynicism, however, was
ill-timed in an America entrenching against
radicalism and intellectualism (whatever impression the handful of neo-realist 'conscience'
films of Kramer and company might be giving)
and *Monsieur Verdoux* flopped in the States. In
Europe, it fared much better.

John Ford allied his own brand of sentimentalized comedy to a war theme in *When
Willie Comes Marching Home* (1950), the story
of a small-towner (Dan Dailey) who quickly
and proudly enlists to fight World War II, only
to get stationed, somewhat humiliatingly, back
in his own home town. When his pleas for
action are answered, he is sent on a dangerous
mission to France – but it is over so quickly
that no one believes he ever went. The film was
double-layered, the war scenes being played
completely straight ('Well, that was my racket
for a while,' said Ford, quoted by Peter Bogdanovich, 'and there wasn't anything funny
about it. I wonder what s.o.b. will be the first
to make a comedy about Vietnam?').

As the war receded and a sense of perspective
could be achieved, the more thoughtful writers
and directors began to produce some effective
studies of men in battle. These were not anti-
war films in the polemic sense, nor did they
glorify the conflict or give it any chauvinistic
emphasis. They simply portrayed the war as a
happening and attempted to show how it
affected the men caught up in its alien web. Two
of the best examples of this were Henry King's
Twelve O'Clock High (1949) and *Battleground*
(1950), directed by William Wellman.

King's film was a compelling, realistic examination of the strain of command, focusing on
the strict CO (Gregory Peck) of an American
bomber group stationed in England who re-
stores morale to his battle-fatigued unit, but at
the cost of a nervous breakdown. With its
intelligent script and convincingly austere
atmosphere (beautifully sustained from the
tense opening shots of a deserted, overgrown
airfield, reminiscent of the fighter-plane scrap-
yard in *The Best Years of Our Lives*) this remains
one of Henry King's most satisfying films. And
as in *The Gunfighter*, King was able to draw the
very best out of Gregory Peck, who was supported by a strong all-male cast which included
many stalwarts, such as Dean Jagger, Paul
Stewart, Millard Mitchell, Hugh Marlowe and
Gary Merrill.

Battleground re-created the Battle of the
Bulge, the Germans' audacious final offensive
in Europe, as experienced by the men of the
second squad, third platoon, 'I' Company of the
101st Airborne Infantry division. 'This,' said
the 'Motion Picture Herald', 'is a war without
drums and without bugles. . . . This is the way it
was. This is how the boy next door, the grocery
clerk, the telephone lineman, the banker, the
broker, the garage mechanic, your own brother,
son or you yourself saw the war from an infantry foxhole.' Wellman's camera concentrates
on the ordinary guy fighting for survival in a
bewildering war. It picks up his casual conversation, captures his foibles (one infantryman
clicks his false teeth infuriatingly throughout
the film), glimpses his scrappy skirmishings
with the enemy, monitors his courage, his fear
and his cowardice, and records his death. And
like the soldier, it sees no further than the particular neck of the woods it happens to find
itself in; beyond that the war is a confusion of
noise and second-hand information. Grim,
compassionate, compelling, *Battleground* is
one of those rare, timeless war films which
manage to celebrate the resilience of the
human spirit without resorting to mock heroics
or false philosophizing; sustained in this case
by a convincing, self-effacing, perfectly inte-
grated set of performances from (among others)
John Hodiak, Ricardo Montalban, George
Murphy, Marshall Thompson, Don Taylor,
James Whitmore, Richard Jaeckel and (unforgettable for his continually frustrated efforts
to scramble some eggs in his tin helmet) Van
Johnson.

Films like *Battleground* were, however, exceptional and, as a trend, short-lived. Another
picture made at this time, Allan Dwan's *Sands
of Iwo Jima* (1949), anticipated the new vogue
for action-packed, flag-waving war films which
were to become a preoccupation of the early
and post-Korea 'fifties. This one had John
Wayne in the familiar role of the tough, pitiless

commanding officer who wins the respect and affection of his men by his leadership and innate decency. The film's best moments are its reproductions of the battles of Tarawa and Iwo Jima, fortified with generous injections of authentic combat footage. Otherwise, to quote the 'Monthly Film Bulletin', 'it is on the acting of John Wayne that the film is hinged, and on him entirely: the rest are only a bunch of familiar types, square-jawed, wide-eyed specimens of American manhood, all talking avidly of women, all uninteresting. When Wayne appears, interest revives. He is a stalwart of the screen, an outwardly unemotional actor whose every move is worth watching, every word carefully timed. *Sands of Iwo Jima* would be very rough without him.'

Britain produced hardly any war films between 1945 and the revival of the genre in the 'fifties, apart from a handful of spy stories (*Night Boat to Dublin, I See a Dark Stranger, Teheran*), three or four melodramas centring on war technology and scientific work, such as radar (*School for Secrets*), bomb disposal (*The Small Back Room*), and test flying (*Landfall*), a couple of resistance adventures (*But Not in Vain, Against the Wind*), and a solitary look at the plight of displaced persons (*The Lost People*). There were also one or two comedies, like Alexander Mackendrick's *Whisky Galore* (1948), which satirized every sacred cow in sight with its story of wartime whisky-looting, and *Private Angelo* (1949), Peter Ustinov's patchy adaptation of the Eric Linklater novel about a cowardly Italian soldier aiding the British at the time of the German retreat. Perhaps the most thoughtful war movie of this reticent period was Vincent Sherman's *The Hasty Heart* (1949), a melancholic portrait of an embittered Scottish corporal (Richard Todd) dying in a Burmese sanatorium who discovers that friendship is more important than self-pity.

Russia's immediate post-war preoccupations were largely propagandist in the dullest official sense, varying between Cold War tracts, such as Romm's *The Russian Question* (1948) and *Secret Mission* (1950), and Alexandrov's *Meeting On the Elbe* (1949), and glorifications of communism in general and Stalin in particular. Among the more acceptable of these was Gerassimov's *The Young Guard* (1947), a stylish, good-humoured tribute to the Young Communists which tells of a group of young people who sacrifice themselves in their efforts to sabotage the Nazis occupying their village. The film was notable for having a cast selected largely from budding new actors such as Sergei Bondarchuk.

The Soviet prestige productions of this period were Mikhail Chiaureli's *The Fall of Berlin* (1949) and Petrov's *The Battle of Stalingrad* (1950), both of which were extremely long and ponderous, alternating between uncompromisingly brutal battle scenes and elaborate, painstaking reconstructions of summit meetings, complete with caricatures of foreign statesmen like Hitler and Churchill – all designed to glorify Stalin and show him as the

effortless solo genius behind the ultimate victory. Kruschev later condemned Chiaureli's film in specific terms: 'Let us recall the film *Fall of Berlin*. In it only Stalin acts, issuing orders from a hall in which there are many empty chairs . . .'. Yet it was an impressive film visually, re-creating the events of Russia's war saga-like through the eyes of a typical Soviet family, and achieving some splendidly epic images. *The Battle of Stalingrad* was equally baroque, a stylized monument to Russia's most emotional victory of the war, viewing the scenes of combat in huge, abstract panoramas and mythologizing Stalin in god-like images. Chiaureli painted his sycophantic portrait of Stalin as the infallible Olympian, saviour of the Russian people, in two other films, *The Vow* (1946) and *The Unforgettable Year 1919* (1951).

Elsewhere behind the Iron Curtain, the satellite countries were busy adjusting to their new socialist world and film production was both sparse and reticent. In Hungary, just prior to the nationalization of its film industry, Géza Radványi made one notable film about the war,

John Ericson and Pier Angeli in *Teresa* (Fred Zinnemann, 1951).

163

Robert Ryan as the homicidal anti-Semitic GI in *Crossfire* (Edward Dmytryk, 1947), with Steve Brodie (*left*).

James Edwards as the Negro troubled by prejudice in *Home of the Brave* (Mark Robson, 1949), with Lloyd Bridges (*left*) and Frank Lovejoy.

Somewhere in Europe (1947), a moving fantasy about the reclamation of war orphans, very like Nikolai Ekk's Russian film, *The Road to Life*.

The Czechoslovakian film industry was nationalized as soon as the war ended and was thus immediately subject to the pressures of socialist realism, under which some fairly unremarkable war stories, such as M. Cikán's *The Heroes are Silent* (1946) and Jiri Weiss's *Stolen Frontiers* (1947), were produced. Again, however, one good film did emerge from the ideological stranglehold, Alfred Radok's *Distant Journey* (1949), an austere, nightmarish study of daily life in a concentration camp.

This was the theme also of the Polish film, *The Last Stage* (1948), though its director, Wanda Jakubowska, used a quite different style to portray the courageous life and horrific death of the prisoners in Auschwitz. She and her co-writer and several of the actresses had themselves survived Auschwitz, and a powerful, realistic documentary style was employed to re-create their terrible experiences. Other films from the healthier, more enterprising Polish film industry offered portraits of war-torn Warsaw and the occupation, including Aleksander Ford's stylized but humane *Border Street* (1948), about the children of the Warsaw Ghetto, the Jews' desperate uprising, and the razing of the district; Antoni Bohdziewicz's *Others Will Follow* (1949); Jan Rybkowski's *House of the Wastelands* (1950); and Jerzy Zarzycki's *Unvanquished City* (1950).

Another new communist nation, the People's Republic of China, was making films about the war at this time, the best-known example being Ling Tsu-Feng's and Ti-Chiang's *Daughters of China* (1949), which told of the heroic lives and deaths of eight young girl-partisans in the Sino-Japanese War. This period of Chinese history, suitably slanted, continued to occupy the Republic's film-makers for many years. *Tunnel*

War, for instance, made in 1965, was about guerrilla resistance against the Japanese – a more than competent movie about the Chinese partisans' trick of going (literally) underground to outwit and surprise the enemy.

Ironically it was Germany, shattered and divided, which produced some of the most compelling films about the war's effects in the first years of peace. This was especially true of the Russian-controlled Eastern Zone, where an acute social awareness gave birth to a brief but distinguished cycle of what came to be known as 'rubble films' (because of the devastation of the country's cities). One of the first and best was Wolfgang Staudte's *Murderers Are Among Us* (1946), which revealed the talents of its then unknown director and the actress Hildegarde Knef (later changed to Neff), and dealt with the problem of detecting war criminals who reverted to respectable, anonymous citizenship. Effectively set in the ruins of Berlin, this was an unhysterical, imaginatively directed drama about a German's attempts to bring to justice an ex-Nazi who liquidated a Polish village. Later, Staudte made *The Underdog* (1951), a satirical analysis of the growth of a *petit bourgeois* fascist at the time of the Kaiser, which lashed out savagely at conformism, authoritarianism and militarism. *Murderers* was followed by Gerhard Lamprecht's *Somewhere in Berlin* (1946), which dealt with the problems faced by German soldiers returning from the war, and Kurt Maetzig's *Marriage in the Shadows* (1947), about the persecution of Germans married to Jews, based on the actual case of an actor, Joachim Gottschalk, who committed suicide with his Jewish wife when threatened with separation from her.

The film-makers of West Germany also showed an awareness of contemporary problems, including refugees (*Birds of Migration*), disillusion with Nazism (Wolfgang Liebeneiner's *Love '47*, 1947), disruption of the social

Gary Cooper in Fritz Lang's atom spy-thriller, *Cloak and Dagger* (1946).

order (Rudolph Jugert's and Helmut Käutner's *Film Without Title*, 1947), and the shadow of the concentration camps (Arthur Brauner's *Morituri*, 1946). Here, too, satire was used to defy the hardships of living under occupation in a defeated, depressed, debris-strewn Germany – most notably in Robert Stemmle's revue, *The Ballad of Berlin* (1948), with Gert Fröbe. *The Last Stage* was anticipated in H.B. Fredersdorf's and M. Goldstein's Jewish-made *Long is the Way* (1947), a realistic portrayal of Warsaw, Auschwitz, and the post-war displaced persons' camps, spoiled somewhat by a tedious plot (a mother's search for her son) and a superfluous commentary. And the rise and fall of the Third Reich was recounted in Käutner's *In Jenen Tagen* (*In Our Days*, 1947), which used the

Dan Dailey as the small-towner suffering from frustrated heroics in *When Willie Comes Marching Home* (John Ford, 1950), with William Demarest (*left*) and Evelyn Varden.

Gregory Peck as Savage, the forceful bomber squadron CO, in *Twelve O'Clock High* (Henry King, 1949), with (*from left*) Gary Merrill, Hugh Marlowe and Dean Jagger.

Listening for friendly engines in *Battleground* (William Wellman, 1950) are Van Johnson, George Murphy, John Hodiak and Douglas Fowley.

linking device of an old car to tell a series of seven stories depicting life under the Nazis.

After the initial flurry of resistance movies, France made few war films until the pacifist revival of the 'fifties. There were three, however, all made in 1947, which had some impact. Claude Autant-Lara's *Le Diable au Corps* used a World War I setting to deliver a polemic against war in general. It told of a student (Gérard Philipe) who falls in love with a woman (Micheline Presle) whose husband is

away at the war. They are separated and she dies giving birth to his child. A beautifully acted, moving, tragic, atmospheric film, it was nevertheless condemned as repulsive and insulting by many critics, following which it enjoyed a *succès de scandale* and turned Gérard Philipe into a star. *Le Silence de la Mer*, Jean-Pierre Melville's first feature, was an equally downbeat affair based (faithfully) on a short story by Vercors, about an aristocratic Nazi officer in occupied France who slowly wins over

166

an old man and his niece, and then is ordered to the Eastern Front. *Les Maudits* (*The Damned*), another of René Clément's original studies of war, imagined a group of Nazis in 1945 kidnapping a French doctor and fleeing in a submarine to South America. A few of them are fanatical enough to believe they still have a mission and try to sink a freighter from which they have refuelled. Tense, claustrophobic and exciting, this was a skilful adventure-thriller, considered by many to be among Clément's best films, made early in his career.

Perhaps the most remarkable group of films to emerge in the immediate post-war period were those which made up the neo-realist movement in Italy. Taking the resistance or the after-effects of the war as their principal theme, these were fresh, vibrant, rough-hewn, intensely humanistic portraits of a tragic but resilient society. The movement was launched by Roberto Rossellini in 1945 with his influential, epoch-making *Rome, Open City*, which

Arno Paulsen and Hildegarde Knef in *Murderers Are Among Us* (Wolfgang Staudte, 1946).

Crude, improvised, and put together piecemeal under the most trying conditions (the film was begun with the Germans still in occupation), *Open City* is nevertheless a powerfully realistic tribute to Italy's freedom-fighters, portraying ordinary people in a full-blooded manner hitherto unknown in Italian (or anyone else's) films.

Rossellini followed *Open City* with the equally impressive *Paisà* (1946), a six-part dramatized journal depicting incidents in the battle for Italy from 1943 to 1945. These ranged from an encounter between an American Negro and a shoeshine boy in Naples to a brilliant, desolate drama of partisans and parachutists fighting a hopeless battle in the dreary wastes of the Po delta. Rossellini used a largely non-professional cast picked from inquisitive on-lookers at his various locations, and although this policy, combined with his improvisatory techniques, led to an occasional clumsiness and naïvety, the over-all result was a universally acclaimed human document of rare quality and compassion. Georges Sadoul wrote that Rossellini had 'damned the horrors that war had brought to his country and his heart cry was emotionally and enthusiastically understood around the entire world.'

re-created in genuine settings the experiences of the resistance workers who defied the Nazis' tyrannical occupation in 1943–44. The hero is a priest (played by Aldo Fabrizi and based on an actual cleric, Father Don Morosini) shot by the Nazis, and the heroine is a proud, dignified partisan (Anna Magnani, at her flamboyant, scene-stealing best) who meets a similar fate.

Rossellini failed to recapture the rough magic

Paisà (Roberto Rossellini, 1946).

168

of *Open City* and *Paisà* in his next film *Germany, Year Zero* (1947), the tragedy of a young boy driven to murder and suicide in the ruins of post-war Berlin. But it was spasmodically effective and tends to be underrated by comparison with the two masterpieces.

The inspiration and influence of Rossellini led to a spate of notable films in the neo-realist vein. Vittorio De Sica made *Shoeshine* in 1946, a poignant study of the corrupting effect of the war and poverty on friendship, in which the innocence of two shoeshine boys in Rome, and their betrayal by a degraded, avaricious adult society, lead them into crime, prison and death.

In the same year, Aldo Vergano directed his excellent resistance story, *The Sun Still Rises*, about the wartime exploitation of peasants in Lombardy, and in 1947 Giuseppe De Santis (who went on to make the phenomenally successful *Bitter Rice*) contributed his lively, melodramatic *Caccia Tragica* (*The Tragic Hunt*), a return to the Po delta, where the peasants pursue a bandit who has stolen money from the co-operative.

Another director to cut his teeth on neo-realism was Alberto Lattuada, who joined the Rossellini ranks with *Il Bandito* (1946) – about men who, trained to kill in wartime, could find no alternative occupation in peacetime – and followed up with his anti-racist film, *Senza Pietà* (*Without Pity*, 1948), the tragedy of an Italian prostitute and a Negro deserter involved with black-marketeers.

By 1950, however, the new wave in Italy was declining as rapidly as it had risen and was being replaced by an opulent glamour symbolized by Gina Lollobrigida and other well-built pin-ups. In all the film-making countries concerned with the war, in fact, five or so years of sensitive soul-searching and counting the cost were coming to an end, and in the English-speaking industries at least, the action war movie was about to stage a considerable comeback.

Florence Marly, Anne Campion and Henri Vidal in *Les Maudits* (René Clément, 1947).

No Peace for the Wicked

America Sees Red

Hollywood's brief honeymoon with 'new realism' and its flirtation with tolerance came to an abrupt but inevitable end in the early 'fifties. The serious doubts expressed after armistice about the validity of war had been eroded by the nationalistic neuroses of the Cold War, and then swept aside by the eruption of the Korean conflict. The war movie, with all its traditional trappings, bounced back into favour, dividing its attention between Korea, anti-communism, and rose-tinted reminiscences of the 1939–45 nightmare. The revival has scarcely subsided after twenty or more years, but, sadly, a majority of its many manifestations have been characterized by a marked lack of integrity and insight, and an increasing tendency towards blatant exploitation of the 'production values' (i.e. the action and violence) of war.

The Korean War had a profound effect, both socially and politically, on the American people, who were puzzled by its remoteness and the fact that the United States was involved in it at all. It led to the beginnings of a collective neurosis and sense of insecurity which has since been exacerbated by the Vietnam confrontation. None of this, though, is reflected in the films inspired by the Korean War, among which can be found scarcely one that could be called an outstanding example of the genre. They were mostly coarse imitations of World War II movies, tough, clamorous, violent and jingoistic.

The tone was set by Samuel Fuller, 'an expert practitioner in the art of gratuitous violence' (John Gillett), whose two savage, anti-Red contributions were *The Steel Helmet* (1950) and *Fixed Bayonets* (1951). Fuller himself has complained that 'you can't show war as it really is on the screen, with all the blood and gore' – but he has certainly tried, setting up an ambivalence between what he has often said about war and the way he has depicted it. Such implicitly anti-war statements as 'The reaction I would like to my pictures from an audience is: "Only an idiot would go to war"', or 'Since I don't believe in war, I don't believe in rules for war', sound a little hollow in a man who extracts the full dramatic value out of armed conflict, emphasizing its excitement, brutality and destruction. His characters and plots (small units of men undertaking hazardous missions) are generally stereotyped and, despite a great deal of butchery and death, have an heroic flavour which suggests a crude glamorization of war rather than an abhorrence of it. Fuller's supposed objectivity is undermined, too, by his overt anti-communism, which leads inevitably to a good versus evil, heroes versus villains set-up. *The Steel Helmet* and *Fixed Bayonets* are unquestionably exciting, skilfully made films, but it is difficult to equate them with a man who has said: 'I make war films because I have met some wonderful men and through them I can dramatize a dislike of war. If fifty pictures a year were made like mine, perhaps people wouldn't go to war.'

Fuller's subsequent output included a number of war or political dramas. In 1954 he made *Hell and High Water*, an anti-communist adventure with Richard Widmark. Patriotism and racialism were added ingredients of *China Gate* (1957), about a Eurasian agent (Angie Dickinson) married to an American during the conflict in Indo-China. The following year, he directed the rarely seen but (in France) critically acclaimed *Verboten*. And in 1961, he sensationalized the Burma campaign in *Merrill's Marauders*, which starred Jeff Chandler.

Films about the Korean War continued to be churned out long after peace was agreed, but with only a few exceptions, they were strictly routine, stressing discipline and the toughness of the American leadership. These included John Farrow's *Submarine Command* (1951) with its familiar cast (William Holden, Don Taylor, William Bendix); Tay Garnett's *One Minute to Zero* (1952) with Robert Mitchum; Joseph H. Lewis's *Retreat, Hell!*, with Frank Lovejoy; Richard Brooks's *Battle Circus* (1952) with Humphrey Bogart and June Allyson; Robert D. Webb's *The Glory Brigade* (1953), with Victor Mature and Lee Marvin; *Battle Taxi* (1954), with Sterling Hayden; Raoul Walsh's *Marines, Let's Go* (1961); Davis Sanders's *War Hunt* (1961), with John Saxon and a

Humphrey Bogart as Captain Queeg in *The Caine Mutiny* (Edward Dmytryk, 1954).

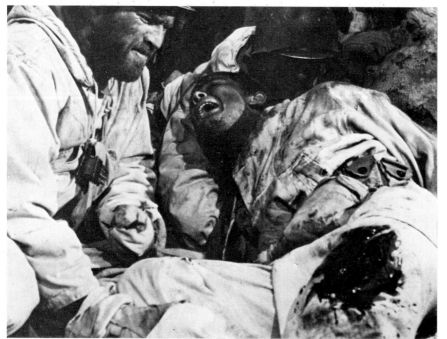

(*Left to right*) Neyle
Morrow, Richard Loo,
Richard Monahan, Robert
Hutton and Steve Brodie in
The Steel Helmet (Samuel
Fuller, 1950).

Gene Evans (*left*), assisted by
Richard Basehart, tends the
agonized Richard Hylton in
Fixed Bayonets (Samuel
Fuller, 1951).

budding Robert Redford; Buzz Kulik's court-martial melodrama, *Sergeant Ryker* (1963), with Lee Marvin; and dozens of B-feature potboilers directed by such conveyor-belt filmmakers as Lew Landers, Lesley Selander and Fred Sears.

A developing theme was the brainwashing of American prisoners, as portrayed in Andrew Marton's *Prisoner of War* (1954), with Ronald Reagan; Karl Malden's *Time Limit* (1957), with Richard Widmark and Richard Basehart; and *The Rack* (1956), Paul Newman's second film – all of which anticipated *The Manchurian Candidate* (1962), John Frankenheimer's brilliant political fantasy about a brainwashed Korean war hero transformed into an automaton programmed for assassination.

Only a meagre handful of Korean war films attempted to say anything meaningful about the conflict or about war in general. The glossiest was *The Bridges at Toko-Ri* (1954), an efficient and whole-hearted tribute by Mark Robson to the heroism of the jet-bomber pilots and the helicopter rescue service ('Where do we get such men?' rhetoricizes Rear-Admiral Fredric March from the bridge of his aircraft-carrier), but one which gave some serious thought, within its conventional confines, to the attitudes of fighting men and their families and the tragedy of war. Finely judged downbeat playing by March, William Holden and Grace Kelly was a strong contributing factor.

Anthony Mann's *Men In War* (1956) was anti-heroic and clearly aimed to be honest, humanistic and realistic (again, strengthened by excellent acting, this time from Robert Ryan and Aldo Ray), but relapsed into a string of repetitive, albeit well-staged battle scenes. Julian Amyes's tribute to National Servicemen, *A Hill in Korea* (1956), the only notable British film about the Korean War, also seemed to be striving for something more than simple heroics with its plausible narrative and unsentimental attitude towards the conflict. But it failed to free itself sufficiently from a familiar plot formula (ill-assorted patrol caught behind enemy lines) acted out by conventional character types (tough, unflappable regular NCO; misfit who dies heroically; inexperienced but instinctively talented leader, etc.) to make any fresh comment on human aggression. As a roll-call, however, of British actors of the 'fifties most at home in uniform, *A Hill in Korea* takes some beating: among those on parade were

George Baker, Harry Andrews, Stanley Baker, Michael Medwin, Ronald Lewis, Stephen Boyd, Victor Maddern, Robert Brown and Percy Herbert, with unknowns Robert Shaw and Michael Caine bringing up the rear.

Hollywood's penchant for hero-worship manifested itself most strongly at this time in Douglas Sirk's *Battle Hymn* (1956), the story of flyer Colonel Dean Hess, who rescued a large number of Korean war-orphans. This was a pseudo-psychological drama with high saccharine content, blithely mixing fact and fiction, war and religion, in its efforts to show that, in any fight, God was on America's side. 'The real-life hero becomes a Hollywood symbol; the experience of war is translated into the language of the box-office' (John Gillett). Equally repellent was Hall Bartlett's half-hearted race drama, *All the Young Men* (1960), in which Sidney Poitier triumphs over North Koreans and colour prejudice alike, meanwhile finding time to contribute some of his blood to hostile amputee Alan Ladd.

Perhaps the best American film about Korea (though by the director's standards a relatively minor movie) was Lewis Milestone's *Pork Chop Hill* (1959), a half-cynical, half-heroic account of the loss and recapture (at considerable cost) of a worthless piece of strategic ground during ceasefire negotiations. Smooth, competent, austerely good-looking, and capably acted (especially by Gregory Peck and Harry Guardino), this comment on the pointlessness and absurdity of war nevertheless lacked the humanity and quiet passion of Milestone's best war films, qualities lost in the over-emphasis on excitement and feats of bravery. Among a bleak collection of second-rate movies, however, it stands out.

A Hill in Korea (Julian Amyes, 1956), with (from left) David Morrell, Barry Lowe, Harry Landis, Harry Andrews, George Baker and (at rear) Michael Caine and Michael Medwin.

Although the Korean War was ostensibly a United Nations operation, few film-making countries outside America took much cinematic interest. One foreign film which, though little known, has a reputation, however, is the Franco-Korean *Moranbong: Chronique Coréene* (1959), directed by Jean-Claude Bonnardot, which describes a love-affair disrupted by the hostilities. Banned from exhibition in France for five years, *Moranbong* has been described as a 'profoundly pacifist film' and as 'perhaps the *Paisà* of Korea'. Apart from this, portrayals of Korea outside the United States have more often been in documentary form, such as the Canadian *Thunder in the East* (1950, director Douglas Tunstall) or the Australian recruiting film *One Man's War* (1952, director Tom Gurr).

American documentaries about Korea have included two (for the War Department) by John Ford (*This is Korea!*, 1951, an account of what the war was like, and *Korea*, 1959, an orientation film for American Occupation personnel); the semi-fictional *Cease Fire* (1953, director Owen Crump), shot in Korea and acted by American, British and Korean combat troops; and the very odd *The Ultimate Weapon – Men's Minds*, narrated by Ronald Reagan, which caused controversy by claiming that Americans captured by the North Koreans gave up too easily, and this was because of an insufficient moral buttressing in the formative years by

families, schools and churches back home.

There was, simultaneously with the Korean War, a vogue in Hollywood for political, mainly anti-communist films which persisted for more than a dozen years. The more prominent of these included *The Woman on Pier 13* (1949 – originally called *I Married a Communist*); the naïve, despicable Leo McCarey film, *My Son, John* (1952), a sad farewell to Robert Walker, who died during its making; *Never Let Me Go* (1953), in which Clark Gable rescues Gene Tierney from Russia; Elia Kazan's *Man On a Tightrope* (1953), in which Fredric March and Gloria Grahame escape from Czechoslovakia and Adolphe Menjou; Nunnally Johnson's story of communist kidnapping in Berlin, *Night People* (1954), with Gregory Peck and Peter Van Eyck; Mark Robson's ambivalent *Trial* (1955), with Glenn Ford, Arthur Kennedy and Dorothy McGuire; *Storm Centre* (1956), which starred Bette Davis as a librarian; *The Fearmakers* (1958), with Dana Andrews; another rabid Leo McCarey tract, *Satan Never Sleeps* (1960), about the sufferings of two missionary priests (Clifton Webb, William Holden) at the hands of Chinese communists; *The Secret Ways* (1961), with Richard Widmark; and *The Counterfeit Traitor* (1962), with William Holden. These were reflected more mildly in Britain in films like Roy Boulting's *High Treason* (1951), about a plot to blow up Battersea power station, and

Michael Anderson's *Yangtse Incident* (1957).

Hollywood's mainstream war movies after 1950 – those perpetuating and fictionalizing World War II and even older conflicts – were numerous, intense, and characterized by a superficial toughness and relish for the bloody excitement of combat. Under the surface, however, lay a fairly complex neurosis, stemming perhaps from the political and intellectual insecurity of the films' creators. Writing about 'fifties war films in 'Sight and Sound', John Gillett offered a plausible analysis of this trend: 'Many liberal Hollywood talents, caught up in an atmosphere of fear, have taken refuge in a sort of hysterical negation of responsibility . . . it has led to an acceptance of war as an inevitable part of the human condition. . . . War is presented as almost a natural phenomenon, something to be lived with, in fact, for like the poor it will always be with us. It is a long way from the revulsion of *All Quiet*, and it is not perhaps surprising that communist critics have lost no opportunity to accuse the West of inculcating its youth with a taste for and acceptance of war as an integral part of existence . . . the American post-war cinema's view of the human implications of an experience touching a whole generation has been both jaundiced and opportunist.'

The most revealing manifestations of Hollywood's state of mind were Robert Aldrich's *Attack!* (1956) and Nicholas Ray's *Bitter Victory* (1957), though the latter was actually made in France. *Attack!* was a violent exposé of cowardice and corruption among American officers fighting the Germans in Belgium; a thoroughly anti-romantic expression of disgust with war, and, more particularly, the war machine, with

its degradation and its own absurd brand of bureaucracy. Jack Palance and Eddie Albert played, at varying pitches of high-tension hysteria, two officers who conflict on the battlefield – the one a strong, straightforward, but disillusioned hero-type, the other a cowardly sadist. Lee Marvin was the cynical superior officer who treats war as a political game, mindless of the sufferings of the ordinary soldier. Despite an inevitable over-fondness for the dramatic values of combat and the savagery of men at arms, this was a powerful, honest attempt to de-mythologize war – which, had it been pitched in a lower key with fewer psychiatric reverberations, would have come nearer to being what Aldrich was striving to achieve, 'a sincere plea for peace'.

Nicholas Ray also blunted his message with an excess of shocking but stimulating violence in *Bitter Victory*. Curt Jurgens (in the unlikely role of a British officer) played the commander of a desert patrol in Libya in 1942. During the course of his mission he allows a scorpion to sting his wife's lover (Richard Burton) to death and then eliminates the witness (Raymond Pellegrin) to his crime, finally returning to a hero's welcome. The futility of it all is finally underlined by Jurgens's cynical gesture of pinning a medal on to the chest of a dummy used for bayonet practice. Again, the characters are riddled with neuroses (the tough-seeming soldier is really a coward; the realist is too sensitive to put his wounded comrades out of pain) and are thus more difficult to identify with than if they had been ordinary men thrust into an

Jack Palance in *Attack!*
(Robert Aldrich, 1956).

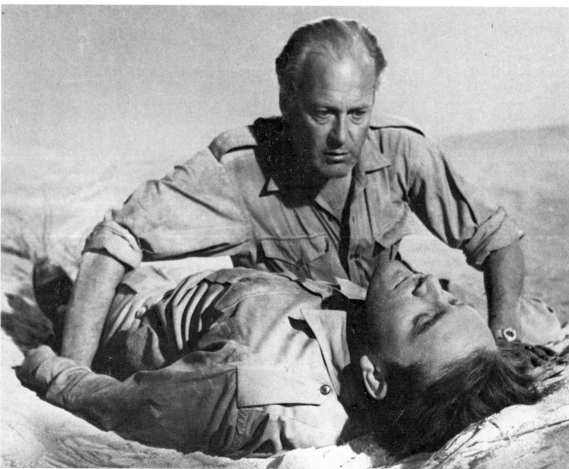

Curt Jurgens supervises the death by scorpion sting of comrade Richard Burton in *Bitter Victory* (Nicholas Ray, 1957).

176

insane situation. And again, this is a distractingly photogenic war and not the hell on earth which the great pacifist movies like *All Quiet* manage to convey.

The desert provided the setting for a number of 'fifties war films, the most familiar being Henry Hathaway's *Rommel – Desert Fox* (1951), an ultra-respectful biography of the German general in his latter days, distinguished by James Mason's effective performance in the name-part. Although directed with an authentic feel by Hathaway, this sober drama tended to over-simplify Nazi politics and contemporary events in its efforts to paint an unsullied portrait of its hero, but the final scenes of Rommel's touching farewell to his family prior to suicide lifted the film out of the rut of mere competence. James Mason repeated his impersonation briefly in Robert Wise's sequel, *The Desert Rats* (1953), a conventional action piece devoted to the part played by the Australian forces at Tobruk. Richard Burton breathed new life into the clichéd role of the unpopular martinet officer who ultimately wins the respect of his men, but on the whole character came a poor second to pyrotechnics. Robert Wise chose a less familiar desert for *Destination Gobi* (1953), a fact-based but unconvincing story, rather frivolously handled, about military weather observers (led by rugged Richard Widmark) escaping from the Japanese with the help of Mongol tribesmen.

The suggestion implicit in *Rommel – Desert Fox* that the Germans weren't all bad became a modish theme in the 'fifties (although the

James Mason as *Rommel – Desert Fox* (Henry Hathaway, 1951).

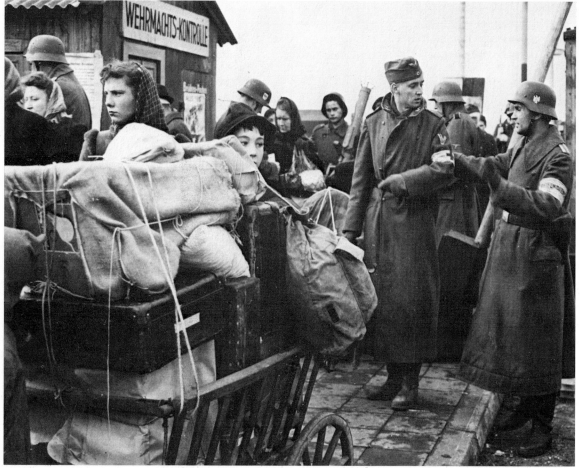

Oskar Werner in *Decision Before Dawn* (Anatole Litvak, 1951).

177

Curt Jurgens in *The Enemy Below* (Dick Powell, 1957).

virulence of some anti-Nazi films, such as *Decision Before Dawn*, was still strong enough to arouse voices of protest in West Germany). As the Russians and communists took over the villainous roles, so the former enemy, now a NATO ally, began to be painted in pleasanter colours, all blame for the war and its excesses being placed on the unscrupulous, unfeeling politicians (i.e. the Nazis). German officers (and

other ranks) were elevated to the status of honourable heroes and their characters senti- mentalized and romanticized in such films as John Farrow's *The Sea Chase* (1955), Dick Powell's U-boat drama *The Enemy Below* (1957), *The Last Blitzkrieg* (1958), Douglas Sirk's *A Time to Love and a Time to Die* (1958), Edward Dmytryk's *The Young Lions* (1958), *Under Ten Flags* (1960), and J. Lee-Thompson's hagio- graphy of rocket scientist Werner von Braun, *I Aim at the Stars* (1960). This new, clean image was endowed with even further respectability by the casting in sympathetic German roles of major Hollywood and continental stars, namely (and respectively in the films mentioned above) John Wayne, Curt Jurgens, Van Johnson, John Gavin, Marlon Brando, Van Heflin, and Curt Jurgens again. One film, Henry Koster's *Fraulein* (1958), went further by purifying the German civilian, attractively and romantically represented by ill-used, war-ravaged Dana Wynter, whose latent virtues are recognized by good Americans James Edwards and Mel Ferrer.

The most thoughtful and ambitious of these whitewashing exercises were *A Time to Love and a Time to Die* and *The Young Lions*, both literary adaptations, the former from a story by Erich Maria Remarque, the latter from Irwin Shaw's massive novel. Sirk returned to his native Germany to shoot his film, a tragic love story set in Berlin and on the Russian front, in which a young Wehrmacht soldier loves and marries a childhood sweetheart (Lilo Pulver) during a brief leave in Berlin, dutifully rejoins his comrades, and is killed while exercising a new, humane attitude to the enemy. It was a

John Gavin and Lilo Pulver in Erich Maria Remarque's *A Time to Love and a Time to Die* (Douglas Sirk, 1958).

178

muted, melancholic sequel to Remarque's *All Quiet on the Western Front*, quietly effective but lacking the latter's epic power and depth of compassion.

Dmytryk's film, an interweaving of stories from opposite sides of the war, was a fusion of the ideas he had aired in *Hitler's Children* and *Crossfire*. A blond-coiffured, impeccably accented Marlon Brando played, in saintly fashion, an idealistic Nazi whose eyes are finally opened to his country's conduct in the war, and Montgomery Clift played a Jew beset by fierce anti-Semitism among his fellow Americans. Apparent rival bids for martyrdom on the part of Brando and Clift tended to iron out many complexities and ironies in the novel, but superficially, at least, it was an effective film, helped along by impressive acting from Brando, Clift, Dean Martin and Maximilian Schell, and by the genuine impact of such sequences as that of the discovery of a German concentration camp during the Allied advance.

The hate content in war films which had up to this point been reserved mainly for the Germans was now temporarily re-channelled in the direction of the Japanese, and the Pacific War was revived in a number of old-fashioned exercises in aggressive patriotism. Allan Dwan, as already noted, began the trend with *Sands of Iwo Jima*. This was followed by a disappointing contribution from Fritz Lang called *I Shall Return* (1950), a portrayal, with Tyrone Power, of American-led guerrilla resistance in the Philippines prior to the islands' promised recapture by General MacArthur. Nicholas Ray also lapsed with *Flying Leathernecks* (1951), a relentlessly violent action melodrama of fighter-pilots at Guadalcanal, with John Wayne and Robert Ryan as officers in conflict with each other's methods.

Even Lewis Milestone succumbed to the prevailing political atmosphere with his *Halls of Montezuma* (1950). This characteristically efficient account of a Marine mission to knock out a Japanese rocket-launching site was no more than a Hollywood potboiler, in which action was made to speak louder than words, God was shown to be clearly on the American side, the characters all solved their hang-ups with bouts of heroism, and Richard Widmark was on hand to lead the final charge with a rousing howl of 'Give 'em hell!' – all a far cry from the impartial humanity of Milestone's other war films.

Don Siegel was yet another noteworthy director called upon to add his quota of petty patriotism to this outpouring of anti-Asian propaganda. His *China Venture* (1953) was an unenterprising Fuller-style adventure about soldiers on a special mission to acquire a captured Japanese admiral from untrustworthy Chinese guerrillas. Despite the presence of dependables like Barry Sullivan and Edmond O'Brien, it was no better than routine. Siegel redeemed himself subsequently with the far more honest *Hell is for Heroes* (1962), a superficially straightforward action war movie which, thanks to skilful, perceptive direction, made

valid visual comments on the effects of warfare on young Americans. Siegel's own comment on the film is revealing: 'I refused to direct certain scenes which I thought were too anodyne, too delicate for a war film. I think that war is a sordid thing. I tried to defuse it and my film has, I think, a very powerful realism.' Steve McQueen, confirming his claim to stardom after *The Magnificent Seven*, led an offbeat

Marlon Brando expresses his disillusionment with the war by smashing his gun against a tree-stump in *The Young Lions* (Edward Dmytryk, 1958).

John Wayne in *Flying Leathernecks* (Nicholas Ray, 1951).

179

Richard Widmark and Neville Brand in *Halls of Montezuma* (Lewis Milestone, 1950).

Steve McQueen's brutal demise in *Hell is for Heroes* (Don Siegel, 1962).

cast which included Bobby Darin, Bob Newhart and Fess Parker.

One of the best of the old-fashioned war melodramas made in the 'fifties was Robert Wise's *Run Silent, Run Deep* (1958), a submarine adventure lifted from efficient mediocrity by documentary-like attention to detail and the pairing of Clark Gable and Burt Lancaster as incompatible but mutually respectful naval officers. The hate-your-enemy attitude remained undiluted, however.

Less satisfactory as a film, but worth mentioning for its unusual variation on the anti-Japanese theme was Robert Pirosh's *Go for Broke!* (1951), a tribute to the heroism in the Italian and French campaigns of the Japanese-American, or Nisei, troops. Van Johnson played a Texas Division lieutenant who is given the job of training the Niseis and, though reluctant and resentful at first, comes to admire and respect them. Unfortunately, with its stereotyped, insensitive treatment and patronizing script, the film did less than justice to its worthy theme.

The war against Germany was not an entirely taboo subject at this time, but it was rarely tackled and then only in shallow fashion. *To Hell and Back*, for example – a re-creation by Audie Murphy himself of the legendary exploits which made him America's most decorated soldier – was a display of heroics of the most uncomplicated kind, nullified by having absolutely nothing revelationary to say about Murphy as an individual, and cheapened by the introduction of obviously fictional scenes.

The death-or-glory sentiments of *To Hell and Back* were in direct contrast to the attitudes

180

portrayed by Murphy in the film he made for John Huston in 1951, *The Red Badge of Courage*. This memorable adaptation of Stephen Crane's novel of the American Civil War fell victim to the crass commercial demands of its producers, MGM, had its budget drastically cut, and was hacked down to sixty-nine minutes of disjointed narrative containing a good deal more action than exposition. Nevertheless, Crane's (and Huston's) theme – fear, or as Sadoul expressed it, 'the fear of fear' – just about survived, along with an uncommonly sensitive performance by Murphy as the confused Northern recruit whose cowardice turns to courage and resolve after his first traumatic experiences of battle. The Civil War also formed the background to Denis and Terry Sanders's neat twenty-two-minute anecdote, *A Time Out of War* (1954), an adaptation of the ironic Robert Chambers story 'Pickets', in which two soldiers from the North, seduced by the summer heat, agree on a one-hour truce with a like-minded Confederate. This was a muted, slightly precious comment on the uselessness of war, but an effective one.

Meanwhile, America's story-book concept of World War II continued in a series of melodramas, comedies and best-seller adaptations. Gary Cooper impersonated another real-life war hero in Otto Preminger's *The Court-Martial of Billy Mitchell* (1955). James Mason followed one alien hero (Rommel) with another ('Cicero', the British Embassy valet in Ankara who sold secrets to the Germans) in Joseph Mankiewicz's *Five Fingers* (1952), a film seen by Leslie Halliwell as regenerating the interest in spying which led to the Bond boom. The poignant experiences of the Jewish girl who

Audie Murphy collects his medals in his autobiography, *To Hell and Back* (Jesse Hibbs, 1955).

Audie Murphy in an earlier skirmish, Stephen Crane's story of the American Civil War, *The Red Badge of Courage* (John Huston, 1951).

stayed hidden with her family in an attic in occupied Holland were rather clumsily dramatized in *The Diary of Anne Frank* (1959), with Millie Perkins in the name-part. And an even more ham-fisted attempt to mix sociological and moral issues with war heroics was made in Delmer Daves's *Kings Go Forth* (1958), which had charming GI Tony Curtis spurning besotted Natalie Wood when he discovers she's half-coloured, but conveniently and climactically sacrificing himself for his nice buddy,

Frank Sinatra, while on a vital mission behind enemy lines.

Service comedies enjoyed a brief vogue, beginning with the John Ford/Mervyn LeRoy adaptation of Joshua Logan's stage success, *Mister Roberts* (1955), about a cargo ship in the Pacific in World War II. This brought Henry Fonda back to the screen after an absence of seven years (at the insistence of John Ford, who then promptly fell out with him over directorial methods), was spasmodically funny thanks mainly to James Cagney's puritanical, tantrum-throwing martinet, and won Jack Lemmon a Best Supporting Actor Oscar. LeRoy was also responsible for *No Time for Sergeants* (1958), a theatrical farce in the *Private Hargrove* mould, with Andy Griffith as a naïve, hill-billy conscript. Griffith was good, but the comedy was static and unsubtle. *Operation Petticoat* (1959), with Cary Grant and Tony Curtis, was a more active affair with some good jokes and decent camerawork, but its tired comic theme (women – and their underwear – on board a submarine) blended uneasily with realistic war scenes.

Best-selling war novels proved to be a rich source of cinematic supply at this time, though some adaptations, such as that of Norman Mailer's searing portrait of war, *The Naked and the Dead* (1958), fell far short of their ambitions. One of the more successful (at least, from a box-office point of view) was Fred Zinnemann's multi-Oscar version of James Jones's anti-military melodrama, *From Here to Eternity* (1953), which combined an intensely

erotic love story (Burt Lancaster seducing ice-capped volcano Deborah Kerr on a Pacific beach) with the Japanese attack on Pearl Harbor. Much of the virulence of Jones's attack on army mores was lost in Zinnemann's otherwise skilful direction, and the film is chiefly remembered for its steamy sex, for its spectacular climax as the Japanese bombers go to work, and for Frank Sinatra's comeback performance as Montgomery Clift's gutsy little soldier buddy, beaten to death by a sadistic sergeant (Ernest Borgnine). Sinatra won an Academy Award (Supporting Actor), and so did the film itself, Zinnemann, Donna Reed (Supporting Actress), Daniel Taradash (Scriptwriter) and Burnett Guffey (Photography). As usual, the accolade was excessive.

Herman Wouk's Pulitzer-prize novel, *The Caine Mutiny* (1954), received tighter, less flashy treatment at the hands of Edward Dmytryk (director) and Stanley Kramer (producer), who dealt seriously and sympathetically with

The Diary of Anne Frank (George Stevens, 1959), with (*from left*) Joseph Schildkraut, Gusti Huber, Lou Jacobi, Millie Perkins (as Anne Frank), Shelley Winters, Richard Beymer and Diane Baker.

Frank Sinatra and Tony Curtis in *Kings Go Forth* (Delmer Daves, 1958).

Wouk's theme of the mental breakdown of the disciplinarian skipper of a minesweeper. Humphrey Bogart gave a memorable performance as the paranoiac Captain Queeg with his petty obsessions and much-mimicked catch-phrases, and strong support from José Ferrer, as the cynical naval lawyer, Van Johnson, as the stolid chief mutineer, and Fred MacMurray as the bookish moral coward, rounded off an absorbing, adult film.

Hollywood's more familiar production values were in evidence in *Exodus* (1960), Otto Preminger's blockbusting adaptation of the Leon Uris novel about the Palestinian War of Liberation and the birth of modern Israel, which plodded on for nearly four hours. ('Otto!' Mort Sahl is alleged to have said to the director after three hours of a Hollywood preview. 'Let my people go!') Good performances by Paul Newman and Ralph Richardson, and a literate script by Dalton Trumbo (the first under his own name since his imprisonment as one of the Hollywood Ten) made it bearable.

Out of Hollywood's collective insecurity and ideological confusion in the 'fifties came one clear, committed, unequivocal statement about the nature of war – Stanley Kubrick's *Paths of Glory* (1957), a film which influenced a whole new attitude to war in American movies, particularly when, in retrospect, it was observed

Henry Fonda (*centre*) as *Mister Roberts* (John Ford and Mervyn LeRoy, 1955), with James Cagney, Jack Lemmon and William Powell.

Arthur O'Connell
explains to Virginia Gregg
that a ship's engine-room is
not a good place to hang
one's smalls in *Operation
Petticoat* (Blake Edwards,
1959).

to contain uncomfortable parallels with Vietnam. Set in World War I and derived from an actual incident involving French soldiers, which caused it to be banned in France (though it could, said Kubrick, 'have happened in any other army in the world'), *Paths of Glory* told of the court-martial of three men, picked arbitrarily from the ranks and accused of cowardice after a futile attempt by their regiment to advance against an impregnable German strongpoint. They are to be tried and executed *pour encourager les autres* (or as arch-cynic General Adolphe Menjou remarks: 'There are few things more stimulating than seeing someone else die'), and in spite of impassioned pleading from their Colonel (Kirk Douglas) this is indeed their fate. One of the men, already dying from other causes, is even carried out on a litter to be shot.

'My aim,' said Kubrick, 'was to make an anti-war film', and most observers would probably agree that he succeeded. Some critics, however (notably Colin Young in his essay 'Nobody Dies', a plausibly argued thesis on the spuriousness and ambivalence of the Hollywood 'anti-war' films), are of the opinion that, while *Paths of Glory* is indisputably a brilliant and beguiling film, it is not so much an indictment of war as an attack on the *conduct* of war, on the gulf which exists between the leaders and

Cary Grant joins the Women's
Army Corps in *I Was a Male
War Bride* (Howard Hawks,
1949), with Ann Sheridan.

Aldo Ray in familiar threatening pose in Norman Mailer's *The Naked and the Dead* (Raoul Walsh, 1958), with Robert Gist.

Frank Sinatra and Montgomery Clift in James Jones's *From Here to Eternity* (Fred Zinnemann, 1953).

186

the led; in other words, it only condemns the politicians, the generals, the cynical war-mongers who feed innocent men to the cannon, and not the fact of war itself. Even if this is accepted as true, it needn't matter, since it is the impact of Kubrick's film which counts. If its effect is to fill the spectator with an awareness of the futility and obscenity of war, then its method (and its attractiveness as a movie) are not important factors, except in so far as they make the film more popular and thus help it to reach a wider audience. By focusing on the power struggle of a corrupt politico-military élite, any member of which can on a whim or in a fit of pique send thousands of men to their deaths, Kubrick emphasizes the tragic impotence of ordinary people to control their own destinies or to decide whether peace may not after all, even *in extremis*, be preferable to war.

However it is interpreted, *Paths of Glory* remains one of the best American films of the 'fifties from one of the screen's most exciting directors. Skilfully staged, intelligently scripted, and flawlessly acted by Douglas, Menjou, George Macready (as the most inhumane of the generals) and Ralph Meeker (as one of the victims), it made Kubrick's reputation and virtually redeems a whole decade of desultory and generally impoverished war-movie making in the United States.

Stanley Kubrick's *Paths of Glory* (1957), with Kirk Douglas (*left*) and (*below*) Richard Anderson and George Macready.

Fight the Good Fight

'The British . . . enthusiastically specialize in movies about triumphant ingenuity, stiff-lipped gallantry under fire and nervy prison camp escapes.' This comment by Martin S. Dworkin admirably summarizes the character of the British war film of the 'fifties, which enjoyed a revival sufficiently intense and sustained to beg a number of questions about the post-war national temperament. The most convincing explanation for this preoccupation with World War II (reflected also in the contemporary popularity of books on the subject) has been offered by Lindsay Anderson, who sees in it a wish to 'evade the complex uncertainties of the present, and the challenge of the future'. In other words, with Britain's position as a world power becoming less and less assured and her traditional political values beginning to be questioned (as evidenced by the break-up of the Empire and the mishandling of the Suez affair), there was an apparent instinctive desire on the part of the public to have its national confidence and pride bolstered by some substitute means. Hence the nostalgic harking back to a time in the recent past when issues were clear-cut and Britain's greatness, though under threat, was self-evident and confirmed by victory.

The mainstream British war film of the 'fifties was thus a simple adventure story with few subtleties and little concern for moral issues or the reasons for the war: an attenuated tribute to heroes and machines. It stressed the courage and stoicism of the British soldier and his loved ones back home; it found and exploited a 'good' side to the war in the British defence of freedom and tradition; it adopted a stern but charitable attitude towards the enemy; and it sustained the 'cult of the stiff upper lip'. Rarely, in fact, did an individual human being break through the stereotyped character shells.

Australian critic Allen Boase (quoted by Dworkin) put it obliquely but neatly by remarking that 'the war film of Britain has its Hollywood counterpart in the Western'. And in the same way that there is no such thing as an anti-Western, so Britain did not at this time even contemplate such a thing as an anti-war film.

The most characteristic examples of this indigenous genre were those films depicting prisoner-of-war camps and escape therefrom. These had a curious way of making what must have been a pretty dismal experience seem quite jolly and the camps appear almost cosy – no worse, really, than being back at public school. The camps' resemblance to boarding-school, in fact, may explain why the officers, at least, took to them so readily. They also afforded a splendid opportunity to indulge in some ripping adventures (i.e. escaping), with the added piquancy that one might get shot, plus a chance to demonstrate the effortless intellectual superiority of Albion over Prussia along with the ineffable, irrepressible and almost inexplicable British sense of humour.

On the whole, these films were absorbingly well made and decently performed by what at times seemed almost like a permanent repertory company. The precursor, and in many ways the best, was Basil Dearden's *The Captive Heart* (1946), which, while it stayed in the camp, stuck to a sober, totally convincing documentary approach never subsequently matched. Concentrating (again unusually) on the lives and emotions of the 'other ranks' (expertly played by such stalwarts as Jack Warner, Jimmy Hanley, and the eternally ill-fated Mervyn Johns), this told the story of a Czech (Michael Redgrave), posing as a British officer whom he knows to have been killed in action, who conceals his identity by corresponding tenderly with the dead man's wife (Rachel Kempson) and consequently falls in love with her. The fault of the film is in allowing this, and other sub-plots, to cut loose from the camp and dissipate themselves on visits back to Britain. The Czech's love-affair, though beautifully rendered, becomes particularly incongruous to the main theme of life in captivity – as one critic put it, 'it's rather like finding an oyster in a fruit salad'. All the same, this remains a superior example of its genre, seriously intentioned and genuinely moving.

More typical was Jack Lee's *The Wooden Horse* (1950), a smooth, cheerful, authentic account of how three British prisoners (Leo Genn, David Tomlinson and Anthony Steel) tunnelled to freedom under a wooden vaulting-horse used for physical exercise.

Similar in theme and approach (and also starring Anthony Steel) was Lewis Gilbert's *Albert RN* (1953), a true story of how naval prisoners of war used a life-like dummy to cover their escapes, marred somewhat by giving the hero unconvincing motives for wanting to stay in camp. The ubiquitous Anton Diffring made one of his early appearances as a villainous Nazi in this escape drama, and turned up again in Guy Hamilton's *The Colditz Story* (1955), an efficient adaptation of Major Pat Reid's memoirs about his trail-blazing escape from the supposedly escape-proof Colditz Castle. John Mills impersonated Reid, and Eric Portman co-starred. The *Colditz* saga was eventually resuscitated as an immensely popular series on BBC Television, part of a general revival of interest in World War II heroics in the early 'seventies. The last of the essentially British escape pictures was Don Chaffey's *The Danger Within* (1958), scripted by Bryan Forbes and starring (in descending order of rank) Richard Todd, Bernard Lee, Michael Wilding and Richard Attenborough. This was a stylish, exciting account of a mass break-out from a camp in Northern Italy, ingeniously plotted and strong on detail and atmosphere.

Roy Baker gave the genre an original twist by dramatizing the true story of Luftwaffe

Lieutenant Fritz von Werra, the only German prisoner of war to escape British hands in World War II, in *The One That Got Away* (1957). Hardy Kruger played von Werra, who managed his final escape, after several fruitless attempts, by fleeing from Canada to the then-neutral United States.

Experiences in Japanese camps were recreated in a few British movies, which concentrated more on the cruelty and atrocities perpetrated by the captors than on escape adventures. These were fictionalized in Val Guest's Hammer production, *The Camp on Blood Island* (1958), which generated some excitement with its story of a prisoner-of-war colonel (André Morell) trying to keep news of the Japanese surrender (heard on a hidden radio) from the camp commandant for fear of a massacre. A 1964 sequel, *The Secret of Blood Island*, directed by Quentin Lawrence, was merely exploitative and wasted good actors like Jack Hedley and Patrick Wymark. More effective and atmospheric was Jack Lee's adaptation of the Nevil Shute novel, *A Town Like Alice* (1956), which starred Virginia McKenna and Peter Finch in a harrowing story about the deprivations suffered by a group of British women in Malaya forced to march to a Japanese camp.

A more recent production, *The Hill* (1965), directed by Sidney Lumet, dealt with a different kind of prison camp, one used to incarcerate army wrongdoers in North Africa. Intended as an indictment of military brutality (the 'Hill'

is a mound of gravel up which prisoners are forced to run as a special punishment), it diluted its impact by concentrating too much on cynical humour. But excellent photography, quirky direction, and fine performances by Sean Connery, Harry Andrews, Ian Hendry, Roy Kinnear and Ossie Davis made it enjoyable.

The Hollywood view of prisoner-of-war camps was harsher, bleaker and less tolerant than Britain's, although the best of the American prisoner-of-war films, Billy Wilder's *Stalag 17* (1953), contained a fair proportion of sentimentality and horseplay. This tough, exciting

Michael Redgrave in The Captive Heart (Basil Dearden, 1946), with Sam Kydd (right).

The Wooden Horse (Jack Lee, 1950), with (standing, left to right) David Tomlinson, Bill Travers, Peter Burton, Michael Goodliffe, Bryan Forbes, and (crouching) Leo Genn, Anthony Steel and Dan Cunningham.

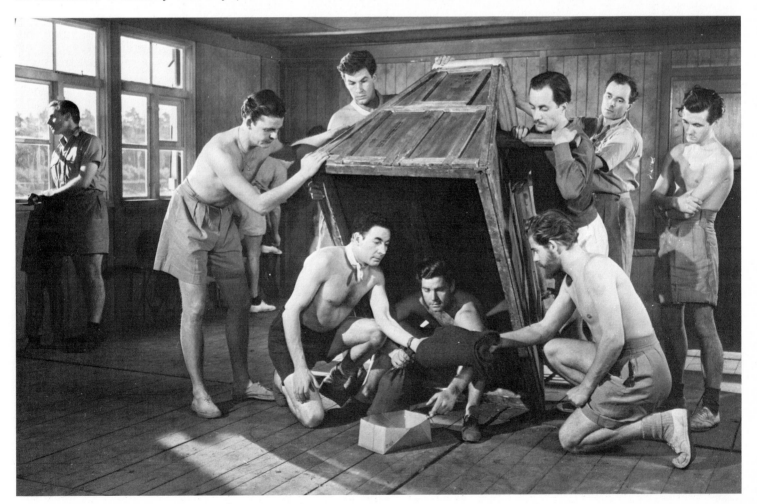

Peter Jones (*left*) is taken in by *Albert RN* (Lewis Gilbert, 1953), to the satisfaction of Robert Beatty, Guy Middleton and Anthony Steel.

Bryan Forbes (*left*) in *The Colditz Story* (Guy Hamilton, 1955).

melodrama of the discovery of an informer in an American hut had, as major assets, Wilder's cynicism, Preminger doing his camp commandant impersonation, and a fine, Oscar-winning performance by William Holden as a smart prisoner snubbed by his compatriots because of his ability to make the most of a lousy situation. (The Americans were, on the other hand, responsible for the absurd TV series, *Hogan's Heroes*, which depicted a camp controlled by the prisoners and staffed by the ultimate in block-headed 'Fritz' stereotypes.)

The last word in prisoner-of-war films was also American. John Sturges's *The Great Escape* (1962) lasted for nearly three hours and threw together the pick of Britain's prison-camp connoisseurs (Richard Attenborough, James Donald, Gordon Jackson, Nigel Stock) and the cream of Hollywood's new star set (Steve McQueen, James Garner, Charles Bronson, James Coburn). It re-created the actual mass break-out, by tunnel, of seventy-six Allied prisoners, whose flight diverted the attention of five million Germans (but ended with fifty of them being shot on recapture), and tarted the whole thing up with fictionalized 'fun' incidents (a camp-wide booze-up on home-made hooch arranged by the American contingent to celebrate the Fourth of July; a spectacular escape attempt on a motor-cycle by McQueen) and beguilingly attractive characterizations, not excluding a sympathetic German commandant. The result was an uncomplicated, marvellously entertaining adventure movie, lifted out of the rut by clever editing, quite serious undertones

and a truly riveting performance by McQueen.

The best serious films about prisoners of war (after Renoir's *La Grande Illusion*) have been those which have used the segregated, microcosmic setting as more than an end in itself. Bryan Forbes's *King Rat* (1965), for example, depicted the dispiriting squalor and futility of life in the Singapore prison camp, and, at the same time, attempted some comment on the nature of human relationships under these abnormal circumstances. The key lay in the character of Corporal King (George Segal), elevated to cock-of-the-roost by his singular self-sufficiency and opportunism, who incongruously befriends a young English officer (James Fox) but cannot sustain the relationship after his fragile kingdom has been shattered by the arrival of the Allies.

The Danger Within (Don Chaffey, 1958), with Donald Houston, Richard Todd and Richard Attenborough.

Hardy Kruger as Fritz von Werra in *The One That Got Away* (Roy Baker, 1957).

Stalag 17 (Billy Wilder,
1953), with William Holden
(*left*), Robert Strauss (*right*)
and Harvey Lembeck
(*second from right*).

A Japanese prison camp was also the setting
for David Lean's resoundingly successful, epic-
proportioned adaptation of Pierre Boulle's
anti-heroic war novel, *The Bridge on the River
Kwai* (1957), though its story of a stubborn,
blimpish British colonel (Alec Guinness) unwittingly aiding the Japanese war effort by
regarding a bridge-building project as good for
his men's morale, was merely symbolic of
broader issues. The film differed crucially
from the book by allowing (for the sake of a
spectacular climax as much as anything else)
the bridge which the British prisoners have
carefully constructed under orders from the
Japanese to be blown up, thus compromising
Boulle's concept of the bridge as an ironic
monument to the utter madness of war. Many
critics have maintained, with some validity,
that in spite of its pretensions, Lean's movie is
no more an anti-war film than (to extend an
earlier parallel) *The Magnificent Seven*, say,
is an anti-Western; that it is merely a sumptuous
adventure story in a war setting, anti-
militaristic certainly, but ultimately a triumph
for Us over Them rather than a defeat for
Everybody, despite the death of the film's one
obvious hero (played with pleasing cynicism by
William Holden).

All the same, *The Bridge on the River Kwai*
has reached a vast audience and its accom-
panying propaganda has always emphasized its
pacifist intentions as well as its spectacle and

action, giving hope that some provocation of thought may occasionally have permeated the production values. And it is, without doubt, a superbly entertaining and brilliantly executed film, a worthy winner (in Hollywood terms) of its seven Academy Awards, at its best, perhaps, in its accurate, witty portrayal of the obsolete British and Japanese military characters.

Kwai was at least against the general trend of British war films, which were mainly simple, smug, uniformly efficient tributes to British heroism, administering a rather meretricious boost to national pride. Real-life heroes were frequently portrayed. Anna Neagle gave a moving, if somewhat regal, impersonation of the courageous French agent, Odette Churchill, in husband Herbert Wilcox's *Odette* (1950), with Trevor Howard as Captain Peter Churchill. Virginia McKenna played another woman resistance worker, shopgirl Violette Szabo, who died in Ravensbrück, in Lewis Gilbert's *Carve Her Name with Pride* (1958), with Paul Scofield in support. Kenneth More played the resolute legless flyer Douglas Bader (and, according to Bader himself, exaggerated his limp rather insultingly) in an earlier Gilbert film, *Reach for the Sky* (1956), based on Paul Brickhill's biography. Dirk Bogarde went one better by portraying both Major Patrick Leigh Fermor – who helped to capture a German general (Marius Goring) in Crete in 1944 – in Michael Powell's and Emeric Pressburger's

Steve McQueen and James Donald (with stick) in *The Great Escape* (John Sturges, 1962).

Tom Courtenay as the despised Provost-Marshal in *King Rat* (Bryan Forbes, 1965).

Alec Guinness as Colonel Nicholson in Pierre Boulle's *The Bridge on the River Kwai* (David Lean, 1957).

The production crew relax during shooting of *The Bridge on the River Kwai.*

moody *Ill Met by Moonlight* (1957), and prison-camp escape expert, Sergeant-Major Charles Coward, in Andrew Stone's enjoyably light-hearted *The Password is Courage* (1962). And, in a pre-war setting (China, 1930) but in the same spirit, Ingrid Bergman played the English missionary, Gladys Aylward, who saved a group of children from Japanese attack, in Mark Robson's *The Inn of the Sixth Happiness* (1958).

True wartime exploits were also re-created – and romanticized – with varying degrees of veracity. The spirit of the defence of Malta was personified by Alec Guinness's introspective reconnaissance pilot in Brian Desmond Hurst's unsung *Malta Story* (1953). Tribute was paid to the paratroopers in Terence Young's *The Red Beret* (1953), which had strong supporting players (Harry Andrews, Donald Houston, Stanley Baker, Anton Diffring) but was spoilt by the star-casting of stodgy Alan Ladd as a Yank in Canadian clothing. The inconceivably courageous marines who raided the Bordeaux docks with limpet-mines in flimsy canoes were even more lovingly glorified in José Ferrer's *Cockleshell Heroes* (1953), the last words of which, spoken by Captain Trevor Howard as he and his comrades are about to be executed by firing-squad, encapsulate the exact mood of the British war film of the 'fifties: 'Keep the line

194

Anna Neagle as *Odette* (Herbert Wilcox, 1950), with Trevor Howard as Peter Churchill.

Virginia McKenna as Violette Szabo in *Carve Her Name with Pride* (Lewis Gilbert, 1958).

straight, men!' Similar praise was bestowed on the men who operated the midget submarines which sank the German battleship Tirpitz in a Norwegian fjord in Ralph Thomas's *Above Us the Waves* (1955), with John Mills, John Gregson and Donald Sinden among the heroes. And the work of Air/Sea Rescue was honoured in Lewis Gilbert's *The Sea Shall Not Have Them* (1954), which didn't quite match up to its first-division cast, led by Michael Redgrave, Dirk Bogarde, Anthony Steel, Nigel Patrick and Bonar Colleano.

The intriguing story of the corpse primed with false plans for an invasion of Sicily and planted on the Germans was skilfully told by director Ronald Neame and scriptwriter Nigel Balchin in *The Man Who Never Was* (1956). Clifton Webb and Gloria Grahame were borrowed from Hollywood to make the cast a little more starry, but the film was stolen by a burgeoning Stephen Boyd as a German spy. An equally remarkable deception practised on the gullible Germans by British intelligence was reproduced in John Guillermin's *I Was Monty's Double* (1958), the story of how a humble actor, M.E. Clifton-James (played with engaging modesty by himself), was persuaded to impersonate Field-Marshal Montgomery and make an appearance in North Africa in order to fool the Germans into thinking that the imminent Allied invasion of Europe would come from the Mediterranean. John Mills and Cecil Parker played the Intelligence officers, and Marius Goring was the man they deceived.

Major incidents of the war were given appropriate prestige treatment in a number of successful productions, the most celebrated of

Kenneth More as Douglas Bader escaping from a prison hospital in *Reach for the Sky* (Lewis Gilbert, 1956).

Marius Goring as the captured German general in *Ill Met by Moonlight* (Michael Powell and Emeric Pressburger, 1957).

which was *The Dam Busters* (1955), directed by Michael Anderson. Good acting (especially by Michael Redgrave as superboffin Dr Barnes Wallis), a superior script (by R.C. Sherriff), excellent aerial sequences, and sober treatment (including some comment on the human cost involved in a large-scale operation) gave an unaccustomed seriousness and adult authority to this account of how Wallis's invention of a powerful bouncing bomb enabled the RAF's best bombers to destroy the Ruhr dams. Unfortunately, a conventionally bombastic march tune and Richard Todd's two-dimensional portrait of Wing Commander Guy Gibson, leader of the raids, kept the film rooted in cliché-land, and it took a long time to reach its splendid action climax.

The Battle of the River Plate (1956), directed by Powell and Pressburger, was an equally ambitious account of the sinking of the German pocket-battleship Graf Spee off Montevideo. This was a conventionally smooth, exciting piece of work, but it took the mythological chivalry of war to extremes, extolling the naval traditions of stoicism (serious wounds are disregarded by their recipients; the destruction of a ship is turned into a wry joke) and fair play, and depicting the Germans (particularly their captain, Hans Langsdorff, played by Peter Finch) as brave, honourable men who dole out Christmas presents to their British prisoners and know when they're beaten.

Michael Anderson's *Yangtse Incident* (1957) recounted a post-war episode in which the British warship, HMS Amethyst, trapped in the Yangtse River in 1949, ran the gauntlet of heavy Chinese communist bombardment and escaped out to sea. The mood, however, was the same, fortified by a characteristic performance from Richard Todd as Lieutenant Commander Kerans, and bags of phlegm and British understatement.

Another triumphant naval exploit was recalled by Lewis Gilbert in *Sink the Bismarck!* (1960), in which Kenneth More, unflappable and highly disciplined, plots the destruction of the famous German battleship from the Admiralty War Room. His task is made easier by the fact that the Bismarck's skipper (Karel Stepanek) is a dissipated, unstable, over-confident Nazi fanatic marked out for a major comeuppance. Overblown and rather tedious, this was a near-parody of its type, scripted entirely in clipped understatements and played with detectable embarrassment by a vintage cast.

More acceptable was Leslie Norman's respectful re-creation of *Dunkirk* (1958), which dramatized Britain's most glorious defeat through the adventures of a corporal (John Mills) as he retreats to the beach-head, and the moral dilemma of a non-combatant (Richard Attenborough) who finds self-respect by joining the armada of small boats which crosses the Channel to perform the most celebrated miracle

Muriel Pavlow and Alec Guinness in *Malta Story* (Brian Desmond Hurst, 1953).

Alan Ladd in *The Red Beret* (Terence Young, 1953).

197

José Ferrer and Anthony Newley – two of the *Cockleshell Heroes* (Ferrer, 1953).

Above Us the Waves (Ralph Thomas, 1955), with midget submarine crew William Russell, Lee Patterson (*at rear*), John Mills and Anthony Wager.

of World War II. Effective detail (business with civilian gas-masks, and so forth) and convincing beach scenes make it watchable.

Fictional war stories on a major scale were rarer but occasionally noteworthy. George More O'Ferrall's *Angels One Five* (1952), which turned Jack Hawkins into a star and gave John Gregson his first big part, was a thoroughly sentimentalized portrayal of the Battle of Britain, told through the training,

career and death of one particular pilot (Gregson). Jeffrey Richards has summed it up nicely as 'a sort of *Dawn Patrol* of the Second World War'. J. Lee-Thompson's *Ice Cold in Alex* (1958), about the flight of a group of officers (led by John Mills) and nurses (headed by Sylvia Syms) by ambulance across the Libyan desert to Alexandria, was lifted by the excellent acting of Harry Andrews, as a reliable NCO, and Anthony Quayle as a thickly

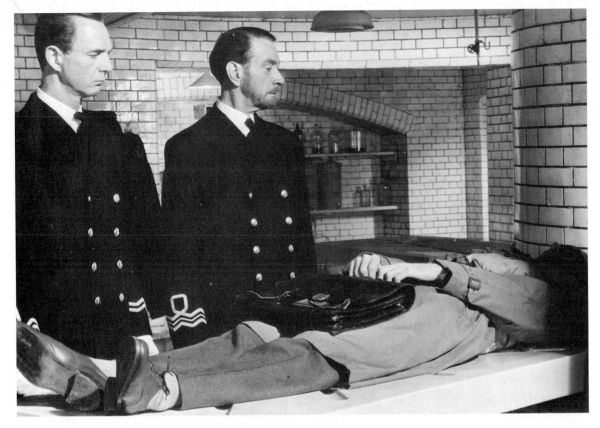

accented, pseudo-South African spy. Ralph Thomas's *Appointment With Venus* (1951), about the rescue from the occupied Channel Isles of a prize cow, was a popular bit of whimsy which starred David Niven and Glynis Johns, and helped to push Kenneth More's career along.

Anthony Asquith returned to the war-movie arena with two decently made contributions: *Carrington VC* (1954), another David Niven

vehicle, which confirmed, by means of a court-martial drama, the honour and integrity of the true British officer and gentleman; and *Orders to Kill* (1958), an absorbing melodrama with Eddie Albert and Paul Massie, about a plot to assassinate an agent suspected of being a Nazi.

By far the best of the 'fifties crop of fictional re-creations of the war was Charles Frend's adaptation of Nicholas Monsarrat's novel, *The Cruel Sea* (1953), scripted by Eric Ambler,

I Was Monty's Double (John Guillermin, 1958), with M.E. Clifton-James (playing himself impersonating Field-Marshal Montgomery) and John Mills.

The officers of HMS Ajax — Patrick MacNee (*left*), Anthony Quayle and Ian Hunter — keep watch for the Graf Spee in *The Battle of the River Plate* (Michael Powell and Emeric Pressburger, 1956).

which launched one very promising film-acting career (that of Donald Sinden) and confirmed several others (Jack Hawkins, Denholm Elliott, Stanley Baker). This atmospheric, anti-heroic, downbeat production depicted with force and realism the anguish of a corvette captain (Hawkins) who has a ship torpedoed under him, and is later forced to run down British survivors from another wreck in his determination to stay on the trail of a marauding U-boat. The plot was peopled, for once, with convincing characters instead of officer stereotypes, men with irritating habits and troubled home lives, and the harshness of war at sea was effectively visualized.

Another film to show some rare compassion and concern for the victims of war was Charles Crichton's *The Divided Heart* (1954), which told how a Yugoslavian refugee mother (Yvonne Mitchell) reclaims her son (Martin Stephens) from his Austrian foster-parents (Cornell Borchers, Armin Dahlen) after first regaining his love.

World War I was recalled in one of the great popular and critical successes of the decade, John Huston's *The African Queen* (1951), which paired Katharine Hepburn's English spinster with Humphrey Bogart's rough, gin-swilling riverboat captain in a German East African setting at the outbreak of war. Despite an improbable plot and weak finale, Huston concocted in this, one of his own favourite films, a perfect blend of romance, humour, fine acting (Bogart won an Oscar for his performance),

Richard Todd and William Hartnell negotiate with the Chinese for the release of HMS Amethyst in *Yangtse Incident* (Michael Anderson, 1957).

suspense, and brilliant location photography (by Jack Cardiff), all parcelled up as an oblique comment on the stupidity of war.

Huston tried to repeat the success of *The African Queen* by transposing his theme to World War II in *Heaven Knows, Mr Allison* (1957), but the combination of Deborah Kerr, as a novice nun, and Robert Mitchum, as a tough GI stranded with her on a Japanese-infested South Pacific island, was less magical, and the story veered towards soppiness and bad taste.

British service comedies were mostly rooted in rock-bottom farce, the general standard of which can be gauged by the fact that Ken Annakin's *You Know What Sailors Are* (1954),

Laurence Naismith, Geoffrey Keen, Kenneth More and Dana Wynter plotting to *Sink the Bismarck!* (Lewis Gilbert, 1960).

Dunkirk (Leslie Norman, 1958).

with its nudging Peter Rogers screenplay, was one of the funnier examples. Four years later, Rogers launched his vulgar *Carry On . . .* series (directed by Gerald Thomas) with *Carry On, Sergeant*, a zany, spasmodically amusing romp about incompetent National Servicemen, in which it was hard to tell which was lower, the comedy or the budget. This had been preceded by a far superior send-up of National Service life in the first of the Boulting Brothers' anti-Establishment comedies, *Private's Progress* (1956), which starred Ian Carmichael as an innocent student tangled up in Army red tape and corruption. The vulgarity was much

John Gregson inspects the remnants of his first 'kill' in *Angels One Five* (George More O'Ferrall, 1952).

202

slicker, the playing (by Carmichael, Richard Attenborough, Dennis Price, Terry-Thomas, and just about every farce-player in British films, from Thorley Walters to John le Mesurier) sharp and light, and the satire apt. Also better than the norm was Jack Arnold's whimsical satire on international diplomacy, *The Mouse That Roared* (1959), in which a mythical, bankrupt mini-Ruritania declares war on America, and wins. Peter Sellers played three parts in the days when he obviously enjoyed doing such things, and the film acquired a surprising (and slightly more than justified) critical reputation.

A few minor but noticeable individual statements about war and aggression saw the light of the projector-lamp from time to time in the 'fifties. Exile Norman McLaren made *Neighbours* (1952) for the National Film Board of Canada, a brief but highly original parable on the futility of violence for settling arguments, which employed to good effect McLaren's own technical innovation, pixilation (the animation of actors), and synthetic music and sound effects. Thorold Dickinson realized a pet project by making in Israel, with a mainly Israeli crew and a largely non-professional cast, *Hill 24 Doesn't Answer* (1955), an authentic, deeply moving account of the establishment of modern Israel, directed with a shrewd eye for its mythical values. Dickinson was also responsible for the deeply pacifist United Nations documentary, *Power Among Men* (1958), which took Eisenhower's hollow 'Atoms for Peace' proposal seriously and won armfuls of awards, but was shunned by the cinema circuits after it had been shown in part on British television.

At the end of the decade the British war movie at last began to take on a harsher, more cynical, more realistic tone, synonymous with the wave of astringent social realism which was shaking the British theatre out of its tired

complacency. Val Guest's *Yesterday's Enemy* (1959), adapted from Peter Newman's TV play, was stagey and superficially routine, but its story of a patrol in Burma which shoots hostages for information and later finds itself in the same position at the hands of the Japanese was uncompromisingly stark and unheroic. An

John Mills and Sylvia Syms start a desert romance in *Ice Cold in Alex* (J. Lee-Thompson, 1958).

Jack Hawkins in Nicholas Monsarrat's *The Cruel Sea* (Charles Frend, 1953).

Katharine Hepburn, Humphrey Bogart and *The African Queen* (John Huston, 1951).

efficient, hard-working cast, including Stanley Baker, Leo McKern and Richard Pasco, played with gritted teeth and helped one to forget the studio sets.

Disastrous *mis*casting proved the downfall of Leslie Norman's similar *The Long and the Short and the Tall* (1961), a pallid adaptation of Willis Hall's caustically tragi-comic play about a cynical, insubordinate private who tries to prevent his colleagues from shooting a captured Japanese soldier. Richard Todd looked ill-at-ease with stripes instead of pips as the patrol sergeant, Laurence Harvey's screen private wasn't a patch on Peter O'Toole's stage version, and the eternal Nippon fall-guy of British war films, Kenji Tagaki, was simply over-familiar as the victimized Jap.

The newly discovered realism, laced with

Carry On, Sergeant (Gerald Thomas, 1958), with Charles Hawtrey, Eric Barker, Terence Longdon, Kenneth Williams and William Hartnell.

Innocent Ian Carmichael
meets corrupt Richard
Attenborough in *Private's
Progress* (John and Roy
Boulting, 1956).

disillusionment and anti-war sentiments, has
continued in British war movies throughout
the past decade, though their numbers have
declined and the industry continues to indulge
its deplorable addiction for tasteless, totally
unfunny military farces such as the Danny La
Rue drag vehicle, *Our Miss Fred* (1972), and
the Boulting Brothers' abysmal *Soft Beds, Hard
Battles* (1973), with Peter Sellers doing a series

of weary character impersonations in a French
brothel.

Peter Collinson directed an interesting failure from a Charles Wood script, *The Long Day's
Dying* (1968), which depicted the brutality of
war rather too lip-smackingly and with an
over-fondness for spectacular stunt-work. More
successful were two studies of the persecution
of ordinary soldiers (both played by Tom

Thorold Dickinson's *Hill 24
Doesn't Answer* (1955).

Yesterday's Enemy (Val Guest, 1959), with Stanley Baker, Percy Herbert (on bed) and Philip Ahn.

Courtenay) who fail to conform, or crack up under fire – Casper Wrede's *Private Potter* (1962), about an infantryman who has a religious experience while on active duty in Cyprus, and Joseph Losey's quietly compassionate *King and Country* (1964), in which a Passchendaele deserter in World War I is unsuccessfully defended by a sympathetic captain (Dirk Bogarde) and sentenced to death.

Bitter satire was employed by Richard Lester – and misunderstood by critics and public alike – in *How I Won the War* (1967), which appeared to be ridiculing the unfortunates who did the fighting (and dying) in World War II, but was really aimed at militarism and the exploiters of war, not the ordinary soldiers. Some of its barbs struck home, but it was ultimately too long and unwieldy. The comedy was broader in John Dexter's enjoyable adaptation of Leslie Thomas's National Service novel, *The Virgin Soldiers* (1969), which described the first experiences of war (and sex) of a group of British soldiers fighting the terrorists in Malaya in 1950. Hywel Bennett played the randy hero, Private Brigg, and Lynn Redgrave was the sergeant-major's temporarily virginal daughter.

The most original evocation of World War II was the courageous first film by semi-professional movie-cum-military enthusiasts Kevin Brownlow and Andrew Mollo, *It Happened Here* (begun in 1957 and finished in 1964), which imagined an England invaded and occupied by the Germans in 1942. The grim, disquieting fantasy was vividly constructed through brilliantly faked newsreels and audacious set-ups (such as the Nazi rally in a Trafalgar Square bedecked with swastikas and eagles), and there was, refreshingly, no attempt to preach or moralize.

Britain's peacetime army was portrayed in several good films, more often to expose the abuses of militarism rather than its virtues. In Ronald Neame's *Tunes of Glory* (1960), this

Laurence Harvey and Richard Harris in Willis Hall's *The Long and the Short and the Tall* (Leslie Norman, 1961).

aspect was incidental to the main theme of the conflict between two colonels in an old-established Scottish regiment, the one an ascetic martinet (John Mills) who is driven to suicide, the other a drunken ruffian (Alec Guinness) who goes mad. There was a suggestion, though, that the army could be a fun place given the right type of officer to run it.

John Guillermin's *Guns at Batasi* (1964), an ironic examination of the ambiguous role played by British troops in an emergent African state, also contained a portrait of a traditional army type – this time a stiff-necked, dyed-in-the-wool regimental sergeant-major (surprisingly well played in bull-terrier fashion by Richard Attenborough) who can't understand the diplomatic reasons why he and his men have to stay out of a local uprising. He fails to resist the temptation to participate and is cashiered – but again, behind the film's superficial attack on army traditions one can detect a nod of approval for this throwback to the imperial past.

The bitterest and most telling attack on British militarism to date has been Jack Gold's compelling film, *The Bofors Gun* (1968), adapted from John McGrath's play about the clash between two National Servicemen in Germany, one a violent, suicidal Irishman (Nicol Williamson), the other a weak NCO (David Warner) who foolishly covers up for him while on guard duty. With its unremittingly oath-strewn dialogue and turbulent atmosphere, this powerful study in humiliation and the brutalizing effect of army life is an unpleasant but riveting piece of cinema, studded with memorable performances from Williamson, Warner, Ian Holm, John Thaw and Peter Vaughan.

While the war film has, in the British cinema at least, become less common and more committed to a pacifist point of view, there has, by contrast, been an escalation of World War reminiscences on television, which has, since its inception, shown itself to be particularly adept at reconstructing past events and using actuality film to good effect. A reminder, therefore, of the more notable contributions shown on British TV might be appropriate here.

Peter Watkins has done his best work for BBC Television with *Culloden* (1964) – a modernistic, 'you-are-there' re-staging of one of the most ferocious engagements in the history of warfare, the battle between the Scottish Jacobites and the Duke of Cumberland's army in 1746 – and *The War Game* (1966), a controversially horrific portrayal of nuclear bombardment (described more fully in due course). A different concept of modern warfare – the use of chemical and biological weapons – was vividly and disturbingly reported by David Plowright and Ingrid Floering in the subsequent Granada TV documentary, *The Silent War* (1967).

Other documentaries have included an Italian *History of the Atomic Bomb* (1964); an NBC compilation of newsreel material describing *That War in Korea* (1965); the

ambitious NBC series, *Victory At Sea* (1961), about World War II naval battles; David Wolper's series, *The Rise and Fall of the Third Reich* (1969); Granada's *Cities at War* series (1968), describing the fate of London, Berlin and Leningrad; the BBC's *Battle for Cassino* (1969); the earlier *Command in Battle* series (1958), describing important battles like Alamein, Normandy, etc.; *The Commanders* (1972), the BBC's very thorough portraits of such

Dirk Bogarde in *King and Country* (Joseph Losey, 1964).

John Lennon and Lee Montague in Richard Lester's *How I Won the War* (1967).

German soldiers relax by the Thames in Kevin Brownlow's *It Happened Here* (1964).

Richard Attenborough as the sergeant-major in *Guns at Batasi* (John Guillermin, 1964).

Nicol Williamson (*left*) and John Thaw drunkenly hack down the flagpole in *The Bofors Gun* (Jack Gold, 1968).

eminent wartime leaders as Rommel, Sir Arthur Harris, General Zhukov, and Eisenhower; and many, many more. In fact, just about every battle, every personality, every incident and every issue of World War II has been depicted in some form on the television screen.

The best television presentations of war have usually been the pointed, personalized views of a battle or incident, and the major World War compilations. Of the former, Robert Vas's semi-dramatized account of the Katyn Forest massacre in Poland, . . . *The Issue Should be Avoided* (1971), conducted in the form of an international tribunal, stands vividly in the memory. Equally unforgettable was the Franco-Swiss study of resistance and collaboration in wartime France, *Le Chagrin et la Pitié* (1970), a careful and compassionate *tour de force* by Marcel Ophüls (son of Max) constructed mainly from the reminiscences of those who experienced the dreadful times. And the euphoria of Italy's entry into the war was imaginatively reconstructed in the RAI production, *10th June, 1940* (1970), a collaboration of three leading directors, Alessandro Blasetti, Franco Rossi and Florestano Vancini. Of the latter, ABC's ambitious visualization of Winston Churchill's memoirs, *The Valiant Years* (1961), with Richard Burton giving a creditable imitation of the war leader's voice, demands mention. So do the three principal World War I compilations – France's *'14–'18* (1963), produced originally for the cinema by Jean Aurel and adapted for Granada, Britain's *The Great War* (1964), produced by Tony Essex and Gordon Watkins, and the CBS series *World War I* (1964). Aurel's seventy-five-minute film stressed the futility and wastage of the Great War, the shambles of the trenches, the criminal ineptness of the generals and politicians, the slaughter, and the growing despair, and made effective use of the superb archive footage held in France. The BBC's twenty-six-part series was a strongly atmospheric evocation of the cumulative tragedy of the war, intensified by Michael Redgrave's tremulous, melancholic narration, a careful choice of stark, poignant images, and the surreal, balletic effect of 'stretching' film shot at a slower speed and normally seen projected in rapid jerks. *World War I* was the best edited and most lucid of the three histories, in spite of a florid script delivered somewhat melodramatically by Robert Ryan. This was divided into clear, compact episodes, richly illustrated with archive film, the best of which included an excellent account of the siege of Verdun, an objective look at America's part in the war, and a brilliant description of life – and death – in the trenches.

The latest and best war-compilation series to be made for television is Thames's *The World at War*, in which producer Jeremy Isaacs has emphasized, by means of reminiscent interviews and incidental home-front detail, the effect of World War II on the ordinary citizens of all the nations involved. In addition, the major events of the war are clearly and dramatically described, with a full awareness

of the ironies, absurdities and tragic nature of the conflict, while Laurence Olivier's subtly delivered narration strikes a happy balance between deadpan commentary and histrionic licence.

Apart from odd plays, TV's fictional treatment of war has been as diverse as the cinema's. Among the more popular and enduring series (all produced since 1968, reflecting the current nostalgia for the war years) have been the resistance drama, *Manhunt*, with Robert Hardy; an overblown eulogy to the Lancaster bomber, *The Pathfinders*, with Jack Watling and Robert Urquhart; a rather theatrical reminder of imperial soldiering, *The Regiment*; the calculatedly nostalgic *A Family at War*, a piece of superior soap-opera disguised as a serious sociological saga; and one of the BBC's most remarkable hits, *Dad's Army*, a gentle, witty, pleasantly inconsequential running joke about the Home Guard which has found its comedy in character and period detail rather than cheap gags.

The depiction of war is one aspect of moviemaking in which, it would appear, television can match and even surpass the cinema. For one thing, television is able, because of its capacity to serialize, to take the time it needs to cover the broad canvas of war and to give epic history its due. A film about World War II destined for the cinema would be pushing its luck if it ran for as much as three or four hours. *The World at War* is twenty-five hours long and still leaves plenty to say.

The BBC's popular and nostalgic TV comedy series, *Dad's Army*, with James Beck, Bill Pertwee, Clive Dunn, John Le Mesurier, Arthur Lowe and Ian Lavender.

Phil Silvers as *Sergeant Bilko*, the best of the TV army comedy series.

C'est la Guerre...

Beyond the impregnable, insular boundaries of Britain and America, the post-war cinematic attitude to the '39–'45 conflict was, on the whole, more serious, more rueful, and more redolent of the suffering brought on by invasion, defeat, or fascist infestation.

France, humiliated and horrified by the war, made very few films about it, and then only to emphasize an earnest desire for sanity in the future. Alain Resnais, the most articulate of France's film-making pacifists, built up to his highly acclaimed first feature, *Hiroshima Mon Amour*, with two important short documentaries about the destruction and suffering of war. In the earlier of these, *Guernica* (1950), co-directed with Robert Hessens, Resnais expressed his feelings through a camera-study of Picasso's fresco from the Spanish Civil War, 'Guernica', and other of the artist's works, combined with collage effects, a lyrical commentary and highly evocative music. *Nuit et Brouillard* (*Night and Fog*, 1956), which followed, is considered by many of the people who make such judgments to be one of the greatest anti-war films ever made – indeed, one of the few *genuine* anti-war films. Its technique is deceptively simple and brilliantly, disturbingly effective: it contrasts archival footage (in black and white) of the Nazi extermination camps in wartime with quiet, unblinking travelling shots (in colour) of Auschwitz as it stands today, grassy and deserted. In many ways, because they avoid mind-blowing visual facts and inconceivable mathematics (six million dead) of the Jewish slaughter, the modern shots are more horrifying than the newsreels: it is possible to shield the eyes, without shame, from explicit visual horror, but one is compelled to look at the empty shell of Auschwitz, and acknowledge its existence and purpose. In the same way, Resnais concentrates on the human trappings of the camps – the mounds of spectacles and shoes and dentures – rather than the corpses themselves: again, there is no excuse to look away. Whereas many atrocity documentaries lose their audience by showing too much and closing the shutters of credibility, Resnais' film shows just enough and grips tight.

Ten years later Resnais made *La Guerre est Finie* (*The War is Over*), about a professional revolutionary (Yves Montand) keeping faith with his ideals by continuing the fight to bring revolution to Spain. He followed this in 1967 with an episode of *Far From Vietnam*, a collaborative venture with William Klein, Joris Ivens, Agnès Varda, Claude Lelouch, Jean-Luc Godard and Chris Marker, which virulently attacked America's Vietnam policy and the perpetuation of war. Ivens made an earlier film about Vietnam, *Threatening Skies* (1965), which echoed his *Spanish Earth* in its sympathetic portrait of the peasants of North Vietnam.

Another short film which attacked the idealization of war was Georges Franju's *Hôtel des Invalides* (1952). Sponsored by the French Army as a prestige documentary, it was turned by its director into an anti-militaristic exercise by contrasting formal scenes of the French War Museum with shots of the real effects of war.

The same year, René Clément made one of the most distressing poignant of all war films, *Les Jeux Interdits* (*Forbidden Games*), about an orphaned five-year-old girl who is adopted by peasants and becomes strongly attached to their eleven-year-old son. The children, influenced by the carnage of war, create a cemetery for dead animals and spend all their time tending it. When the grown-ups discover their obsession they punish the girl by handing her back to the Red Cross. Apart from the main theme, gently and lyrically realized, the film is justly famous for its opening sequence, the strafing of a column of refugees which kills the girl's parents and her puppy, and the unbearably moving finale in which the girl is left, labelled and abandoned, on a bench at a refugee assembly-point.

In direct contrast to this was Robert Bresson's austere, economical, unique evocation of the spirit of French Resistance, *Un Condamné à Mort s'est Echappé* (*A Man Escaped*, 1956), a story told, says a prologue, exactly as it happened, 'sans ornements' – which is as good a description as any of Bresson's remarkable style. This authentic account of a wartime escape by a prisoner of the Gestapo from a Lyons prison was made with a carefully directed, non-professional cast, and concentrated on simple but telling detail – the artefacts required for the escape (a sharpened spoon, bed springs and blankets made into ropes, and so on), the painstaking work of cutting through the cell door, the peripheral sounds in the prison – to sustain tension and encourage sympathetic identification with the prisoner. The understated visuals and the dispassionate voice of the hero narrating his thoughts were contrasted with luxuriant Mozart on the soundtrack, creating an emotional involvement which the formality of the proceedings might otherwise have prevented.

No subsequent French war film could match up to the masterpieces of the early 'fifties. Christian-Jaque directed Brigitte Bardot in *Babette Goes to War* (1959). Charles Aznavour and Georges Rivière starred in André Cayatte's *The Crossing of the Rhine* (1960), a superficial, pretentious morality tale of two Frenchmen, one humble, the other ruthless, buffeted by the war. Jean-Luc Godard made *Le Petit Soldat* (1961), about the struggle between French and Algerian terrorists in Geneva, and *Les Carabiniers* (1963), an irritating anti-war 'fable'. And Jean Renoir revamped the ambiguities of *La Grande Illusion* in the pleasingly comic *Le Caporal Epinglé* (*The Vanishing Corporal*, 1962), about the relationship between three French soldiers held in a German detention camp.

Italian film-makers became even less responsive to war themes after the decline of

Nuit et Brouillard (Alain Resnais, 1956).

Georges Poujouly and Brigitte Fossey in René Clément's *Les Jeux Interdits* (1952).

211

François Leterrier in Robert Bresson's *Un Condamné à Mort s'est Echappé* (1956).

neo-realism, although Rossellini and De Sica returned to the genre. De Sica in fact starred in Rossellini's ironic *Il Generale della Rovere* (1959) – about an actor who impersonates a general and ends up fatefully in front of a firing-squad – before making his own *Two Women* (1961), adapted from a novel by Alberto Moravia. This emotional drama of a refugee mother and daughter suffering deprivation and abuse (including rape) after the Allied invasion of Italy, was a temporary revival of De Sica's talent and an international success, earning an Oscar for Sophia Loren. De Sica made nothing to match this until his 1970 film, *The Garden of the Finzi-Continis*, a sad, beautiful account of the erosion of Ferrara's Jewish community under the fascists.

One of the prestige productions of 1959, sharing a Venice Festival prize with *Il Generale della Rovere*, was Mario Monicelli's questionable tragi-comedy of World War I, *The Great War*, a would-be satire centring on the antics of two incompetent soldiers (Alberto Sordi and Vittorio Gassman) in the Austro-Italian campaign. The film upset the Italian military élite, but flopped leadenly outside Italy, its pacifist intentions acknowledged but its parochial humour lost on foreign audiences.

A better, though somewhat cold and abstract,

Brigitte Bardot in *Babette Goes to War* (Christian-Jaque, 1959), with Jacques Charrier.

polemic against war was *Thou Shalt Not Kill* (1961), directed by Claude Autant-Lara in Yugoslavia with Italian backing (though temperamentally a French production). This depicted an army trial in which a German priest (Horst Frank) is acquitted of killing a resistance fighter, while a conscientious objector (Laurent Terzieff) receives an indefinite prison sentence. Made at the time of the Algerian War, it was banned in both France and Italy.

Perhaps the cleverest and most significant film to issue from an Italian director in recent years was Gillo Pontecorvo's *The Battle of Algiers* (1965), a brilliant, beguiling, totally convincing reconstruction of the Algerians' fight for freedom against the French. Pontecorvo had given little hint of his technique of superficially objective, authentic 'reportage' in *Kapó* (1960), the story of a Jewish collaborator in Auschwitz (played by Susan Strasberg). In *The Battle of Algiers* he perfected it, while subtly winning the spectator's sympathy for the freedom-fighters (although they, like their military oppressors, commit atrocities) as well as his belief. Said Max Kozloff in his review of the film: 'When a movie especially compels the illusion that one is witnessing "live" events, yet at the same time heightens them by its art, when, moreover, its subject is recent and highly

sensitive, then it has truly inflammatory possibilities.'

Japan's output of films about the war has also been slender since the conflict ended, but it has included some interesting reflections on the atomic bomb (outlined in due course) and a

Vittorio De Sica in Roberto Rossellini's *Il Generale della Rovere* (1959).

Sophia Loren and Eleanora Brown as a refugee mother and daughter raped by Allied troops in Alberto Moravia's *Two Women* (Vittorio De Sica, 1961).

213

The Battle of Algiers (Gillo Pontecorvo, 1965).

few notable anti-war statements, beginning effectively with Sekigawa's *Listen to the Roar of the Ocean* (1950). This was followed by Satsuo Yamamoto's potent *Vacuum Zone* (1952); a whitewash job on *General Yamashita* (1952), with Sessue Hayakawa; and Imai's *The Tower of Lilies*, a tragedy about the death of young nurses in the war.

Three later productions stand out, however: *The Burmese Harp* (1956) and *Fires on the Plain* (1959), both directed by Kon Ichikawa from scripts by Natto Wada, and Masaki Kobayashi's epic trilogy, *The Human Condition* (1958–61). *The Burmese Harp*, set in Burma during the Japanese collapse, told of a young Japanese soldier, wounded and separated from his unit, who becomes a Buddhist monk, committed to

wandering the countryside and burying the unknown dead. It was a fierce, heady, occasionally over-emotional plea for humanity and peace, effectively contrasting the horrors of war with pastoral lyricism. *Fires on the Plain* was an even more savage indictment of war, set this time in the Philippines and following the desperate, terrified wanderings of a starving soldier who eventually resorts to cannibalism. Most powerful of all, if only by virtue of its immense scale (it lasts, *in toto*, for over nine hours), was *The Human Condition*, the tragic adventures of a young pacifist forced into military service in Japanese-occupied Manchuria, who tries to improve the harsh lot of the Chinese labourers and army recruits under his command: he is captured by the Russians,

214

The Burmese Harp (Kon Ichikawa, 1956).

Maria Schell in Helmut Käutner's *The Last Bridge* (1953).

escapes, and dies in the snow as he tries to make his way back home to his wife after the Japanese collapse. Said Kobayashi: 'I wanted to bring to life the tragedy of men who are forced into war against their will. . . . I wanted to denounce the crimes of war, but I also wanted to show how human society can become inhumane.'

In West Germany, economic recovery began to stifle the committed cinema in favour of escapism, but a number of strong anti-war statements were made in the 'fifties. One of the best was Helmut Käutner's *The Last Bridge* (1953), in which a German nurse (Maria Schell), taken prisoner by Yugoslav partisans, comes to sympathize with her captors and is killed as she tries to bring medical supplies to them.

Käutner also made *The Devil's General* (1955), an unequivocal attack on Hitler's war, about a Luftwaffe air ace (Curt Jurgens) whose contempt for the Nazis causes him to be persecuted by the SS and leads him eventually to crash his plane on purpose.

Bernhard Wicki, who appeared as an actor in *The Last Bridge*, himself directed one of the most effective of German anti-war films, *The Bridge* (1959). This highlighted the absurdity and tragic irony of the last days of the war in Germany by focusing on seven boys, drafted into what is left of Hitler's army, who are ordered to defend a strategically useless bridge against American tanks. They do so to the last boy, and the war ends two days later.

Other prominent war features made at this

Marianne Cook and Curt
Jurgens in *The Devil's
General* (Helmut Käutner,
1955).

Vladimir Ivashov and
Shanna Prokhorenko in
Ballad of a Soldier (Grigori
Chukhrai, 1959).

Tatyana Samoilova in *The
Cranes are Flying* (Mikhail
Kalatozov, 1957).

time in the Federal Republic included Kurt
Hoffmann's *Wir Wunderkinder* (*Aren't We
Wonderful*, 1958), a saga of the sons of two
families, one fascist, the other liberal, from the
Kaiser's time to the present, played out in the
style of a German satirical cabaret; Frank
Wysbar's reconstruction of the German collapse at Stalingrad, *Battle Inferno* (1959); and a
subtle political comedy by Wolfgang Staudte
(originally an East German director), *Roses
for the Prosecutor* (1959), in which a one-time
Nazi prosecutor is confronted by a petty thief
whom he had previously sentenced to death at
the war's end.

The most prominent of the East German
directors concerned with the war was Konrad
Wolf, who made *Lissy* (1957), a perceptive study

of a lower-middle-class woman of the 'thirties who decides to oppose Nazism in defiance of her husband; *Men With Wings* (1960), an ambivalent study of an aeronautical engineer's refusal to work on Nazi war projects, which falls into the same moral traps as *I Aim at the Stars*; and the celebrated *Sterne* (*Stars*, 1959), a sensitive, lyrical study of tragic love between a German soldier and a Greek-Jewish girl being transported through Bulgaria to a concentration camp.

Elsewhere behind the Iron Curtain, Stalin's death in 1953 brought a measure of liberation to Soviet and satellite cinema. The signs became apparent in Russia with Grigori Chukhrai's first film, a remake of Protazanov's *The Forty-First* (1956), about a Bolshevik girl

partisan's love for a White Russian officer. The trend was followed and confirmed by veteran Mikhail Kalatozov's internationally acclaimed *The Cranes are Flying* (1957), a mini-saga about a girl who marries another man while her fiancé is away at the war, but cannot shake off her guilt even after she learns of his death at the front. This stylish film brought realism, and the role of ordinary, fallible people, back into the Russian war film, and it dared to depict, once again, individual suffering and the loss of liberty against the rousing, epic sweep of the war.

The emotionalism (and occasional melodrama) of *The Cranes are Flying* was converted into unashamed sentimentality by Chukhrai in his romantic *Ballad of a Soldier*

217

Kanal (Andrzej Wajda, 1956).

A Generation (Andrzej Wajda, 1954).

Measuring out meagre prison-camp rations in *Eroica* (Andrzej Munk, 1957).

(1959), but the technical bravura and incidental commentary on the true nature of war remained. Nothing which happens afterwards quite matches up to the opening sequence in which the hero, a young soldier, in a state of abject panic (superbly conveyed by turning the camera on its head) knocks out two Nazi tanks and earns six days' leave. But the subsequent love story, punctuated with subtle and ironic indications of the horror and tragedy of war, was sensitively and realistically handled by Chukhrai and showed that romanticism was not Hollywood's exclusive preserve.

In the same year, the actor Sergei Bondarchuck directed his first film, *Destiny of a Man* (and starred in it himself), which traced the wartime sufferings of a soldier captured by the

Nazis. This tribute to the indefatigable Russian spirit continued the fresh, realistic approach of the post-Stalin films, which was evident in the contemporary work of most of the younger directors – notably Andrei Tarkovsky, whose *Childhood of Ivan* (1962), though marred by over-lyrical dream sequences, is an original, tragic study of a twelve-year-old boy, aged by the war, who acts as a scout and spy for the Russian Army. Tarkovsky later turned to epic treatments of the past (*Andrei Roublev*) and the future (*Solaris*).

Another heroic but humanistic panorama of the war, *The Flaming Years* (1961), was created by Yulia Solntseva from a script by her late husband (Dovzhenko). This story of a courageous Ukrainian soldier lacked the master's touch but contained some spectacular battle scenes. Chukhrai's third war film, *Clear Skies* (1961), was, as its title indicates, politically more explicit in its story of a pilot, unjustly persecuted by the Party for alleged defeatism in the war, who is reinstated after the death of Stalin.

Towards the end of the 'sixties there was evidence of a return to tighter artistic control in Russia and interesting films became rarer, particularly those prepared to take a nonconformist view of war. Typical of a new propagandist tack was M. Bogin's *Zozia* (1967), which depicted the affection of the Poles for the Russian soldiers who came to liberate them from the Nazis.

The healthiest cinema behind the Iron

Zbigniew Cybulski in
Ashes and Diamonds
(Andrzej Wajda, 1958).

220

Curtain blossomed in Poland, where need for individual expression was recognized and many major talents emerged. One of the first was Andrzej Wajda, who launched his tragic, profound, unplanned war trilogy with *A Generation* (1954), a portrait of young resistance workers in Nazi-held Warsaw and their divergent attitudes towards the occupation. This was followed by *Kanal* (1956), the film which brought Wajda into the international limelight. In this, a group of partisans take to the sewers during the Warsaw Uprising of 1944, become separated, and are trapped and killed. The most romantic as well as horrific part of the trilogy (in spite of its setting), *Kanal* gave eloquent expression to Wajda's most common theme, the heroic martyrdom of the Polish people. The set was completed by *Ashes and Diamonds* (1958), which gave the enigmatic actor, Zbigniew Cybulski, his first major role, as a right-wing assassin ordered to murder a communist district secretary on the first day of peace. His dilemma, whether to obey orders or stifle at conception a cause which will force Pole to kill Pole, was symbolic of the confusion experienced in Polish society at this crucial moment in its history. In the end, the assassin performs

his duty, and is himself shot to death on a rubbish-dump, Wajda's final symbolic image of disillusionment.

Wajda returned periodically to war themes, notably in *Lotna* (1959), another nostalgic portrayal of Polish heroism and self-sacrifice which re-created the Polish cavalry's futile resistance to the invading German Panzers in 1939; *Samson* (1961), which recalled the Biblical legend in its story of the life and death of a young Jew in Warsaw during the German occupation; and *Landscape After Battle* (1970), about a poet in a concentration camp who finds adjustment difficult when the war ends and he is forced to stay on in the camp.

Andrzej Munk saw another side to the Polish heroic tradition, which he gently ridiculed in his two-part film, *Eroica* (1957). In the first episode, a disillusioned volunteer returns home but finds he prefers the Resistance to his wife's company. In the second, set in a German prisoner-of-war camp for Polish resistance fighters, the prisoners' morale is sustained by the one 'successful' escape which has taken place. In fact, the escapee is hiding in the roof and slowly going mad. When he dies and is discovered, the Germans and Poles quietly

Josef Kroner in Jan Kadar's *The Shop on the High Street* (1965).

221

smuggle his body out, the Germans to save face, the Poles to maintain morale. Where Wajda found romantic dignity in the Polish devotion to heroic gestures and lost causes, Munk saw only foolishness and senseless dramatics.

In his last film, *Passenger* (1963), completed with stills after his tragic death in a car accident, Munk explored the theme of guilt as experienced by a German woman who recalls her days as an SS guard in Auschwitz. It was a rare portrayal of an extermination camp from the point of view of the captors.

As in Russia, much of the creative flair seeped out of the Polish cinema at the end of the 'sixties, and recent war films, such as those by Jerzy Passendorfer (*Scenes of Battle, Direction Berlin, The Last Days*, etc.) have mostly been routine recollections of World War II.

Czech film-makers also enjoyed a period of creativity after the communist thaw, the chief exponent of war themes being Jiri Weiss, whose *No Middle Road* (also known as *Life is the Stake*, 1956) and *Romeo, Juliet and Darkness* (1960) were very close in plot and treatment to Wolf's *Lissy* and *Sterne*. The first of these concerned an engineer who collaborates with the Nazis while his wife is working for the Resistance. The second was about a Prague student who hides a Jewish girl with whom he falls in love. Both were notable for their depth of debate and their confined, claustrophobic settings.

Another veteran director, Jan Kadar, won Czechoslovakia's first Academy Award with *The Shop on the High Street* (1965), a sensitive study of a man's impotent sympathy for a Jewish button-shop owner in German-occupied Slovakia in 1942, and the bungling guilt which causes him eventually to hang himself. At its best, an affectionate, poetic film, it was not without its *longueurs* and passages of whimsy.

Noteworthy films from younger directors included Jan Nemec's *Diamonds of the Night* (1964), about the escape from a train of two young Jewish prisoners, and the visions and dreams they experience brought on by their hunger and fear. More widely celebrated was Jiri Menzel's gentle, humorous, and ultimately tragic *Closely Observed Trains* (1966), which set the sexual initiation of a young railway porter in World War II against a background of resistance and sabotage. Like Kadar's film, it won an Oscar.

In other communist countries the war received scant attention. In Hungary, Andras Kovacs made *Cold Days* (1967) – a compelling dramatized investigation of a notorious massacre in Yugoslavia – and Miklos Jancso came into prominence with his pleasantly moody *My Way Home* (1964), but the Hungarian cinema was otherwise dominated by Jancso's carefully choreographed, increasingly elliptical political allegories (*The Round-Up, Silence and Cry*, etc.). And in Rumania, Liviu Ciulei recalled the fate of a deserter in World War I in his poignant *The Forest of the Hanged* (1965).

In the independent, non-aligned communist state of Yugoslavia, whose war had been one of

brave and determined resistance led principally by the country's future President, Marshal Tito, most of the films about the war dealt, naturally, with the heroic internal struggle. Characteristic examples were Branko Bauer's *Don't Look Back, My Son* (1956), about a partisan who works to rescue his son from the moral corruption of a Nazi-organized school, and Veljko Bulajic's *Hill of Death* (1962) noted for its vivid action scenes, in which the partisans, against superior odds, force the Germans back

Closely Observed Trains (Jiri Menzel, 1966).

from the mountain village of Kozara.

One young Yugoslav director, France Stiglic, tackled less typical themes. *The Valley of Peace* (1956) told the moving story of two war orphans who avoid deportation by running away across country, and meet a Negro airman, who has bailed out of his plane. He dies while saving them from a German patrol and they continue their search for a mythical 'valley of peace'. *The Ninth Circle* (1960) painted a terrifying picture of Nazi atrocities against which was set the tragic story of a student's love for a Jewish girl who is put into a concentration camp and then deported ('one of the best works of the young Yugoslav cinema', according to Sadoul).

Among other European films depicting aspects of World War II, the Finnish epic, *The Unknown Soldier* (1955 – director Edvin Laine), an account of Finland's struggle against the Russians, stands out as a powerful portrayal of the futile, unrelenting bloodiness of war and the bewilderment of the men drawn into the

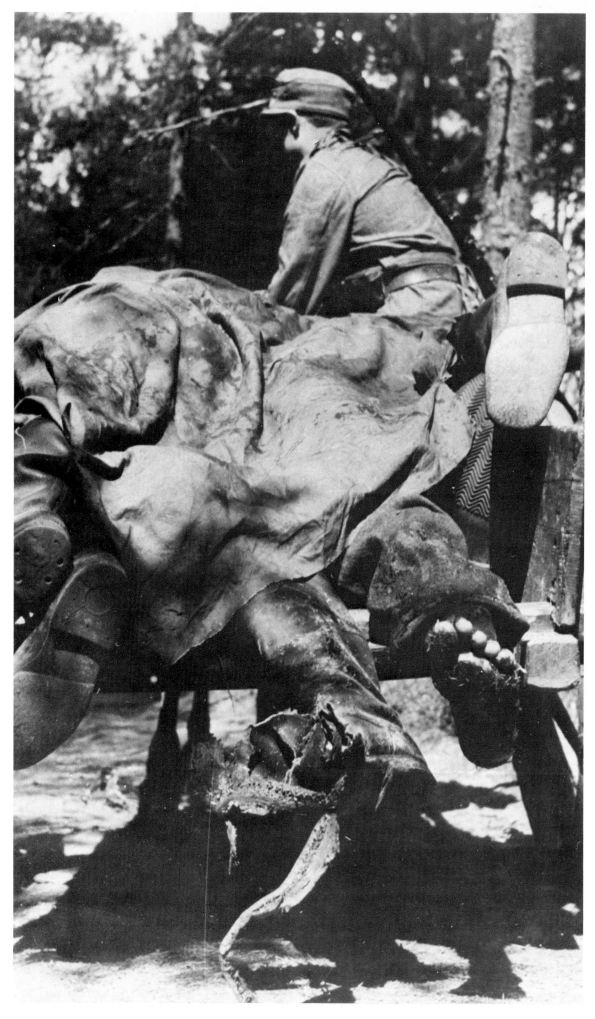

The Unknown Soldier
(Edvin Laine, 1955).

224

deadly conflict. More recently, Satyajit Ray's intensely sad *Distant Thunder* (1973) has shown how a remote Bengali village is affected by the war. The villagers never see the war, apart from an occasional sight of planes flying picturesquely overhead, but slowly and inexorably their contented existence is eroded away by famine, looting and other deprivations and abuses. It is a melancholically beautiful, finely perceptive understatement on the intrinsic and inevitable sufferings of the innocent during war, and by no means a minor work by Ray.

The innocent also suffer in Ingmar Bergman's haunting film, *The Shame* (1968), which depicts an unidentified civil war of the near future and its brutalizing effect on a sensitive, devoted couple (Max Von Sydow and Liv Ullmann) forced to become refugees. In the end, they feel only mutual contempt, but remain dependent on each other for survival. A disturbing premonitory reminder of man's baser instincts and the frailty of civilization.

Max Von Sydow and Liv Ullmann in Ingmar Bergman's *The Shame* (1968).

225

...But He Won't Lie Down

One of the cinema's more morbid but easily understandable preoccupations has been with the character of Hitler and the nature of Nazism. Understandable because the Nazis' own fascination for the ciné-camera caused them to create a thorough, detailed film record of their philosophy and deeds, along with the public (and private) image of their beloved leader. This material has been constantly reworked into film portrayals and condemnations of the Nazis and their era.

The Nazis (as opposed to the German people) have, since the 'fifties, constantly been cinematically skinned, hacked up and nailed to the fence of history as an awful warning to posterity of the lengths to which dirty politics can go. And Hitler has proved the greatest heavy the cinema has known.

One film-maker consistently committed to the exposure of Nazism, past and present, has been the East German documentarist, Andrew Thorndike, who, in collaboration with his wife Annelie, was responsible for *The German Story* (1956) and the subsequent series, *The Archives Testify*. The Thorndikes' technique has been to utilize the mass of archive material available in order to attack didactically the alleged corruption of authority in West Germany and the elevation of surviving Nazis to positions of influence. One of the Thorndikes' fiercest indictments of the Federal Republic was *A Diary for Anne*, which used shots of atrocities in the concentration camps alongside footage of the war criminals, still at large, supposedly responsible for the death of Anne Frank and other European Jews.

The Thorndike films are strictly propagandist in the political sense. Other film-makers have used the archives to create relatively more objective studies of Nazism, fascist atrocities, and the Hitler period. Alain Resnais' *Nuit et Brouillard* has already have mentioned. There have also been the West German compilation, *The Nazi Crimes and Punishments* (also called *The Nuremberg Trials*, 1958), made by a group of journalists; *Mein Kampf* (1960), a history of Germany from before World War I related to Hitler's life, made in Sweden by the exiled German, Erwin Leiser; Mikhail Romm's Russian film, *Ordinary Fascism* (1964), an attempt to discover the motivations behind Nazism and its mystique by focusing on the people who observed it, fed it and were hypnotized by it; the Polish documentary *Under This*

Burt Lancaster as a remorseful war-criminal in *Judgment at Nuremberg* (Stanley Kramer, 1961).

Same Sky, a depiction of the Warsaw Ghetto and its destruction; and Leiser's *Germany, Awake!*, a demonstration of Nazi propaganda techniques liberally illustrated with clips from feature films like *Morgenrot* and *Hitlerjunge Quex*.

Fictional portrayals of Nazism and its effect on people's lives have ranged from the dubious (like Hollywood's opportunistic *Operation Eichmann*, made in 1961, which was banned in West Germany for being 'over-simplified') to the routine (such as the 1966 Sophia Loren vehicle, *Judith*, about the rooting out of secret Nazis who still oppose Israel) to the worthily sincere. Best in the last-named category were Stanley Kramer's *Judgment at Nuremberg* (1961) and Sidney Lumet's *The Pawnbroker* (1964). Kramer's long, solid, commercially successful dramatization of the Nuremberg trials was a drastic simplification of the issues, peopled with stereotypes (guilt-ridden war criminal, indignant prosecutor, incipiently fascist defence lawyer, etc.), but a marvellous cast made it immensely watchable, particularly Spencer Tracy as the judge, Maximilian Schell as the defence lawyer, and Judy Garland, Montgomery Clift and Marlene Dietrich as witnesses. *The Pawnbroker* starred Rod Steiger as a Jew haunted by his experiences in a concentration camp where his wife and children

were murdered: a rather empty debate on human responsibility lifted by Steiger's convincing performance.

Hitler himself has been portrayed many times, in both fact and fiction – never more frequently, though, than in the early 'seventies, which saw a veritable glut of investigations into the character and myth of the Fuehrer. Among the first serious dramatizations of

Adolf Hitler and Albert Speer captured on Eva Braun's home movies – revealed publicly for the first time in Philippe Mora's *Swastika* (1973)

Albin Skoda as Hitler and Willy Krause as Goebbels in G.W. Pabst's *Ten Days to Die* (1954).

Rod Steiger as *The Pawnbroker* (Sidney Lumet, 1964), with Geraldine Fitzgerald.

Hitler's career were the two films by G. W. Pabst, *Ten Days to Die* (also called *The Last Act*, 1954), a reconstruction of the last days in the bunker, with Oskar Werner as a 'good' German officer and Albin Skoda as Hitler, and *The Jackboot Mutiny* (*It Happened on 20th July*, 1955), which re-created Count Stauffenberg's abortive attempt on Hitler's life in 1944. Among the best impersonations of the Fuehrer have been Alec Guinness's, exact down to the last minute gesture, in *Hitler – The Last Ten Days* (1973), and Frank Finlay's, more introverted and neurotic, in a 1973 television play about the final hours in the Berlin bunker.

Actuality portraits of Hitler built up from archive material have included Paul Rotha's straightforward, condemnatory *The Life of Adolf Hitler* (1962), and a curious documentary, *The Black Fox*, which attempted to present Hitler as a creature of fable. The most revealing documentaries about the Fuehrer and his works, however, are the two recent VPS productions, *Swastika* and *The Double-Headed Eagle* (both 1973). Philippe Mora's *Swastika* benefits mainly from the extensive use made of the several hours of colour home movies

Above and left: The twenty-five-year-old Hitler as a face in the crowd at a political meeting in 1919 — part of Lutz Becker's portrayal of the rise of Nazism in *The Double-Headed Eagle* (1973).

shot in Obersalzberg, Hitler's mountain retreat, by Eva Braun and other Hitler associates. These above all else demonstrate the 'banality of evil', the surface ordinariness of the Nazi leaders (Hitler shifting his feet nervously, Speer looking shy and embarrassed) and their women (Eva Braun revealed as a rather attractive, giggling coquette), heightened by being contrasted with a rich supply of cleverly edited Nazi newsreel and official film, full of the familiar pomp and bombast. One would quarrel only with Mora's decision to dub lip-read dialogue on to the home movies, in order to make them rather more palatable.

Lutz Becker (with Mora as co-writer) directed *The Double-Headed Eagle*, a skilful survey of Hitler's rise to power from 1918 to 1933, using rare newsreel material (including a glimpse of Hitler in a crowd in 1919) combined, sometimes ironically, with excerpts from contemporary escapist feature films. This is the more disturbing of the two films, a clear visual expression (if not an explanation) of the Nazi mentality. Its best achievement is in conveying the charisma and oratorical skills which hid the intrinsic absurdity of Hitler and Goebbels.

Spectacle and Holocaust

Hollywood's policy towards war films in the 'sixties was simple: to make them as big, noisy, colourful and spectacular as possible. Even the 'message' movies took on a new epic scale. Allied to this was another tacit policy decision: to ignore the issues raised by Vietnam and to leave the reporting of it to television.

British film-makers (with a little financial assistance from America) went along with the idea of spectacle and, indeed, the first of this genre of giants bore a British imprint. This was the long, popular, pyrotechnic adventure-fantasy, *The Guns of Navarone* (1961), directed by J. Lee-Thompson and scripted by Carl Foreman from an Alistair Maclean novel about a special army mission to destroy a battery of enormous, radar-controlled guns overlooking a vital sea channel in Greece. The film wasted a lot of time making simple-minded comments about the futility of war and ironing out discontent among the usual mixed bag of stereotypes (played by a prestige cast led by Gregory Peck), but eventually it plodded its way to one of the biggest and loudest bangs seen and heard on a cinema screen, earning an Oscar for Best Special Effects.

Darryl Zanuck, with the help of co-directors Andrew Marton, Ken Annakin and Bernhard Wicki, plus fifty stars, twenty thousand extras and several million dollars, followed this with his three-hour adaptation of Cornelius Ryan's *The Longest Day* (1962), a would-be realistic (i.e. shot in black and white with the Germans speaking German, and so on) reconstruction of the Allied landings in Normandy on 6 June 1944. Financially one of the most successful war movies ever made, it threw together every British and American tin-hat hero on the books (Richard Burton, Henry Fonda, Richard Todd, John Wayne, Kenneth More, etc., etc.) but could not prevent its complexity of settings (British, German and American) and parallel sub-plots (beach landings, glider landings, paratrooper landings) from becoming ultimately tiresome. It was certainly inferior to Jean Grémillon's *Le Six Juin à l'Aube*, and in many ways less enjoyable than Henry Koster's more modest *D-Day the Sixth of June* (1956), starring Robert Taylor and Richard Todd.

After this, British films again made the running, first with David Lean's brilliantly filmed *Lawrence of Arabia* (1962) and then with Carl Foreman's highly personal *The Victors* (1963). *Lawrence* picked up seven Oscars ('one every half-hour', quipped a Hollywood wag) and sundry other awards and still stands, in Leslie Halliwell's words, as the 'supreme example of the modern multi-million dollar international epic'. Assets included superb photography, a fine, intelligent script by Robert Bolt, apt theme music, a captivating performance by Peter O'Toole as Lawrence, and a pleasant début in international movie-making by local Egyptian heart-throb Omar Sharif, who starred in Lean's next film, *Doctor Zhivago*.

The Victors, an episodic study of American soldiers battling their way from Italy to Berlin, was intended by Foreman as the ultimate anti-war film ('War, any war, big or little, just as well as unjust, degrades the victors equally with the vanquished, and inevitably sows the seeds of still another war') but its clumsy size and unconvincing characterizations (inadequately put across by leads George Peppard and George Hamilton) let it down. It had, nevertheless, many effective sequences, some horrifying, some ironic, and some a combination of both, such as that in which a deserter is executed in the snow on Christmas Day with Frank Sinatra crooning 'Have Yourself a Merry Little Christmas' on the soundtrack. It also acquired the virtue of rubbing right-wing elements in America up the wrong way, causing it to be condemned as 'a massive, sordid, anti-military film slanted to shock us into believing soldiers defending our country are cruel fools, black marketeers, and murderers'.

There were messages hidden also in John Frankenheimer's *The Train* (1964), a superbly exciting resistance drama in which stars Burt Lancaster, Jeanne Moreau and Paul Scofield were upstaged by the film's real heroes, the hissing locomotives. The plot concerned the attempts of a railway engineer (Lancaster) to prevent a German officer (Scofield) from making off to Germany with a train-load of French art

Burt Lancaster in *Castle Keep* (Sydney Pollack, 1969).

231

treasures. There was some tentative debate about weighing the value of human life against a bunch of old paintings, but it was the spectacular action which counted – the crashes, the strafings, the bombings, all seemingly done without the aid of models.

Mark Robson's similar spectacle, *Von Ryan's Express*, was pure adventure and courted no moral dilemmas in its story of a prisoner-of-war escape by captured train from Italy to Switzerland. Frank Sinatra and Trevor Howard led the bouts of action, which included a superb climax on an Alpine viaduct.

Sydney Pollack's *Castle Keep* (1969), on the other hand, takes the war versus culture issue a good deal further, using it as an excuse for a semi-horrific, semi-hilarious fantasy which

almost succeeds in catching the allegorical essence of William Eastlake's original novel. A group of exhausted soldiers, led by the pragmatic Major Falconer (Burt Lancaster), takes over a Belgian castle filled with priceless art treasures. The soldiers become preoccupied – one with saving the castle, another with the local baker's widow, another with a captured Volkswagen he has come to love passionately – until the Germans advance and they die in an heroic rearguard action which ends with the castle beginning to totter. 'War,' said Eastlake in his book, 'is a Cinderella story where each man turns into a soldier', and it is the fairy-tale element thus implied which works best in the film: Falconer on a white charger; one of the American soldiers discussing Brahms with

a German concealed in the bushes; the Volkswagen floating in the moat; three men lying dead in a withered bed of red roses. The script is economical and intelligent, the dialogue bitterly funny, and the acting (particularly by Al Freeman, as an aspiring Negro novelist, Peter Falk, as a Brooklyn baker, and Scott Wilson, as the car-lover) flawless.

Three celebrated incidents of the war formed the subject of a like number of spectaculars in 1965: Otto Preminger's *In Harm's Way*, which starred John Wayne and Patricia Neal, re-created the Japanese bomb attack on Pearl Harbor; Ken Annakin's *Battle of the Bulge* was a portrayal of the Battle for Bastogne during the last major German offensive of the war; and Anthony Mann's *The Heroes of*

Telemark (Kirk Douglas and Richard Harris) was an epic dramatization of the successful bid by resistance workers in Norway to prevent the Germans moving their stocks of heavy water to Berlin.

In 1967, Robert Aldrich made the most profitable war movie of them all, *The Dirty Dozen*, described by critic Stephen Farber as 'one of the most vicious, though one of the craftiest movies I know'. This violent, much-imitated adventure story employed a plot formula which had already been used to good effect in the modest and little-known Roger Corman film, *The Secret Invasion* (1964, with Stewart Granger). A dozen dangerous criminals (thieves, murderers, rapists, psychopaths) are assigned to a hazardous mission under the

The Guns of Navarone (J. Lee-Thompson, 1961), with (*from left*) James Darren, Stanley Baker, David Niven, Gregory Peck, Anthony Quinn and Anthony Quayle.

Robert Mitchum in *The Longest Day* (Darryl Zanuck, Andrew Marton, Ken Annakin and Bernhard Wicki, 1962).

Peter O'Toole as *Lawrence of Arabia* (David Lean, 1962), with Claude Rains, Jack Hawkins (as General Allenby) and Anthony Quayle.

leadership of an insubordinate major (Lee Marvin). They are to attack a country-house in Brittany used by top-ranking German officers for recreation and kill as many of them as possible. If they succeed, they will be treated with clemency; if they fail, then humanity will be none the poorer. From this promising concept, with its potential for irony and for comment on the insanity of war and its parallels with murder, the film degenerates, alas, into scenes of gratuitous violence and meretricious anti-militarism, revelling finally in a repellently gory climax which has the German officers (and their female companions), trapped in a bomb shelter, being obliterated by a combination of petrol and grenades. And the

apparent liberalism and impudent enlightenment of the Major turns out, in fact, to be just a veneer hiding a fascist hero who is no better than the supposed villains he has been ordered to eliminate. Among those dishing out the sadism were John Cassavetes, Telly Savalas, Jim Brown and Donald Sutherland.

Savalas and Sutherland turned up again, with Clint Eastwood, in a popular comedy adventure called *Kelly's Heroes* (1970, director Brian Hutton), in which a group of unenthusiastic soldiers with criminal tendencies suddenly achieve a fighting spirit when they learn of gold hidden behind the enemy lines. The *Dirty Dozen* formula was also reworked in the British film *Play Dirty* (1968, director André

John Mills, Richard Johnson, Tom Courtenay, Lilli Palmer, Anthony Quayle) in which the Germans are prevented by saboteurs from using rockets and atomic warheads; Jack Cardiff's unpleasant film, *The Mercenaries* (1968), with Rod Taylor, set in the Congo in 1960; and Brian Hutton's and Yakima Canutt's box-office success, *Where Eagles Dare* (1968), a fairly preposterous Alistair Maclean story about a parachute mission into the Alps to rescue a captured officer, with Richard Burton and Clint Eastwood sharing the heroics. Superior to these was Peter Yates's absorbing *Murphy's War* (1970), set in Venezuela in 1944, in which Peter O'Toole played an Irish merchant sailor who takes ingenious revenge on the U-boat that sank his ship and killed his comrades.

One or two films in the 'sixties attempted to show the Germans in a sympathetic light once again, notably Anatole Litvak's lengthy, rather ponderous melodrama, *The Night of the Generals* (1966), about a German Intelligence officer (Omar Sharif!) lumbered with the task of finding out who, among the top brass (he has Peter O'Toole, Donald Pleasence and Charles Gray to choose from) has been murdering prostitutes.

Better was George Seaton's cleverly plotted *36 Hours* (1964), about a German scheme to

Above: Robert Shaw conducting the *Battle of the Bulge* (Ken Annakin, 1965).

Below: The Dirty Dozen (Robert Aldrich, 1967), led by Clint Walker, Telly Savalas, Jim Brown, Donald Sutherland, Charles Bronson and John Cassavetes.

De Toth), in which a company of ex-criminals (among them Nigel Davenport and Nigel Green), led by Captain Michael Caine, destroy a German oil depot in Africa.

Similar mindless comic-book adventures were the principal feature of Michael Anderson's *Operation Crossbow* (1964), a stellar production (George Peppard, Sophia Loren, Trevor Howard,

Philippe Noiret and Peter O'Toole in *Murphy's War* (Peter Yates, 1970).

persuade a US major (James Garner) to reveal the D-Day invasion plans by making him think he has had a lapse of memory, that he is recovering among fellow Americans, and that the invasion has already taken place. Seaton made most of it convincing, got good performances out of Garner and Eva Marie Saint, and marred a good movie only by feeling the need to add one good German (Rod Taylor) who, most improbably, assists the hero's escape.

Also well made but largely routine were Edward Dmytryk's *The Battle for Anzio* (1968), which achieved a measure of realism in its portrayal of the beginnings of the Italian campaign, and John Guillermin's *The Bridge at Remagen* (1968), with George Segal and Robert

Peter Falk and Robert Mitchum in *The Battle for Anzio* (Edward Dmytryk, 1968).

237

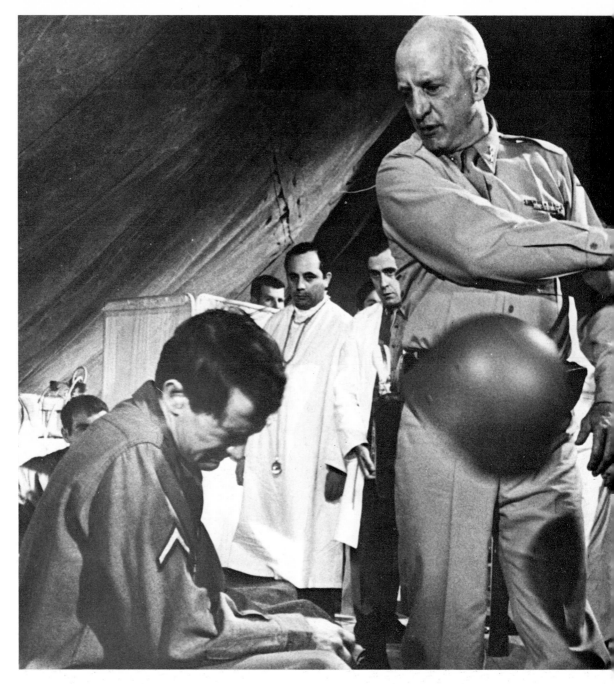

George C. Scott, as General
George S. Patton Jr,
re-creates the famous
slapping incident in *Patton:
Lust for Glory* (Franklin
Schaffner, 1969).

Vaughn, about the German retreat and attempts to destroy the Ludendorff Bridge.

After a brief respite, the war epic was revived with Franklin Schaffner's admirable, though not always likeable, *Patton: Lust for Glory* (1969), a bold attempt to probe in depth, and at some length (three hours), the complex character of America's most colourful and controversial general. In spite of a skilful performance by George C. Scott in the lead role, the man behind the blunt talk and blunter actions (the striking of a shell-shocked soldier is, of course, included) remains elusive, and the characterization is not helped by an exaggeration of his rivalry with Montgomery, outrageously caricatured by Michael Bates. Schaffner's control of his material, however, is impressive, and the various campaign sequences are strikingly photographed through an audaciously wide lens. Ironically, though, the film's most memorable sequence is Scott/Patton's static opening speech ('No dumb bastard ever won a

war by dying for his country . . .') delivered to camera against a backdrop of the Stars and Stripes.

Other biographies of eminent war leaders have included Robert Montgomery's *The Gallant Hours* (1960), with James Cagney as Admiral 'Bull' Halsey, and, on a more modest scale, *PT 109* (1962), Leo Martinson's portrait of John F. Kennedy performing his wartime duties on a torpedo boat, with Cliff Robertson as the future President of the United States.

Britain stayed in the epic stakes with Guy Hamilton's disappointingly shallow *Battle of Britain* (1969), a vague, unconvincing re-creation of Britain's finest hour, redeemed somewhat by one riveting, balletic dogfight sequence which captures both the horror and mystique of the fighter pilot's role, and a quietly superb performance by Laurence Olivier as the reticent Air Chief Marshal Sir Hugh Dowding.

The aim was a good deal clearer in Richard

238

Japanese production *Tora! Tora! Tora!*. Using a similar inter-cutting technique to that employed for *The Longest Day*, Fleischer's film described Japan's attack on the US fleet in Pearl Harbor vividly and clearly from the point of view of both nations, wisely simplifying the complex drama of code-breaking and bungling which permitted the surprise attack and concentrating on the spectacle itself.

An occasional attempt was made in the 'sixties to do more than depict the war as simply a spectacle. A few American films expressed disillusionment or cynicism, or tried to show the degrading effects of armed aggression. The attempt was not always successful. Delbert Mann's *The Outsider* (1961), for example – although a creditable enough essay at a biography of Ira Hayes, the Pima Indian who found himself elevated to the status of a national hero after his fortuitous appearance in the historic news photograph of the raising of the American flag at Iwo Jima – got lost in a muddy script, and suffered badly from the miscasting of Tony Curtis as Hayes. The Indian's breakdown and the hypocrisy of hero-worship were well enough conveyed, but the film failed to keep a rein on all the issues it raised (racial prejudice, patriotism, etc.) and became merely confusing.

Frank Sinatra's *None But the Brave* (1965), about an uneasy temporary truce between American and Japanese soldiers on a Pacific island, must, in the light of its own pretensions, also be accounted a failure. Its simplistic anti-war message, delivered with sledge-hammer blows ('Nobody ever wins,' says a superfluous closing title after a bloody beach battle), is compromised by naïvety, sentimentality and a box-office ending (the American stars survive), and the acting is self-indulgent. All the same, Sinatra's sincerity, as both director and star, occasionally breaks through to hold the attention and help one to believe in his good intentions.

Similar faults occurred in another actor-

Laurence Olivier as Air Chief Marshal Sir Hugh Dowding in *Battle of Britain* (Guy Hamilton, 1969), with Michael Redgrave.

Attenborough's flawed but impressive adaptation of Joan Littlewood's theatrical evocation of the '14–'18 conflict, *Oh! What a Lovely War* (1969), described succinctly by one critic as 'an angry, eloquent obituary for a lost generation'. With a breathtaking cast (Cecil Parker, for what it's worth, was twenty-eighth on the list, and John Mills fourteenth) and the odd stroke of genius (such as converting Brighton Pier into a gleaming white symbol of the madness and euphoria which turned Europe into a death-pit), Attenborough triumphantly solved most of the problems of transforming a poignant musical romp into a screen epic, although the final dazzling result sometimes lacked the soul of the original. Most importantly, the songs survived, and the final image of countless white crosses planted in neat rows multiplying back to the horizon formed a memory difficult to dislodge.

The biggest blockbuster of the early 'seventies was Richard Fleischer's joint American/

director's film, Cornel Wilde's *Beach Red* (1967), an excessively gory, portentous study of an assault by marines on a Japanese-held Pacific island. As the 'Monthly Film Bulletin' frankly put it, 'Cornel Wilde's uncompromisingly pacifist film encompasses every cliché known to the anti-war cinema from *All Quiet* onwards'. It did, however, have a simple, unquenchable honesty of a kind not often shown in the American cinema, and this, together with a few ideas which did actually work (the recurring image of a boot poised over an insect, for instance) combined with technical expertise, resulted in an unusually effective statement about the horror and waste of war. Wilde's directness is more potent, for example, than the intended symbolic subtleties of John Boorman's *Hell in the Pacific* (1968), an allegory of war in which a lone American pilot (Lee Marvin) and a stranded Japanese naval officer (Toshiro Mifune) face each other on a remote Pacific atoll. They skirmish, make a truce, build a raft, quarrel and fight – but their situation is never quite convincing enough and Boorman's film has the cold look of an intellectual exercise rather than a sincere plea for understanding.

One of the best and most underrated war films of the 'sixties was *The Americanization of Emily* (1964), an honourable and highly enjoyable attempt to deflate the cult of war heroism, liberated from Arthur Hiller's stolid direction by Paddy Chayefsky's sharp, literate script and the finely tuned acting of James

Garner and Julie Andrews. Garner played an admiral's aide, based in England, who, despite being an irredeemable coward, is ordered by his deranged superior to be the first Navy man to hit Omaha beach in the Normandy landings. Meanwhile, he has fallen for the prim Miss Andrews, whose mother behaves like a reincarnation of Mrs Miniver. Julie tries to tell him that 'it's the *virtue* of war that's a fraud, not war itself', but he goes off, unconvinced and rolling drunk, to meet his fate on Omaha with a very ill grace. Often caustically funny, this anti-war comedy presented a refreshingly cynical outlook in a decade noted more for its bland exploitation of the war than for its questioning of moral issues.

The freshly derisory attitude of Hiller's film was subsequently copied by Blake Edwards in his intermittently funny *What Did You Do in the War, Daddy?* (1966) with James Coburn and Dick Shawn; and by Norman Jewison's *The Russians are Coming, the Russians are Coming* (1965), about a Red invasion scare on a Massachusetts island, saved from whimsy by a crystalline comic performance from Alan Arkin. Stanley Kramer partly redressed the balance with his sentimental, heavy-handed Anthony Quinn vehicle, *The Secret of Santa Vittoria* (1969).

Latterly, cynicism has become a prime ingredient of the American war film. First used in any appreciable quantity by Stanley Kubrick in *Dr Strangelove* . . ., it has since become the dominating flavour in such films as Robert Altman's *M*A*S*H* (1969), Mike Nichols's *Catch 22* (1970), and Robert Aldrich's *Too Late the Hero* (1970).

M*A*S*H, an anti-war satire set in a mobile field hospital in Korea, broke new ground by introducing total realism into a black-comic situation and by discarding 'theatrical' dialogue in favour of a much more natural speech-sound technique. This meant that, in visual terms, the blood was allowed to flow as thickly as the jokes, while on the soundtrack one heard the speech patterns of real life – unfinished conversations and strands of dialogue filtering in and out of the consciousness. Both techniques are now part and parcel of any film which has any pretension to realism.

M*A*S*H is the American service comedy turned on its head and kicked in the teeth. It is irreverent, irreligious, anti-militaristic, farcical and passionately humanistic. It depicts war as a human-mincing machine, in the face of which the surgeons and nurses whose job it is to reconstitute the ground-up bones and meat of men have to laugh and letch and booze and smoke marijuana and play outrageous charades simply in order to stay sane. War is consequently turned into one great, gory joke which, in hands as skilled and sincere as those of Altman and his talented performers (particularly Donald Sutherland and Elliott Gould), can make for very potent anti-war propaganda indeed. (Little of this comment, incidentally, applies to the television series built round the original *M*A*S*H* idea, which has been bowdlerized and sentimentalized for the small screen.)

Catch 22, an ambitious adaptation of Joseph Heller's despairingly comic portrait of bomber crews desperately trying to survive the war, has some of the atmosphere and bitterness of *M*A*S*H*, a few good visual jokes (best of all, a burning bomber lurching in to land behind two Air Force officers engrossed in the latest black-market dealings) and a fine central performance by Alan Arkin, but it suffers from its

own epic proportions, and its anti-war sentiments are a little on the heavy side. It has visual splendour, however, including some stunning opening scenes of bombers preparing for take-off at dawn, and its more serious effects (Arkin's recurring nightmare, for example) are very telling.

Paradoxically, the black comedies of Altman and Nichols have reintroduced a serious, essentially pacifist note into the American war

Raising the flag at Iwo Jima – re-creation of the famous news photograph in *The Outsider* (Delbert Mann, 1961).

Japanese planes attack Pearl Harbor in *Tora! Tora! Tora!* (Richard Fleischer, 1970).

241

weight (NBC's *Vietnam – It's a Mad War*, 1965, and Pierre Schoendoerffer's *The Anderson Platoon*, 1967, which is, in any case, French), and a host of US government propaganda and training shorts and a like number of equivalent North Vietnamese films.

The explanation for Hollywood's shyness over Vietnam is simply that film-makers have been reluctant to get involved in what is, to the American people, an ideologically very confusing issue, over which there is a great deal of ambivalence and fiery feeling. Television has, moreover, reported the war with immediacy and in reasonable detail, and re-creating such scenes in a fiction film has rightly been regarded as a redundant exercise. Even *The Green Berets*, a shamelessly right-wing, hawkish view of the Vietnam War, is set cautiously in 1963, when the official role of the US forces was to 'advise' the South Vietnamese Army.

All the same, it is surprising – and vaguely alarming – to note that not a single one of Hollywood's more radical film-makers has, so far, shown any sign of wanting to break The Big Silence over Vietnam.

It seems appropriate to end this broad survey of war films with a word or two about those that have treated the one, the unthinkable war which has yet to happen – in the knowledge that if any of them are at all prophetic, then the seventy-five years of conflict recorded and

Frank Sinatra in his own project, *None But the Brave* (1965).

James Garner caught with his pants down in *The Americanization of Emily* (Arthur Hiller, 1964).

film, and one can only hope that, if cinema in the 'seventies and 'eighties continues to show the same preoccupation with war as it has in the past, its exponents will take their cue from these new talents and not from those film-makers of the previous decade who were incapable of regarding war as anything other than a challenge to the box-office and the special effects department.

One of the more remarkable features of war movie-making since the early 'sixties has been the utter dearth of American films on the Vietnam War – a fact noted a few years ago by 'Sight and Sound' in an article entitled 'The Big Silence': 'For Hollywood,' it said, 'the Vietnam war is stuff too hot to handle. Glamourland, which stood up and let itself be counted at the sound of the first clarions of other wars, is sitting this one out.'

Apart from the very occasional foreign propaganda film, normally taking the side of North Vietnam (e.g. the Cuban satire on President Johnson, *Hanoi, martes 13 diz.* made in 1967), and one or two left-wing documentaries such as *Interviews with My Lai Veterans* (1970), there has, to date, been one main feature film (John Wayne's *The Green Berets*, 1968), a couple of forgotten B-features (Marshall Thompson's *A Yank in Vietnam*, 1964; Jack Starrett's *The Losers*, 1970), one major official documentary (John Ford's 'historical' survey of the war, *Vietnam! Vietnam!*, 1971), one independent full-length documentary (Eugene Jones's *A Face of War*, 1968), only two TV programmes of any

242

dramatized by the films described in this book will have been no more than a grim rehearsal for global suicide.

Films about nuclear war fall into two categories – those about the atomic bombs which fell on Japan and ended World War II, and those about some nuclear holocaust of the future, accidental or otherwise.

Japan itself was the first country to reflect seriously on the implications and consequences of the Allied decision to drop atomic bombs on Hiroshima and Nagasaki, and did so in a curiously disarming way by emphasizing, not the horror or the outrageousness of the deed, but the pain and tragedy of it. This, at least, was the initial reaction, contained in such documentaries as *Hiroshima* (1950), *Nagasaki After the Bomb* and *Pictures of the Atom Bomb* (both 1952), and the feature films, *Children of Hiroshima*, *The Bell of Nagasaki* and *I'll Not Forget the Song of Nagasaki* (all 1953).

Hiroshima was a newsreel compilation, an objective, unemotional account of the bombing and its aftermath and a tribute to the survivors. Kaneto Shindo's *Children of Hiroshima* recreated the aftermath in a realistic though rather sentimental way, and its sponsors, the Teachers' Union, rejected it as 'a tear jerker with no political orientation'. This was a reflection of changing attitudes, whereby the guilt of the Americans who were in occupation was beginning to transmit itself to the Japanese.

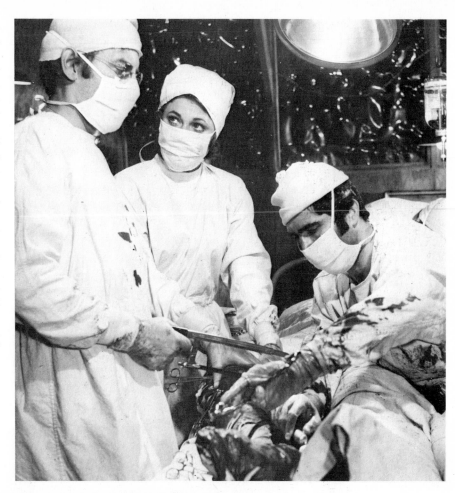

Donald Sutherland and Elliott Gould in *M*A*S*H* (Robert Altman, 1969).

Cornel Wilde's *Beach Red* (1967).

243

Jim Hutton relaxes between takes during filming of *The Green Berets* (John Wayne, 1968).

Alan Arkin as Yossarian in Joseph Heller's *Catch 22* (Mike Nichols, 1970).

Emmanuèle Riva and Eiji Okada in Alain Resnais' *Hiroshima Mon Amour* (1959).

The latter adopted a new attitude of resentment which began to appear in films about the bomb.

The Teachers' Union supported the anti-American documentarist Hideo Sekigawa's *Hiroshima* (1953), which combined a dramatic reconstruction of the explosion with an implicit condemnation of the Americans' motives in causing it. Fumio Kamei followed a similar tack in his highly emotional portrayals of human suffering and disfigurement, *Still, It's Good to be Alive* (1956), *The World is Afraid* (1957), and *Voices of Hiroshima* (1959). In contrast to these was Tadashi Imai's compassionate *A Story of Pure Love* (1957) which avoided Kamei's hysterical tone, and a number of non-political films on the A-bomb, such as

Sotoji Kimura's children's films, *Children of Nagasaki* (1957) and *A Thousand Paper Cranes* (1958), and the satirical *Carmen's Pure Love* (1952), directed by Keisuke Kinoshita, about an old lady who blames all her misfortunes on the bomb.

The best and most responsible Japanese film about the bomb was Akira Kurosawa's characteristically slow-paced *Record of a Living Being* (also known as *I Live in Fear*, 1955), a poignant study of an ageing factory-owner (Toshiro Mifune) who fears atomic war, wants to emigrate to Brazil and begins to go mad.

This is not to exclude, of course, Alain Resnais' celebrated Franco-Japanese film *Hiroshima Mon Amour* (1959), an enigmatic, multi-layered study of the effect of traumatic war experiences on the love-affair of a Frenchwoman and a Westernized Japanese businessman in Hiroshima. It is difficult, though, to see the connection, if any, between the couple's relationship and the atomic devastation of Hiroshima, unless the intention was to contrast the deep scar left on the girl by her singular, personal experience of suffering (shaved and locked up as a collaborator, her German lover shot) with the apparent indifference of the man to his country's collective tragedy.

America has shown a surprising lack of guilt over the dropping of the A-bombs, except indirectly in olive-branch movies like *Sayonara*. The nearest she came to it was in *Above and Beyond* (1952), but that was not so much a study of conscience as of the officer chosen to drop the atomic bomb, Colonel Paul Tibbets (played by Robert Taylor) and his wife (Eleanor Parker). It was easier to believe, in fact, that America was preparing to drop some more when confronted with such films as Delbert Mann's *A Gathering of Eagles* (1962), an overt tribute to

244

America's strike force of giant bombers ready to go into nuclear attack at a moment's notice (although Colonel Rock Hudson took care to stress their strictly defensive purpose).

Prophecies of nuclear holocaust in British and American films have ranged from the dire to the fantastic to the satirical, taking in the odd peripheral piece of political science fiction, such as Frankenheimer's *Seven Days in May* (1963), about a military plot to overthrow the US President after he has signed a disarmament pact. One of the first fictionalizations of a third world war was Ronald MacDougall's *The World, the Flesh and the Devil* (1958), an intriguing but ultimately rather silly triangle drama about the only survivors of an atomic war (Harry Belafonte, Inger Stevens, Mel Ferrer) who find true peace and understanding in front of the United Nations building, but experience none of the probable horrors of an atomic aftermath (radiation, rotting corpses, etc.).

This was followed by Stanley Kramer's celebrated but rather glib and heavy-handed adaptation of Nevil Shute's novel, *On the Beach* (1959), about the last days of the world after an atomic war, in which the survivors prepare for death from radiation sickness. The acting and photography were, however, up to Kramer standard, with Gregory Peck and Anthony Perkins outstanding, and there were some effective things, notably an authentic long-shot

Robert Taylor as Colonel Paul Tibbets, deliverer of the first atomic bomb, in *Above and Beyond* (Norman Panama, 1952), with James Whitmore and Jeff Richards.

Rod Taylor and Rock Hudson time a B-52 training exercise in *A Gathering of Eagles* (Delbert Mann, 1962).

245

Fred Astaire, Gregory Peck and Ava Gardner await death by nuclear fall-out in *On the Beach* (Stanley Kramer, 1959).

and Slim Pickens, the latter whooping with Texan glee as he rides his personally delivered H-bomb down to its Soviet target. Kubrick called it a 'nightmare comedy'.

The only other effective comedy of nuclear war has been Richard Lester's British satire, written by Spike Milligan and John Antrobus, *The Bed Sitting Room* (1969), a kind of black Goon Show, in which the survivors of an H-bomb holocaust find themselves undergoing the most extraordinary metamorphoses.

A year after Kubrick's film, Sidney Lumet made a serious version of *Dr Strangelove*, the unjustly ignored *Fail Safe*, in which an electronic error sets off a chain of events which must culminate in nuclear disaster. The President (superbly played by Henry Fonda) has to offer to swap cities with Russia, i.e. to bomb New York to make up for the destruction of Moscow, in order to keep diplomatic faith. Tight, tense, terrifying and entirely convincing, this is a film which demands reappraisal.

Another underrated nuclear movie was Ray Milland's modest *Panic in Year Zero*, which dramatized the attempts of an average American family to stay alive in the chaos following a nuclear attack on Los Angeles. It was certainly less pretentious than, for example, James Harris's *The Bedford Incident* (1965), which imagined a tragic confrontation in the North Atlantic between the pig-headed skipper of a destroyer (Richard Widmark) and his opposite number in a Russian nuclear submarine (Eric Portman, returning to a familiar old role).

Perhaps the most devastating portrayal of an imagined nuclear explosion is Peter Watkins's documentary reconstruction, *The War Game*,

of San Francisco completely deserted, and a car-race in which the participants commit suicide.

Kramer's film was made to look particularly solemn and portentous by the first nuclear black comedy, Stanley Kubrick's *Dr Strangelove: Or, How I Learned to Stop Worrying and Love the Bomb* (1963), a sharp, very funny satire on H-bomb diplomacy in which a mad general creates panic by pressing the vital button. Peter Sellers played (successfully) three roles, including a manic German scientist, George C. Scott was perfect as a hawkish adviser, and there were marvellous, wild-eyed cameos from Sterling Hayden, Keenan Wynn

Director Stanley Kubrick sizes up his next shot with Sterling Hayden and Peter Sellers in *Dr Strangelove: Or How I Learned to Stop Worrying and Love the Bomb* (1963).

246

made for BBC Television in 1965 but banned from the small screen because of its horrifically explicit simulation of the physical effects of a missile attack. It was eventually released for showing in cinemas, but has still not been as widely seen as it deserves. Using powerful shock effects and a totally convincing 'instant newsreel' technique to build up its vision of human devastation and social collapse, *The War Game* is strong, manipulative propaganda of the most justified kind, which could and should be shown where it was intended – on television. To borrow the final ironic message from *On the Beach* – 'There is still time, brother.'

The War Game (1965), Peter Watkins's concept of a nuclear attack on Britain.

247

Acknowledgments

Of the many people who contributed in large or small measure (and sometimes unwittingly) to the preparation of this book, I owe a particular debt to Rosemary Stark, who typed the manuscript and generally maintained morale. 'A Pictorial History of War Films' is dedicated to her.

Special thanks are due also to the Information Department and Book Library of the National Film Archive, without whose staff and facilities a project of this kind would be unthinkable; to Sheila Whitaker and the Archive's Stills Department; and to Mary Jackson.

I am no less grateful to the following for their help and advice: Lutz Becker, Kevin Brownlow, Clive Coultass, David Meeker, Al Reuter, Markku Salmi, Frances Thorpe, and Victoria Wegg-Prosser.

Although war films have been much written about from a political and analytical point of view, there has, until now, been no attempt to survey the whole genre factually and chronologically (unlike, for example, Westerns or Musicals). The sources for this book have, therefore, been wide-ranging and often scattered, fragmented and obscure. It would be impractical to try to document all of them, but the following books, chapters from books, pamphlets, essays and articles proved more or less indispensable:

'A Million and One Nights' (two volumes) by Terry Ramsaye. Simon and Schuster, New York, 1926.
'History of the Film' by Maurice Bardèche and Robert Brassilach, translated by Iris Barry. Allen and Unwin, London, 1938.
'The Rise of the American Film' by Lewis Jacobs. Harcourt, Brace, New York, 1939.
'Twenty Best Film Plays' edited by John Gassner and Dudley Nichols. Crown, New York, 1943.
'Best Film Plays of 1943–44' edited by John Gassner and Dudley Nichols. Crown, New York, 1945. (Includes chapter: 'The Motion Picture Industry and the War Effort' by Walter Wanger.)
'The Factual Film', a survey by The Arts Enquiry. Oxford University Press for Political and Economic Planning, 1947.
'From Caligari to Hitler' by Siegfried Kracauer. Princeton University Press, Princeton, 1947. Dennis Dobson, London, 1947.
'Magic and Myth of the Movies' by Parker Tyler. Henry Holt, New York, 1947. Secker and Warburg, London, 1947.
'An Index to the Films of Ernst Lubitsch' by Theodore Huff (Index Series No. 9). British Film Institute, London, 1971.
'The History of the British Film' (four volumes) published in London by Allen and Unwin: 'Part I: 1896–1906' by Rachael Low and Roger Manvell (pub. 1948); 'Part II: 1906–1914' (pub. 1949); 'Part III: 1914–1918' (pub. 1950), and 'Part IV: 1918–1929' (pub. 1971) all by Rachael Low. In New York by Bowker, 1973.
'Anthony Asquith' by Peter Noble (New Index Series No. 5). British Film Institute, London, 1951.
'Documentary Film' by Paul Rotha. Faber and Faber, London, 1952. (Includes chapter: 'The Use of Films by the US Armed Services' by Richard Griffith.)
'The Japanese Film: Art and Industry' by Joseph L. Anderson and Donald Richie. Charles E. Tuttle, Rutland, 1959, and London, 1963.
'Film: Book 2 – Films of Peace and War' edited by Robert Hughes. Grove Press, New York, 1962.
'National Film Archive Catalogue, Part I: Silent News Films 1895–1933'. British Film Institute, London, 1965.
'John Ford' by Peter Bogdanovich. Studio Vista, London, 1967. University of California Press, Berkeley, 1968.
'The Parade's Gone By . . .' by Kevin Brownlow. Secker and Warburg, London, 1968. Knopf, New York, 1968.
'The American Movies Reference Book: The Sound Era', Paul Michael (editor-in-chief). Prentice-Hall, New York, 1969.
'The Movies' (revised edition) by Richard Griffith and Arthur Mayer. Simon and Schuster, New York, 1970. Spring Books, London, 1971.
'Politics and Film' by Leif Furhammar and Folke Isaksson, translated by Kersti French. Studio Vista, London, 1971. Praeger, New York, 1971.
'Dictionary of Films' by Georges Sadoul, translated and edited by Peter Morris. University of California, Berkeley, 1972.
'Studies in Documentary' by Alan Lovell and Jim Hillier (Cinema One Series). Secker and Warburg/British Film Institute, London, 1972. Viking Press, New York, 1972.
'The International Encyclopedia of Film' edited by Dr Roger Manvell and others. Michael Joseph, London, 1972. Crown, New York, 1972.
'The British Film Catalogue 1895–1970' by Denis Gifford. David and Charles, Newton Abbot, 1973. McGraw-Hill, New York, 1973.
'Visions of Yesterday' by Jeffrey Richards. Routledge and Kegan Paul, London, 1973.
'Hollywood at War' by Ken D. Jones and Arthur F. McClure. A.S. Barnes, London and New York, 1973.
'The Films of World War II' by Joe Morella, Edward Z. Epstein and John Griggs. Citadel Press, New York, 1973.

'Featuring Mars' by E.E. Barrett. 'The Picturegoer', July, 1926.
'The War from Three Angles' by Bryher. 'Close Up', July, 1927.
'War' by Marie Seton. 'Sight and Sound', Winter, 1937/38.
'Milestone and War' by Karel Reisz. 'Sequence', New Year, 1952.
'Westfront 1957' by John Gillett. 'Sight and Sound', Winter, 1957/58.
'Nazi Crimes and Punishment' by Peter Wright. 'Motion', Winter, 1961/62.
'Sunflowers and Commissars' by Robert Vas. 'Sight and Sound', Summer, 1962.
'The Old Lie' by David Robinson. 'Sight and Sound', Autumn, 1962.
'One . . . Two . . . Three?' by Richard Whitehall. 'Films and Filming', August, 1964.
'Clean Germans and Dirty Politics' by Martin S. Dworkin. 'Film Comment', Winter, 1965.
'Hollywood Goes to War' by Rory Guy. 'Cinema (USA)', March, 1966.
'World War I on the Screen' by Jack Spears. 'Films in Review', May to October, 1966.
'World War I Aviation Films' by Rudy Behlmer. 'Films in Review', August to October, 1967.
'World War II and the American Film' by Lewis Jacobs. 'Cinema Journal', Winter, 1967/68.
'The Big Silence' by Axel Madsen. 'Sight and Sound', Winter, 1967/68.
'Over the Brink' by Leslie Halliwell. 'Films and Filming', September/October, 1968.

In addition, I delved frequently into the following periodicals: 'The Bioscope', 'Picturegoer','Close Up', 'Kine Weekly', 'Documentary Newsletter', 'Motion Picture Herald','Sight and Sound', and the 'Monthly Film Bulletin'.

Grateful thanks are also due to the following for their help in providing stills: Jeff Fairman; Val Guest; Imperial War Museum, London; John Kobal; National Film Archive, London; Oesterreichisches Film Museum, Vienna; Sovexportfilm, Moscow. And to all the film companies who made the films: Cinema-Allianz, Tobis, Uva; British Lion, Ealing Studios, Eros, London Films, Rank; and Columbia, Disney Corporation, MCA-Universal, MGM, Paramount, Republic, RKO, 20th Century-Fox, United Artists, and Warner Brothers.

Index